FARMHOUSE COOK BOOK

TIM WILSON & FRAN WARDE

Photography by Kristin Perers

MITCHELL BEAZLEY

Tim Wilson, owner of The Ginger Pig chain of butchers, is one of the most respected meat producers in Britain. His shops have received many accolades and prizes, including Best Food Producer in the *Observer* Food Awards. The Ginger Pig's shops stock meat almost exclusively from his three Yorkshire farms. Of his own business, Tim says, 'There is no great secret to what we do: we simply raise the best animals in the happiest of circumstances, on the finest stretch of the Yorkshire Moors we could find.'

Fran Warde is a cook and best-selling food writer. She spent 18 months in the kitchens of the Café Royal before opening her own restaurant in London and then moving into catering and opening a successful cookery school. Fran co-authored the award-winning *The French Kitchen* with Joanna Harris, which was followed by *The French Market*. Her other books include *New Bistro* and *Food for Friends*. She has written for numerous publications, including *The Saturday Times Magazine*, *BBC Good Food* and *Waitrose Food Illustrated* and is the former food editor of *Red* magazine.

This book is dedicated to the RSPCA and Freedom Food, the RSPCA's nationwide farm animal assurance and food labelling scheme, that follows animals' wellbeing from birth to slaughter. Freedom Food focuses solely on improving the welfare of farm animals reared for food, so all members of the Freedom Food scheme meet the RSPCA's strict welfare standards.

Together we both strongly and passionately believe that what the RSPCA does is outstanding both for the welfare of animals and for the future of this country. British farmers produce some of the finest quality meats, off the best land, from native breeds, which can and should continue to improve things for both the animal and the consumer, with the animal always coming first.

'As a farmer and butcher it is my duty to provide my animals with good husbandry, then I can provide my customers with quality items and a clear conscience.'
Tim Wilson

'As a food writer it is my passion to search out provenance ingredients. When it comes to meat this means it must have been looked after well, naturally fed, considerately slaughtered, dry aged and purchased from a reputable butcher in order for me to truly enjoy my work in the kitchen.'
Fran Warde

'It is clear that The Ginger Pig have their hearts and minds in good animal husbandry and are excelling at demystifying where food comes from. I am delighted we were able to recognize them in the RSPCA Good Business Awards 2010 and wish them every success for the future.'
David Bowles, Director of Communications RSPCA

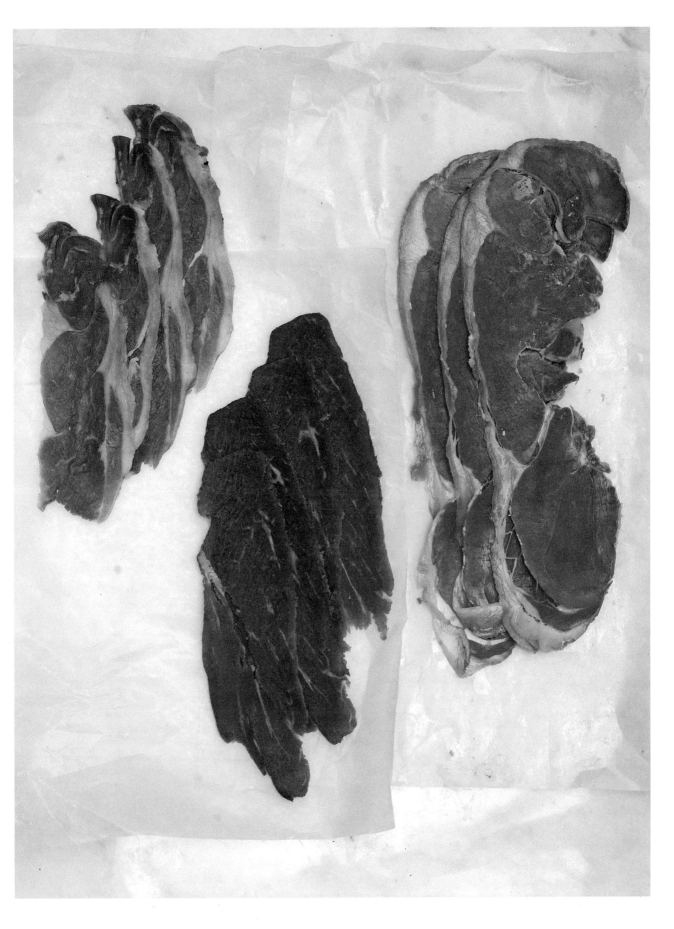

Contents

The birth of The Ginger Pig

As the son of an antiques dealer, perhaps it was inevitable that I started my professional life in the antiques trade. From there, it was a small step to begin buying run-down properties and fixing them up to sell, and in 1990 a farmhouse for sale in Harwell, Nottinghamshire, caught my eye. It was an old eighteenth-century property, with ducks splashing in a pond in the yard, pigs lolling in old wooden sties and a few large outbuildings for storing hay and farm equipment. I thought it was perfect for renovation, and planned to sell it on as an idyllic country home.

The sale went through in the autumn, 1992, and Harwell Manor became mine. I visited the property to start planning all the work that was needed, and what I saw in the cold light of day gave me a real sinking feeling. Without the ducks, the pond was just a muddy hole in the ground, and the pigless sties were nothing more than run-down wooden huts with caved-in roofs. Minus the life and vibrancy of animals, the place was just a near-derelict mess.

Gritting my teeth, I got cracking, and to cheer myself up I installed a pigsty in the front yard and got three pigs, a few ducks and some hens. As I replaced bricks and beams and the renovation gradually progressed, the hens laid eggs and the pigs grew – everything was going pretty well. Then one day I answered a knock at the door. The man on my doorstep claimed to be a retired butcher; he matter-of-factly told me that the pigs in my front yard were almost at full maturity and that I'd need to have them slaughtered soon or they'd start to mate. I duly took them to the abattoir, then dropped the carcasses off with my newfound butcher friend, who stored them in his cold room and turned some of the meat into bacon and sausages.

This experience of seeing how food travelled from field to fork sparked off an interest that became a passion, and I've retained it ever since. It wasn't long before I decided to have a go at breeding Tamworth pigs. I acquired three pure-bred gilts (female sows that have never been pregnant), named them Milly, Molly and Mandy, and started my search for a pure-bred boar. After a false start with a boar we nicknamed Wee Willy from Wootton Wawen – because the poor fella was just not up to the job – a Tamworth breeder in South Wales said he had just the animal for me, so I went to see. A big beast of a pig, Dai Bando, as I called him (after the boxing coach in Richard Llewellyn's 1939 novel *How Green Was My Valley*), was irresistible, so I bought him, and his owner offered to transport him to his new home in Nottinghamshire.

Having a few hours to spare on the day of delivery, I popped into the nearby town of Bawtry for the day's newspapers. In the marketplace I spotted a beaten-up, yellow Land-Rover occupied by what looked like two burly brothers, both with bristly ginger beards and big weathered faces. As I got closer, I realized that the passenger was in fact Dai Bando, sitting beside the driver just as you or I would, and appearing completely at ease. They followed me back to the farmhouse, and Dai Bando climbed out of the vehicle just as neatly as he'd sat in it. I started to ask the owner whether this boar would really work properly, but before I even finished getting the words out, Dai Bando was charging towards the gilts, crashing straight through the electric fence. That's how I became a pig farmer.

The problem with breeding pigs on a relatively small scale is that each female has a litter of around eight piglets, so three gilts very quickly produce about 24 piglets. These piglets reach a good slaughter weight in seven months, and then you have a fair amount of pork to deal with. I solved the problem by teaching myself bacon curing, sausage-making and butchery from two classic books: John Seymour's *Self-Sufficiency* (1973) and Jane Grigson's *Charcuterie* and *French Pork Cookery* (1970). Once I'd mastered these skills, I began selling meat locally, and the proceeds helped me to finish the renovation I'd embarked on nearly two years earlier.

Encouraged by my local success, in 1994 I took on a monthly stall at Borough Market in southeast London, driving down on Friday night in a beaten-up van, selling out each Saturday and driving straight home again. By this time I was farming three types of pig – Tamworth, Berkshire and Gloucester Old Spot – and Longhorn cattle, and I was becoming increasingly sure that, with a bigger farm, The Ginger Pig could become a real part of the London food scene. I had my eye on a farmhouse in North Yorkshire, with a good acreage and grazing rights across beautiful moorland, but the local banks just couldn't see why I would want to farm in Yorkshire and sell meat in London. Eventually, though, a London-based bank took a shine to The Ginger Pig and risked lending the money so I could buy Grange Farm near Pickering and open a shop on Moxon Street, London W1, both of which continue today.

The team and I (about 70 people in total) now farm rare-breed cattle, sheep and pigs over more than 3,000 acres of farm and moorland, and at the time of writing we have five London shops selling our meat, home-made pies, terrines and much more. With the help of the Botterills at Lings View Farm on the Belvoir Estate, we've also brought an old English chicken breed back to the table, a Cornish Game and Light Sussex cross (see page 95), and we make our own chutneys, pickles and preserves using fruits and vegetables from our garden and from locally sourced produce.

Given that my grandfathers were a butcher and a grocer, perhaps my current career was as inevitable as my first one in antiques. Nothing gives me greater satisfaction than rearing the best animals on one of the finest stretches of North Yorkshire, and using each and every ingredient to its full potential. I hope this book will help you to buy wisely, learn some new skills and produce fantastic dishes to add to your repertoire.

A week in the farm kitchen

Here's a taste of the diet that sustains our working farm. It may contain a good deal of meat, butter, animal fat and a splash of cream, but this is countered by the hard physical work and long hours involved in animal husbandry. There's an element of 'rolling eternity' to food on the farm, with something always borrowed from a previous meal, or an ever-present slab of bacon to add life and heart – which it especially does with leftovers.

Sunday is usually roast beef, more often than not a fore rib, and always with more vegetables and potatoes than can be eaten in one meal. Sunday isn't just a day of rest, but about preparing for the week ahead, and a few leftovers give you a meal in hand for Monday.

On Sunday night, any rendered fat from the roasting tin is salvaged and stored, and the remaining meat picked from the bones. The latter go into a pot with any stock we already have and a little water, and the whole lot goes into the oven overnight at around 90°C/gas ¼. There's lots of flavour and gelatine to be extracted from beef bones, and a very gentle simmer overnight will do just this. In the morning the stock goes into the fridge and will be preserved by the fat that sets on the top.

In winter, Monday night's supper will be beef hash. In a frying pan, an onion is softened in butter or dripping and any leftover potatoes added. A can of whole tomatoes goes in next, crushed with a wooden spoon. The leftover beef is shredded and added to the pan, then seasoned and stirred until the liquid is reduced, and served with fried eggs on top. Monday night in summer is beef and salad, with perhaps the cold potatoes and a blob of mayonnaise.

Tuesday on the farm is always trial day for new sausages, pies and terrines, which make a convenient if occasionally curious supper. We often make a casserole-type dish on Wednesday, though when it's warmer – which it is occasionally in the North Yorkshire summer – a few slices of ham, new potatoes and some salad vegetables do very nicely. For a casserole either a big piece of shoulder of pork will be slowly pot-roasted with a little stock and some root vegetables, or I make a 'quick pan casserole'. Pork tenderloin is chopped into large pieces and browned in a pan in butter, then transferred to a plate. Onions and diced red pepper go into the pan and cook until soft and lightly caramelized. In goes a good teaspoon of grain mustard plus a tablespoon of Dijon mustard, the pork is returned to the pan and a generous amount of double cream is added. A quick simmer, then it is served with rice and the calorific content ignored.

A big roast chicken is cooked on Thursday, and any meat left on the carcass is stripped off and put in the fridge. The bones then join the existing stock and go in the oven overnight to create an intensely flavoured liquor that will give life to many dishes. A simple pasta dish rounds off Friday. The leftover chicken is sautéed with onions and bacon, then layered with cooked pasta and tomatoes, topped with lots of cheese and baked. Saturday is a day off from cooking for us, so we often make our way to The Magpie Café in Whitby for truly unbeatable fish and chips.

The farmhouse larder

A kitchen should have preparations
for a meal in its store, as well as a
few flavour-giving ingredients with a
longish life, such as a piece of streaky
bacon or the dripping from your last
roast. Stock will keep a long time if
covered with a layer of fat, and a piece
of beef or pork fat added to the liquid
as it simmers will ensure this.

Essentials

Butter, good quality (unsalted and slightly salted)

Cheese, usually a good Wensleydale
or Cheddar

Cooked potatoes and vegetables

Cream

Dried fruit

Dripping

Eggs

Flour

Ground spices (cinnamon, cloves, coriander seeds,
nutmeg and mace) for baking, stock-making and
curing

Milk

Onions

Root vegetables

Salt

Stock

Streaky bacon, in the piece

Sugar

Useful extras

Capers

Dried pasta

Grains and pulses

Lemons

Natural yoghurt

Preserved fish

Tinned/canned tomatoes

Curing, preserving & smoking

Curing and preserving

Curing is an age-old preserving technique dating back to Roman times – a race to get natural preservatives into food before bacteria have a chance to take hold. Along with bottling, chutney- and jam-making, drying and pickling, curing was the solution to scarcity of food during the winter months, and prevented waste when refrigeration had yet to be invented. With the introduction of the fridge-freezer, artificial preservatives, commercialized canning and the power to move fresh produce around the world at speed, home curing and preserving techniques fell out of fashion, but are once again gaining popularity as people remember the provenance of the food on their plate. Modern ways of preserving have a tendency to remove the soul of the raw ingredient, leaving an insipid, spidery sketch of what once was, whereas traditional methods – curing, storing in fat, bottling – retain the characteristics of what you started with. Yes, bacon is salty where pork is not, but you can still taste the quality of the pig and get the satisfying hit of pork fat.

In basic terms, curing is a form of dehydration, using the deliquescent properties of salt to draw moisture out of food, water – along with warmth, oxygen and time – being the catalyst for bacteria and degradation. Although it is possible to cure meat with just salt, the usual practice is to add nitrates and sugar too, the former to keep an attractive colour, the latter to soften the harshness of the salt and allow you to use a little less of it. This method is known as dry-curing, but there is another method – wet-curing (also known as brining, see page 22).

After chemically removing the moisture using a natural cure, meat needs to be hung to allow it to 'set', to dry a little and firm up enough to slice. Years ago, hams and sides of bacon were hung from ropes strung from the ceilings of pantries and kitchens. The neck of a broken bottle was threaded onto the top of the rope, spiky side up, to keep away rodents – much like a shard-topped wall is designed to deter thieves.

Basic principles of curing and preserving

• Use the freshest meat you can get, preferably within 36 hours of the animal's slaughter. Although you may be used to eating aged beef raw, if bacterial growth has already made good progress, there's little point in wasting your cure on it.

• Size is everything. The larger the piece of meat, the longer and stronger the cure needs to be. The cure must completely penetrate the meat in order to draw out the moisture and preserve the flesh.

• Balance is also key. Too much salt in the curing mix can produce too firm a texture and too harsh a taste; too little and the meat will spoil. Ten per cent is a reliable ratio for the home cook.

• Keep cool and consistent. Curing is a chemical reaction, so excess heat or changes in temperature will affect this reaction. The meat and its cure are best kept in a cool, dryish place, such as a well-insulated garage, shed or cellar.

• Fat is good. Without a decent covering of fat, cured meat won't 'set' properly when it is hung. It is the fat that offers structure and support, with the meat remaining relatively soft and therefore difficult to handle and slice. Ham hocks had nooks and crannies which would have been packed with hard lard to seal.

• Cure in a non-reactive container, such as a large plastic, enamel or porcelain box or dish. Materials like aluminium, copper and cast iron are reactive, meaning that they have properties that may react chemically with an ingredient, therefore tainting the finished dish.

• Smoking does not act as a preservative. While it aids the process of drying the finished product, it is used mainly to flavour.

Bacon and ham

• Even as late as the mid-twentieth century, most of the meat from a pig would be turned into variations on ham or bacon, with very little pork eaten fresh. Pigs were bred for size and a decent covering of fat, which was essential for the curing process as well as fuel for farm workers performing hard physical labour.

• The rule was to kill pigs only in months containing an 'r' – ie, not during the summer – to ensure a suitably low temperature for curing the meat without refrigeration. As observed by John Seymour in *Self-Sufficiency*, the book that inspired Tim to start The Ginger Pig: 'In the morning the carcass will be 'set' (stiff) if the weather is cold enough (and if it isn't you shouldn't be killing a baconer).'

• Bacon is one of the easier cured meats for beginners to start with, and belly – which makes streaky bacon – is very economical for a first attempt.

Making ham the Ginger Pig way

Leg of pork, taken from the hindquarter of the animal, is a plentiful cut and usually quite economical to buy. Although it makes a decent roast, it pales in comparison to shoulder, belly and loin, and it's in its cured form – ham – that it really begins to shine.

Although we use a dry cure for our bacon, we use a wet cure – submersing the meat in a brine bath – for our ham. A whole leg is a big joint and requires a lot of salt, and a lot of time in it, in order for the cure to penetrate right to the bone. If the penetration is incomplete, the flesh near the bone will spoil and you'll lose the whole lot. Loins and bellies, being long and flat, cure much faster than legs; a ham simply becomes very salty if dry-cured for the time required.

Before modern refrigeration, meat had to be cured very aggressively as there were no fridges in which to store the end result. With a very salty cure – and central heating yet to be invented – hams could hang in the kitchen or larder for months on end without spoilage. These pieces tended to come from big, fat animals in order to feed the workforce, and these larger pieces of meat meant even more salt. Although pigs were slaughtered from September to April, the majority would be killed in the autumn, before they started to lose weight as their body fat was turned into energy to keep them warm.

I still remember visiting my aunt as a boy. She would have great big hams hanging from the ceiling, and for Sunday tea would lop off a big piece, boil it for an hour to remove some of the salt, then slice and fry it for us to eat. They weren't too fussy back then about removing the hairs, and the taste of the salty, hairy, over-cured ham remains with me to this day.

Thanks to refrigeration, less salt can be used now for the curing process because chilling helps meat to last a good while. This has done great things for the flavour and texture of British ham, one of the few aspects of modernization that has improved the ham and bacon we eat.

Submerging the pork leg in a wet cure or brine (heavily salted water) uses much less salt than a dry salt rub, and the water allows the salt to penetrate the meat more evenly. This process, somewhat counter-intuitively, still functions as a drying method, drawing out moisture while allowing the salt in. It's only when pork is injected with saline solution that it holds the liquid. Some producers do this to increase the weight and therefore the profit margin, speed up production and give a longer shelf life, but the end result is watery and flavourless. It is this shortcut that has done ham and bacon a disservice, with the meat insipid and producing the unpleasant 'white stuff' that too often accompanies the cooking of cheap products. 'Never take shortcuts' is the unofficial Ginger Pig motto.

We use legs from smallish pigs weighing around 85kg (187lb), which result in finished hams of around 9kg (20lb). We feel that these slightly smaller legs achieve the right balance between size, the salt required and the curing time so that the ham produced is neither too small nor too salty. We brine the legs for a week, then transfer them into a fresh brine for a further 4–6 days to finish the cure. The cured hams are then gently simmered in water (around 20 minutes per lb/450 g) until cooked. After that, the ham can be cooled for slicing, or eaten hot, but we like to finish ours with a sweet glaze (see page 28).

Ham versus gammon

Opinion is mixed over the definitions of 'ham' and 'gammon', though the most common and most contemporary meanings are that ham denotes something that has been cured, possibly hung and then cooked, whereas gammon is sold 'wet' – straight out of the brine – and needs to be cooked before it is eaten. The confusion between the two terms stems from the time before domestic refrigeration, when most of the pig would be cured, and the back leg was known simply as a fresh ham. A gammon was a joint cut from the leg once it had been cured, and was usually tied to make a neat roasting or boiling joint. These days we use 'gammon' to refer to cured but raw products and 'ham' to refer to cooked, so these terms will generally not take you too far wrong when you are ordering meat from your butcher. However, do explain exactly what you're after if you are unsure.

Cure variations

Just as Lancashire has its hotpot and Scotland its broth, so many regions had, and to some extent still have, local recipes for curing and cooking a ham. Some may involve a handful of spices or a heavy-handed smoke, while others might go for pickling in a bath of beer and black treacle, or simply brining and gently steaming. Here are three classic hams:

Shropshire 'black' ham

Originally devised in Buckinghamshire by Lord Bradenham, it is thought that the cure became a stalwart of Shropshire after his lordship's butcher moved to the county, taking the cure with him. The black skin of the ham is produced when the meat is cured for a number of weeks in a heady pickle of stout, black treacle, coriander seeds and/or juniper berries. The ham is then smoked and hung, and has a strong, sweet, smoky taste with a sour back-note from the beer. This recipe is also made in Suffolk, notably by Emmett's of Peasenhall.

Wiltshire ham

Perhaps the most important cure described in this book, and the one that made huge leaps towards a more delicate, softer – yet not wet – more palatable ham. It was the making of a family who would 'innovate' so far as to mechanize and industrialize the ham- and bacon-curing industry, but not all to positive effect.

The innovators were John and Henry Harris, second-generation butchers, whose father, John senior, ran a butcher's shop in Calne, Wiltshire, during the late eighteenth century. After John senior's death, his widow carried on the business, albeit on a much smaller scale, but eventually her sons built it up. John opened a second shop near by, and Henry helped his mother until her death in 1809. Both shops cured their own hams and bacon on site, the pork coming largely from Irish pigs 'driven' on foot through Bristol and on to London in the years before the Great Western Railway. The village of Calne provided a convenient rest stop on this trade route. Pork was plentiful until the failure of the potato crop in 1846 put Irish farmers in a state of crisis. At the time of the famine, one-third of Ireland's population depended on potatoes as food, and without being able to feed the workforce, they could not farm anything else. In desperation, George Harris, son of John junior, travelled to America to explore the feasibility of curing pork there and exporting it back home. His bacon-curing business was brief and unsuccessful, but it led to a discovery that became the saving grace of the business. During his time in America, George studied the use of ice insulation to cure bacon at a lower temperature. This process not only meant that less salt could be used, but also was gentler and allowed hams to be cured throughout the year rather than aggressively dry-cured in just the colder months. The more delicate ham produced by this method proved to be instantly popular with customers more used to tough, very salty cured pork.

In 1856, the Harrises converted their high-street factory in Calne into an ice-house, with a floor of iron providing the base insulation and layers of coal to insulate the walls. During the winter they used ice found locally, and in summer imported it from Norway. Their innovation gave the Harris family a huge advantage over other producers and they became very wealthy. They even patented their production method, and gained a secondary income from selling the licence to other businesses throughout Britain. Financial success made them ambitious, allowing the company to expand and even to invest in the development of the Calne–Chippenham railway in order to move produce and livestock faster.

The family developed their curing technique further, moving to the cold brining method that is now used by most producers today. The end-product of this method is commonly known as Wiltshire ham, although not everything given that name is worthy of it. The Harrises also set about persuading farmers to produce leaner pigs, which they declared to be much better for bacon. Sadly, the pursuit of leaness has escalated to the point where it has obliterated many traditional British breeds and encouraged a consumer taste for very little fat.

By the twentieth century, the Harris family employed approximately 230 staff, were allegedly processing up to 3,000 pigs each week and were exporting their produce as far as New Zealand. It has to be said that their hams and bacon were almost certainly still of a decent standard at that point, but the industrialization they introduced paved the way for the often low-standard mass-production we see today.

York ham

Produced from a very large breed known as the Yorkshire pig or large white, York hams can weigh up to 25kg (55lb). They are heavily dry-cured, so usually require long soaking before they can be cooked. Just a handful of producers are still making real York hams, though the name, having no legal protection, is often misappropriated by others. Some say the genuine article should be smoked, but smoking appears to be a variation within the region.

How to calculate curing time

- The curing time for pork can be calculated according to its density. An old rule says to allow one day per 1cm (½in), so measure the thickness of the meat to work out how long it should stay in the curing salt. A large leg of pork takes on average two weeks in a wet cure.
- Beef cures slightly more quickly than pork because it is less dense: in this case, allow one day per 2cm (¾in).

After the cure

- Wrap cured meat in muslin or a cotton cloth tube to protect it from flies. In times past it was traditionally rubbed with crushed black pepper, which helps keep flies off.
- Check a hanging ham regularly for mould. White mould is fine, but black mould is dangerous and every scrap of it should be cut off.
- Trust your natural instincts: if a ham looks good and smells good, all is well; if something seems amiss, do not take any risks – discard the ham.
- Deboned cured legs become great gammons that can be rolled and tied and cut into manageable smaller pieces to roast.

Wet-cured & hung ham

7kg (15lb 4oz) leg of pork

For the cure
500g (1lb 2oz) curing salt
200g (7oz) molasses sugar
50g (2oz) pickling spice
2 bay leaves

1. Select a plastic box or bucket large enough to hold the pork. Place all the cure ingredients in it and add 10 litres (17 pints) of water in it. Mix gently with a wooden spoon until all the salt has dissolved.

2. Insert a long, thin-bladed knife or skewer into the pork all the way to the bone: this is to ensure that the cure penetrates down to the bone. Repeat several times so the holes are evenly spaced over the joint.

3. Immerse the pork in the brine solution and sit a weighted plastic container on top to keep to keep it submerged. Place in the fridge or other cool place for 12 days, turning and checking it daily.

4. Remove the pork from the brine, rinse well and pat dry. Wrap in muslin and hang in a cool, dark place or the fridge for 28 days. To cook the ham, see page 28.

Serves 20
Takes 40 minutes, plus 12 days to cure and 28 days to hang
While this recipe can be made with sea salt, I like to use curing salt (see page 30) as it always delivers a perfect result.

Dry-cured & hung ham

3kg (6lb 8oz) deboned leg of pork (this is small, so you might need half a leg if the joint is bigger)
1kg (2lb 4oz) curing salt
100g (3½oz) brown sugar
1 tbsp olive oil
1 tbsp cracked black peppercorns
1 tbsp dried oregano

1. Place the pork in a large plastic bowl or box. Mix together the salt and sugar, then pour onto the joint and rub all over, taking extra care to pack the mixture into any crevices and hollows. Place the pork in the fridge for 12 days (a whole leg of pork weighing 7–9kg/15lb 4oz–20lb on the bone will need 20 days). Turn frequently, draining off any liquid that seeps out of the pork and rubbing it with the salt.

2. When ready, rub off any excess salt, then smear the olive oil all over the outside. Mix together the black peppercorns and oregano and rub all over the outside of the meat.

3. Wrap in muslin and hang the joint on a meat hook in a cool, dark place or the fridge for 6–12 months. A white mould may build up on the outside of the ham, but this is normal. If a black mould builds up, it needs to be cut off and discarded (see page 20).

4. When ready, the ham should resemble a dry-cured Parma ham, and is best sliced with a professional wheel carver.

Serves 20
Takes 40 minutes, plus 12 days to cure and 6-12 months to hang
An important part of getting a good dry cure is to hang the ham in a room where the temperature remains cool and steady. A dry, airy larder, cellar or shed is ideal.

Glazing a ham

As a large amount of salt is needed to cure a ham, a little bit of sweetness added to the finished item is highly complementary. You can achieve this by serving the ham with something sweet yet acidic, such as Cumberland or cranberry sauce, or by baking the cooked ham with a glaze. Often the former makes a good base for the latter, and it wouldn't be considered wrong to do both.

To glaze a ham

Peel off the skin (not the fat) while the ham is still hot; this is very tricky to do neatly once it cools, so wear a pair of rubber gloves to guard against the heat. If you're a stickler for presentation, score a neat, criss-cross pattern into the fat, though a few slashes will suffice if you're less particular.

Prepare your glaze and rub it into the fat. The glazes suggested on the right are easy to make and really delicious, but for a very simple alternative, brush a tangy, thick-cut marmalade or redcurrant jelly over the ham.

Stud the surface with cloves if you wish, then bake the ham in a hot-ish oven (200°C/400°F/gas mark 6) for 20–30 minutes, until the fat is wonderfully caramelized. Slice and serve hot, or allow to cool if you prefer it cold.

Mustard and brown sugar glaze

1 tbsp Dijon mustard

1 tbsp grain mustard

3 tbsp soft brown sugar

Black treacle and spice glaze

2 tbsp black treacle

1 tbsp golden syrup

3 tbsp stout

½ tsp ground coriander

½ tsp ground cinnamon

Apricot and ginger glaze

3 tbsp good-quality apricot jam

1 piece of stem ginger, finely chopped

Roasted & glazed wet-cured ham

7kg (15lb 4oz) wet-cured
ham (see page 22)

For the glaze
50g (2oz) brown sugar
50g (2oz) golden syrup
50g (2oz) mustard
30ml (1fl oz) cider vinegar

1. Preheat the oven to 170°C/325°F/gas mark 3.

2. Weigh your ham and calculate the cooking time you need at 40 minutes per kg (2lb 4oz).

3. Place the ham on a rack inside a large roasting tin and add 2 litres (3½ pints) of water. Using large sheets of foil or joining sheets together, make a large tent over the ham (it should not touch the meat), securing it all around the edges to make a steaming chamber that will cook the ham to perfection.

4. Place the ham in the oven and cook for the calculated time.

5. Put the glaze ingredients into a small saucepan and mix over a low heat until the sugar has dissolved and the mixture is smooth. Set aside.

6. Remove the ham from the oven and carefully peel off the skin, leaving the fat in place. Score the fat into a criss-cross pattern, then spread generously with the glaze. Return the ham to the oven and cook for 30 minutes, until the glaze is bubbling and the ham golden. Serve hot or cold with a selection of mustards and pickles.

Serves 20
Takes about 6¼ hours
It is really important to cook a cured ham correctly so that the flavour and tenderness are preserved. Here we have devised a way of locking in that moisture to deliver the perfect ham.

Dry-cured long-back bacon

2kg (4lb 8oz) long-back
pork

For the cure
200g (7oz) curing salt
85g (3oz) demerara sugar
2 tsp pepper

1. Find a plastic container large enough for the pork to lie flat. Mix together the cure ingredients and rub the mixture vigorously all over the pork. Cover and place in the fridge for 5 days, regularly draining off any moisture, then turning the meat and rubbing the cure into it.

2. Remove the pork, wash and dry it well, then hang in a cool, dark and dry place or the fridge for at least 7 days or up to 28 days. The bacon should be firm to the touch.

Makes 5kg (11lb)
Takes 30 minutes, plus 5 days to cure and 7-28 days to hang
This bacon can be sliced as needed, or cut into 'chops' 5cm (2in) thick and grilled or fried like rashers, but for a little longer because of their thickness.

A note on saltpetre and curing salts

Potassium nitrate is the active ingredient that stops meat from turning grey as it cures. The food grade version of this is called saltpetre, which can be bought from specialist retailers online.

Although saltpetre can be used perfectly safely at a very diluted concentrate, using too much can be potentially harmful, so extreme caution and exact measuring is essential. We use saltpetre in our cures at the farm, however we've not included it in the recipes in this book as it's not essential for curing meat and is used purely for appearances' sake and to keep a nice pink colour.

In fact, adding 'a pinch for luck' of saltpetre could prove unsafe, which is why we don't recommend using saltpetre in the recipes in this book. Instead, you can either buy curing salt, which is a pre-mixed formula of salt and nitrates or, better still, we suggest asking your butcher. If he makes his own bacon, he can supply you with some of his own cure, which will have been made from an exact mix of salt and saltpetre —the two basic ingredients of a professional cure.

Sel rose is a weaker version of curing salt, containing saltpetre and colourants, and is more suitable for retaining and enhancing the colour of pâtés and terrines than to use when curing particularly large pieces of meat.

Baked bacon joint

Once you've made your cured, set bacon, why not bake a whole piece for a special dinner? Score the skin and place the joint in a low oven, around 150°C/300°F/gas mark 2, until the flesh is beautifully tender and you have crisp, salty crackling. Serve with Cumberland sauce (see page 282), stewed lentils and a few vegetables.

Ginger Pig pancetta

2.5kg (5lb 8oz) boneless belly of pork (boned weight)

½ lemon

1 garlic clove, cut in half

For the cure

125g (4½ oz) salt

25g (1oz) demerara sugar

1 tsp pink peppercorns, crushed

4 juniper berries, crushed

4 bay leaves

1. Rub all over the pork with the cut side of the lemon, then do the same with the garlic clove.

2. To make the cure, mix the salt and sugar together very thoroughly, then combine with the peppercorns and juniper berries. Work the mixture into the flesh of the pork with your hands, ensuring that everything gets covered.

3. Rub the bay leaves between the palms of your hands to release the oils, then place them on top of the pork flesh.

4. Place the pork skin-side down in a large plastic box, cover with a sheet of paper or a towel and leave in the fridge for 4 days.

5. Using kitchen paper, brush off as much of the cure as you can. Wrap the pancetta in muslin, then hang in a cool and pest-free place, or put it in the fridge, for 2–4 days. (It will need less time if hung.)

6. To serve, slice thinly with a very sharp knife. The pancetta will keep in the fridge for 7–10 days.

Makes 1.5 kg (3lb 5oz)

Takes 30 minutes, plus 4 days to cure and 2-4 days to hang

Traditionally, pancetta is rolled, but I prefer it flat because this makes the preparation of it simpler and faster. It's also easier to slice and chop into cubes, which is useful for starting off risottos, casseroles and sauces.

Sweet-cured shoulder of pork

2kg (4lb 8oz) deboned and rolled shoulder of pork (see recipe introduction)

For the cure
280g (10oz) curing salt
300g (10½oz) soft brown sugar

1. Place the cure ingredients in a plastic container large enough to hold the pork. Add 2–3 litres (3½–5¼ pints) of cold water and stir gently with a wooden spoon until both salt and sugar have dissolved.

2. Place the pork in the brine and sit a weighted plastic container on top to keep it submerged. Place in the fridge for 10 days and turn daily.

3. Remove the pork and rinse in cold water. Pat dry, wrap in muslin and hang in a cool, dark place or the fridge for 14 days.

4. Cook as for the roasting ham on page 28, weighing your pork and cooking for 30 minutes per 500g (1lb 2oz).

Serves 8
Takes 40 minutes, plus 10 days to cure and 14 days to hang
Ask your butcher to bone, roll and tie a whole shoulder of pork. You can then get him to cut off a 2kg (4lb 8oz) piece ready for curing. The remainder can be roasted.

Dry-cured & smoked ham hock

2 ham hocks about 2–2.3kg (4lb 8oz–5lb 1oz) in total

For the cure
100g (3½oz) curing salt
25g (1oz) molasses sugar
2 bay leaves, chopped
6 peppercorns, crushed

1. Combine the cure ingredients in a large plastic container. Add the hocks and rub vigorously with the cure, filling all the cracks and crevices. Place in the fridge for 7 days, turning daily and draining off any excess liquid.

2. When ready, rinse the hocks in cold water, dry well and hang for 1 day. Place in a smoker and smoke according to the manufacturer's instructions.

Takes 30 minutes, plus 7 days to cure, 1 day to hang plus the time specified for your home smoker
At the farm we have a machine in which the hocks are smoked and dried. The smoking part of this recipe can only be done if you have a home smoker, or know a friendly farmer with a similar machine.

Cured and dried pig's cheeks

2 pig's cheeks, skin on

400g (14oz) curing salt

100g (3½oz) soft brown sugar

2 garlic cloves, crushed and peeled

leaves from 2 sprigs of thyme, roughly chopped

1 tsp fennel seeds, crushed

4 black peppercorns

1. Trim any knobbly white bits (the glands) from the cheeks and discard them.

2. Mix together the salt and sugar. Place half in a plastic container and vigorously rub the cheeks with it. Add the remaining salt mixture, then place in the fridge for 7 days. Turn daily, draining off any liquid and rubbing in the salt mixture.

3. When ready, rinse well and soak in a large bowl of water for 1 hour. Remove and dry.

4. Using a pestle and mortar, pound the garlic, thyme, fennel seeds and pepper. Rub the mixture vigorously all over the cheeks. Wrap in muslin and hang in a cool, dark place or the fridge for 20 days.

5. Slice the cheeks very thinly and pan-fry or grill for two minutes on each side for the wickedest and sweetest bacon.

Serves 2

Takes 1¾ hours, plus 7 days to cure and 20 days to hang

This recipe comes from Italy, where it is known as guanciale *or Roman bacon. A grilled slice makes an excellent addition to any burger, as the sweet fat adds moisture and wonderful flavour.*

Home-made cooking chorizo

1kg (2lb 4oz) shoulder of
pork, roughly diced
(N.B. if making a chorizo
'loaf' rather than sausages,
make sure the pork you
use contains 25% fat)
375g (13oz) skinless pork
back fat, roughly chopped
4 tsp table salt
2 tsp demerara sugar
4 garlic cloves, crushed,
peeled and finely minced
50g (2oz) smoked paprika
1 tbsp hot paprika

1. Using your hands or a food processor, mix all the ingredients together for at least 5 minutes, until thoroughly combined. The mixture is ready when you notice tiny white strands starting to form within it.

2. If you are using a sausage-making machine, pass this mixture twice through a mincer on a medium to coarse setting, then use it to fill natural sausage casings according to the manufacturer's instructions. Twist the filled casings at regular intervals to make linked sausages, then cover and place in the fridge for 12 hours so that the flavour can develop. Use within 3 days or freeze immediately.

3. If you are not using a sausage-making machine and would like to make a chorizo 'loaf', simply pack the pork mixture into an airtight container, pressing a layer of clingfilm flush against the surface to ensure it has no contact with the air. Place in the fridge for 24 hours so that the flavour can develop. Use within 2 days, or divide into manageable portions, cover in clingfilm and freeze for up to 2 months.

Makes 1.5 kg (3lb 5oz)
Takes 1 hours, plus 12 hours to chill (sausages) or 15 minutes, plus 24 hours to chill (chorizo 'loaf')

Cooking chorizo is different from cured chorizo in that it cannot be eaten raw. The basic spicy mince mixture can be formed into a loaf, left to mature, then simply sliced or shaped into little meatballs. After that, it can be fried to add to other dishes, sautéed with vegetables and potatoes, or barbecued.

If you'd prefer to make sausages, you will need a mincer, a sausage-making machine and sausage casings, all of which can be bought from www.sausagemaking.org. If you happen to have access to a cold smoker, pop the finished sausages in there for about four hours – it makes them taste even better.

Lardo

500–750g (1lb 2oz–1lb 10oz) pork back fat, skin on, at least 5cm (2in) thick

For the cure
4 tbsp coarse sea salt
2 tsp brown sugar
leaves from 2 sprigs of rosemary
4 bay leaves
2 garlic cloves, bashed twice with a rolling pin

1. Place the fat in a non-reactive container. Combine the cure ingredients in a bowl, then rub them all over the fat. Cover with clingfilm, sit a heavy weight on top and place in the fridge for 15–20 days, turning the fat every 2–3 days.

2. Rinse the fat under running water to remove the cure, then dry thoroughly with kitchen paper. Using a strong skewer, poke a hole in one corner of the fat and thread a length of string through it (you might need to push it through with the skewer). Knot the ends of the string, then hang the fat in a cool, dark place for 21 days. A cellar or dry, dark shed work well, but at a push you can place the fat skin side down on a plate, cover with a bowl and leave in the fridge for the same amount of time. Check every few days, and use kitchen paper to mop up any liquid.

3. To serve, slice very thinly. The easiest way of doing this is to run a vegetable peeler across the fat (keeping the skin side down).

Makes 500–750g (1lb 2oz–1lb 10oz)
Takes 15 minutes, plus 20 days to cure and 21 days to hang

A Tuscan speciality, lardo is a thick piece of fat taken from the back of a pig, which is cured for several weeks. It is then sliced very thinly to be served with warm bread, or wrapped around grissini for a simple appetizer to accompany drinks. It's a useful ingredient too, providing a porky, salty hit to various dishes: use thin slices to bard meat; melt it to sauté potatoes; or chop finely and stir into cooked Savoy cabbage or greens. The difficult part is finding a big enough piece of fat, so the recipe is best made during the autumn, when pigs have the most fat. You'll only be able to get the fat from a good butcher or farm, and you might need to request it in advance to ensure you get a piece thick enough.

Curing beef, veal & lamb

In times past, a family or group of villagers would kill a selected animal, then share the meat between them. What could not be consumed quickly was cured with salt and spices, then carefully stored and eked out over the lean winter months. Most animals were considered worthy of curing, hence the old saying: 'If it moves, it can be cured.' However, beef, veal and lamb were the most usual choices.

The practice of curing meat is common to many countries, even today – the main difference is in the name of the finished product. Americans love their beef jerky, and Italians their bresaola, while South Africans eat the same thing but call it biltong and make it from zebra meat as well as beef. Cured veal and lamb products are less commonplace, but they do exist. Cured veal can be found in fine French delicatessens, and the Italians make a lamb prosciutto, though it is something of a rarity and rather expensive.

High-altitude areas, such as in the Alps and high altitudes of South America, usually make very good cured meats because the air is dry and the daily temperature range is narrow, which ensures a steady cure. Hotter countries tend to finish the air-curing process in caves or cellars, where the temperature has greater consistency.

Spiced leg-of-mutton-cut beef

2kg (4lb 8oz) leg-of-mutton-cut beef joint

4 shallots, peeled and cut into quarters

1 head of garlic, peeled

2 red chillies

6 tbsp olive oil

2 tsp Dijon mustard

leaves from 1 bunch of flat leaf parsley, chopped

For the cure

200g (7oz) curing salt

125g (4½oz) demerara sugar

1 tsp spiced pepper

1 tsp ground cloves

1 tsp ground cumin

½ tsp allspice

freshly ground black pepper

2 bay leaves, chopped

1. Combine the cure ingredients in a bowl, then rub them into the beef. Place in a plastic container and leave in the fridge for 6 days. Turn the beef daily draining off any liquid and rubbing in the cure.

2. When ready, rinse the beef under running water. Dry well, then wrap in muslin and hang in the fridge overnight, then hang somewhere cool or keep in the fridge for at least 7 days and up to 14 days.

3. Heat a large saucepan of water until boiling, then add the shallots, head of garlic and chillies. Place the beef in the pan, making sure it is submerged, then cover and simmer really gently for 3 hours. Remove the beef and set aside to rest in a warm place for 10 minutes.

4. Meanwhile, separate the garlic cloves, snip the end off each one and squeeze the pulp into a blender. Peel and add the shallots, toss in the chillies and blend to a smooth paste. Add the olive oil and mustard and whiz until emulsified.

5. Put the parsley into a bowl, add the emulsified mixture and stir well.

6. Carve the beef and serve topped with a spoonful of the spicy sauce.

Serves 8

Takes 30 minutes, plus 6 days to cure, 8-15 days to hang and 3½ hours to cook

The beef used for this recipe is cut from inside the shoulder of the forequarter. The shape of the muscle resembles a leg of mutton, hence the name of the cut. The meat is both lean and fine-textured, which makes it ideal for slow cooking.

Dry-cured rump cap of beef

1 kg (2lb 4oz) rump cap of beef

For the cure
140g (5oz) curing salt
1 tsp chilli flakes
1 tsp sweet paprika
1 tsp mustard seeds, crushed
1 tsp garlic salt
1 tsp oregano

1. Trim the beef of any excess fat and place in a plastic container.

2. Mix the cure ingredients in a bowl, pour over the beef and rub in vigorously. Place in the fridge for 5 days. Turn daily, draining off any liquid, and rubbing the meat with the cure.

3. When ready, wipe off the cure. Wrap in muslin and hang in a cool, dark place, such as a cellar or larder, or in the fridge for 21 days, checking the beef from time to time for signs of mould, scraping off any that appears.

4. To serve, slice very finely, preferably using a commercial slicer if you can persuade your butcher to cut it for you.

5. Lay a thin layer of the beef over a plate, scatter with peppery rocket and a drizzle of fine olive oil for an elegant starter.

Serves 8
Takes 20 minutes, plus 5 days to cure and 21 days to hang
As its name suggests, a rump cap of beef sits directly over the rump, which means it is richly marbled with fat. The Brazilians call it a picanha, *and often cut it into thick slices, which they cook like steaks. In my version here, it is dry-cured and spiced up to add a twist of fiery flavour.*

Dry-cured veal with rosemary & lemon

1 kg (2lb 4oz) veal shoulder (ask your butcher to try to seam out one muscle)
75g (2½oz) curing salt
leaves from 1 sprig of rosemary, finely chopped
zest and juice of 2 lemons
freshly ground black pepper

1. Trim the veal of any excess sinew or fat. Place in a non-reactive bowl and generously rub all over with the salt, pushing it into any crevices. Place in the fridge for 4 days. Turn the meat daily, draining off any liquid and rubbing it with any salt that's fallen to the bottom of the bowl.

2. When ready, wipe off the cure. Place the rosemary in a bowl, add the lemon zest, juice and pepper and mix well. Spread the mixture on a flat surface and roll the veal in it, pressing it in and working it into the crevices. Put the meat on a plate and place in the fridge for 16 days. Turn it daily, rolling the veal in any herb mixture that falls off.

3. When ready, sharpen your knife and slice the veal very finely, or persuade your butcher to do the job for you on a commercial slicer. Serve it in a very thin layer on a plate.

Serves 6
Takes 40 minutes, plus 20 days to cure
Seaming out meat is a French method of butchery and delivers a neat joint that stays together better during curing.

Corned beef

2kg (4lb 8oz) boneless, unrolled brisket, or 2kg (4lb 8oz) fore rib cap

For the brine
400g (14oz) curing salt
100g (3½oz) demerara sugar
1 tsp mustard seeds
1 tsp coriander seeds
5 cloves

1. Put the brine ingredients into a very large pan and add 4 litres (7 pints) of water. Bring to the boil, stirring until the salt and sugar have dissolved. Allow to cool to room temperature for about 2 hours and then refrigerate for at least 2 hours or overnight until completely cold.

2. Place the beef in a snug-fitting non-reactive container with a lid, pour the cold brine over it and leave in the fridge for 7 days, turning it daily.

3. Drain the beef, discarding the brine, and soak in fresh water for 4 hours to remove the excess salt.

4. Place the beef in a large saucepan, cover with fresh water and bring to a gentle simmer (90°C/195°F). Simmer for 4 hours, until completely tender. Transfer the beef to a board and use the back of a knife to scrape off any jellied fat. At this point you can press the beef into a slicing loaf (see recipe introduction) or carve as it is. It's great served warm with potatoes, greens and mustard.

5. To continue the process of making corned beef, carefully pull the hot meat into a few pieces roughly as wide as a 1kg (2lb) loaf tin. Line the tin with clingfilm, leaving a generous overhang, then tightly layer the meat in it, ensuring that the grain of it runs the length of the tin. Keep layering until the tin looks a little overfull, then fold the clingfilm over it and place a board and some heavy weights on top. Leave to set in the fridge for 24 hours.

Makes 1.5kg (3lb 5oz)
Takes at least 8 hours, plus 7 days to cure, 5 hours to cook and 24 hours to set

A far cry from the tinned stuff, proper corned beef should be made with whole cuts of beef, which are brined and simmered before being pressed. Cuts such as brisket or fore rib cap are good, as the fat and connective tissue break down during the long, slow cooking to produce a wonderfully succulent end result. At the farm we use a large metal press to compact the cooked beef into a slicing loaf, but a loaf tin and a few heavy books are more than adequate for pressing beef in the home kitchen.

Pastrami

2kg (4lb 8oz) boneless, unrolled brisket or 2kg (4lb 8oz) fore rib cap

For the brine
400g (14oz) curing salt
100g (3½oz) demerara sugar
1 tsp mustard seeds
1 tsp coriander seeds
5 cloves

For the coating
3 tbsp coarsely ground black pepper
1 tbsp English mustard powder
75ml (3fl oz) malt vinegar

1. Follow steps 1–4 of the recipe for Corned beef (see page 42).

2. Mix the coating ingredients together and press them right into the the beef while it is still hot. Don't worry too much about the ends, as these will be sliced off.

3. Line a 1kg (2lb) loaf tin with clingfilm, leaving a generous overhang. Press the brisket into it, then fold the clingfilm over it and place a board and some heavy weights on top. Leave to set in the fridge for 24 hours before turning out and slicing.

Makes 1.5kg (3lb 5oz)
Takes at least 8 hours, plus 7 days to cure, 5 hours to cook and overnight setting

The name 'pastrami' derives from a Romanian word used to describe meat (usually beef) that has been brined, smoked and cooked. The most popular cut used for it is beef brisket.

I first had pastrami (on rye) at Katz's Delicatessen in New York, where they have been selling it for the last 120 years. And it was there that I felt inspired to start making pastrami back in Yorkshire.

To be truly authentic, pastrami should be cold-smoked after curing and before it is cooked. This not only adds flavour, but also contributes to its famous texture, which allows it to be sliced so beautifully.

If you or anyone you know has a cold-smoking cabinet at home, or if you live close to an obliging smokehouse, six hours of cold-smoking before cooking makes the finished product the real deal (though it is still a fine cured meat without).

Dry-cured lamb

2kg (4lb 8oz) tunnel-
boned leg of lamb

For the cure
600g (1lb 5oz) curing salt
400g (14oz) golden caster
sugar

1. Combine the cure ingredients in a bowl, then rub the mixture all over the lamb, packing it into the boned-out cavity. Place the meat in a plastic container and leave in the fridge for 12 days. Every 3 days drain away the liquid and rub the meat with the salt mixture.

2. When ready, rinse the lamb in cold water and dry well. Wrap in muslin and tie securely with string.

3. Hang the lamb in a cool, dark place with a good airflow for 6 weeks: in the winter a larder or cellar is ideal, but during a hot summer, a fridge is the best place. When ready, unwrap the meat and carve very thin slices, just as you would a cured ham.

Serves 6
Takes 30 minutes, plus 12 days to cure and 6 weeks to hang
The unusual cure used here is favoured in northern Europe, where there is a long tradition of curing every type of food. The lamb acquires a salty, mellow flavour and is something of a delicacy these days because it is no longer widely made. It is great served in thin slices with a glass of red wine.

Traditionally, dry-cured lamb is served on rye bread with a little horseradish or mustard, but it also can be used to replace ham in a pea and ham soup, adding a different twist to an old favourite.

Smoking

Smoking is commonly believed to be a preserving technique in its own right, but is, in fact, just a process for adding flavour to cured meat and fish. Even when used in small quantities, smoke can flavour a whole dish and combine to great effect with salty cures.

It is a myth that you can simply hang something to smoke in a chimney flue. While this would certainly dry the food, it would make for a sad, soot-covered and potentially harmful end result. Instead, you need an inglenook fireplace, which is large enough to hang the meat in without fear of contamination from soot or, ideally, a proper smoking cabinet or kiln.

Smoked foods are either hot- or cold-smoked. The cold process adds a smoky flavour and perhaps dries the meat or fish a little, while hot-smoking is done closer to the heat source of the smoke so that the meat or fish is cooked as well as flavoured.

There are many different sorts of domestic smoker available but perhaps one of the easiest to use (and clean) is a hot smoker such as the one pictured opposite. It can be used on the hob, on a barbecue, and even on a camp fire. Follow the manufacturer's instructions, but smoking is simple. All you need to do is to put a teaspoon of finely cut culinary wood chips (available online) under the drip tray in the base of the smoker and then put the meat, fish or vegetables that you want to smoke on the wire rack above it. After a relatively short time cooking over a medium heat, your delicious smoked food will be ready to serve. After the smoker has cooled down it can even be cleaned in the dishwasher.

Poultry and game

Smoking adds great flavour to meat. Both poultry and game, such as venison or pheasant breasts, are well suited to this technique as it adds flavour while also keeping the meat tender. However, don't forget there are other ways to preserve poultry and game, some examples of which can be found overleaf.

Brined chicken

2kg (4lb 8oz) really fresh chicken

For the brine

100g (3½oz) brown sugar
175g (6oz) table salt
1 tbsp black peppercorns
1 tsp caraway seeds
2 cloves
1 tsp allspice
1 cinnamon stick
2 star anise
1 tbsp mustard seeds
1 onion, peeled and chopped
5cm (2in) piece of fresh root ginger, peeled and sliced
4 garlic cloves, crushed, peeled and sliced
3 tbsp black treacle
3 tbsp soy sauce
zest and juice of 1 lemon

For the glaze

50g (2oz) butter
2 tbsp soy sauce

1. Place all the brine ingredients in a large saucepan and add 1 litre (1¾ pints) of water. Heat, stirring constantly with a wooden spoon, until all the sugar and salt have dissolved. Transfer the liquid to a plastic container. Add 2 litres (3½ pints) of water, mix well and set aside until completely cold. You must never put your chicken into a warm brine mix.

2. Untruss the chicken and remove the giblets, then submerge the bird in the cold brine. Place a small plastic lid or tray on the bird and sit a weight on top to keep it totally submerged. Place in the fridge or a cold place for 2 days, turning the bird occasionally.

3. Drain the chicken for at least 1 hour before cooking and allow it to reach room temperature. Preheat the oven to 180°C/350°F/gas mark 4. Weigh your chicken and calculate its cooking time (20 minutes per 500g/1lb 2oz, plus 20 minutes).

4. Heat the glaze ingredients in a small pan and mix well. Use kitchen paper to dry it, then place the chicken in a roasting tin and brush some of the glaze all over it. Roast for 20 minutes, then lower the temperature to 170°C/325°F/gas mark 3, brush again with the glaze and cook for the remaining time.

5. When cooked, transfer the bird to a warm plate, cover with foil and rest for 15 minutes.

6. Meanwhile, make a sauce by adding 200ml (7fl oz) of water to the chicken juices in the roasting tin. Place on the hob and simmer for 5 minutes, reducing the liquid by half. Serve spooned over the sliced chicken.

Serves 6

Takes 2¾ hours, plus 2 days to cure and 3 hours to cook

You must always brine in a non-reactive container because otherwise it will erode and tarnish the taste of the brine with rust. I suggest you buy a large plastic storage box, bucket or sturdy zip-lock bag, but do check that it will fit in your fridge.

Brining a chicken adds moisture to the flesh, and the spices give extra flavour that makes a big difference when the bird is roasted. This technique can also be used with a turkey. A bird weighing 4–5kg (8lb 13oz–11lb) will need double the quantities listed.

Confits

Confit is a piece of meat – usually pork, duck or goose – which is cooked in its own fat, then stored in the same fat to preserve it. The principles of making confits are similar to those for curing bacon or ham. In both cases, a dry salt cure is used to draw moisture out of the meat, but for a confit it is then slow-cooked and preserved in fat, where it will keep for months or even years. Like a standard bacon cure, a confit cure contains sugar (usually brown) and also includes aromatics, such as bay leaves and garlic, because they add pep to cut through the rich fat.

Fat

Goose and duck fat are traditionally used to make confits because they add body and flavour as well as preserving the meat. Both are now readily available from butchers, delis and supermarkets, but using them can be costly as a large amount is needed to cover whatever you're preserving. They can be picked up more cheaply in France, but if a trip to the Continent isn't on the cards, it's still worth buying the fat over here. Alternatively, lard bought from a good butcher makes a cheap and delicious alternative. We use rendered fat from our rare-breed pigs, which works a treat and smells divine when cooking.

Meat

Rich meats with good-tasting fat make for the best confit, so duck, goose and pork tend to be the most popular choices. Our recipe for these is on page 52, and here are some ideas for serving them.

• Serve the meat hot, with mash or lentils, greens and pickled red cabbage to cut through the richness.

• Pick the meat from the bones for salad. Redcurrants, blackberries, slices of apple or slivers of red onion add a touch of sharpness to offset the fat, as do peppery leaves, such as rocket and watercress. Tender lentils make a good addition.

• Sweat an onion and some garlic in a little fat until tender, then add a handful of peeled, chopped plum tomatoes. Flake 2 duck legs, 1 goose leg or 500g (1lb 2oz) of the pork into the pan, add 100ml (3½fl oz) of stock and cook gently for 4–5 minutes, until you have a rich, meaty ragù. Serve this with pasta, rice or potatoes, or a green salad if preferred.

Pork, duck or goose confit

1.3kg (3lb) belly of pork on the bone or 4 large duck legs or 2 goose legs

1.5kg (3lb 5oz) rendered pork, duck or goose fat (use whichever type you have available – it doesn't have to 'match' the meat)

For the cure

2 tbsp coarse sea salt

1 heaped tbsp brown sugar

4 bay leaves, bruised by rolling them gently in your hands

2 star anise

1. Combine all the cure ingredients in a bowl. Place your chosen meat in a non-reactive container and rub the cure all over it, ensuring that the bay and star anise get some contact with the flesh. Cover loosely and place in the fridge for at least 12 hours and up to 18 hours.

2. Once the curing time is up, brush any excess cure from the meat and transfer to a roasting tin just big enough to fit everything snugly in one layer. Preheat the oven to 150°C/300°F/gas mark 2. Dollop the fat over the meat and place in the oven until the fat melts (around 10 minutes). After that, spoon the fat all over the meat, adding a little more fat (or flavourless oil, such as groundnut) if necessary to cover it completely. Return the meat to the oven and cook for 3 hours, checking occasionally to make sure it is still covered with fat.

3. Allow the meat to cool a little before handling it, then place in a large, sterilized jar or container (see page 222). Be careful not to break off the flesh at this point, as it is very soft and tender. Pour the fat over the meat, seal the container and store in a cool, dark place or the fridge. Alternatively, place the meat in a vacuum bag with 6 tablespoons of fat, then seal.

4. When you want to use the meat, allow it to come up to room temperature, then dig it out of its fat and place in a roasting tin. Roast at 200°C/400°F/gas mark 6 until the skin is crisp and the flesh heated through – around 20 minutes for duck legs and 30 minutes for belly of pork or goose legs. You can then serve it as suggested on page 51.

Serves various numbers as a main course: the pork belly serves 4; each duck leg serves 1; each goose leg makes a moderate-sized portion for 1 person

Takes 15 minutes, plus 12-18 hours to cure and 5 hours to cook

Making confit is not an exact science: it needs just enough salt and sugar to draw out some of the moisture from the meat, and enough pork, duck or goose fat to completely cover the meat as it cooks. If you're able to cook the meat in fat from the same animal, then all the better, but there's absolutely no harm in using whatever you have available.

Confit meat is wonderfully versatile and a fantastic store-cupboard staple. With jars of it tucked away, you'll always have the makings of a flavoursome meal, and it can be ready within minutes.

Pâtés &
terrines

Pâtés & terrines

Farmhouse living and eating is about thrift. It is not meanness or paucity, but healthy respect for what nature provides and all that you can make from it. Pâtés and terrines are the embodiment of this ethic, often using the less popular parts of an animal, such as liver, kidneys, tongue and trotters, and preserving them for months.

Classically there are three names for pâtés/terrines: pâté that is cooked/shaped in a ramekin, jar or bowl; pâté en terrine that is cooked in an ovenproof dish often with straight sides; pâté en croute, which is wrapped in pastry. The first two dishes' names are often used interchangeably. Mostly made from meat or offal, pâtés can also be made from fish and vegetables but at The Ginger Pig we like to use our produce.

Terrine dishes tend to be made from robust materials, such as cast iron or glazed earthenware, because they conduct heat well, helping cook the contents evenly. They have a tight-fitting lid which, as the mixture inside expands during cooking, presses down to keep the pâté in shape and give it a good, tight texture. Without the weight, the mixture expands too much and takes in air and moisture, making it difficult to slice and serve, and more perishable. If you don't have a terrine dish, use a loaf tin. After filling, wrap it tightly in foil and baking parchment, place in a roasting tin half-filled with water and cook. After cooking, place a board and a heavy weight on top of the wrapped tin and leave until cold.

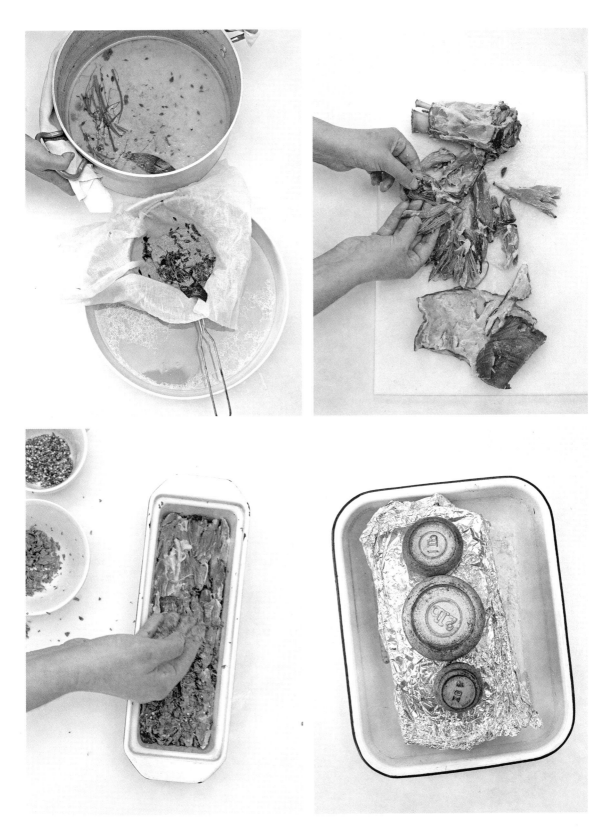

Pork & walnut pâté

600g (1lb 5oz) minced belly of pork

250g (9oz) minced shoulder of pork

200g (7oz) minced lamb's liver

freshly ground black pepper

sea salt

6 juniper berries, crushed

2 garlic cloves, crushed, peeled and diced

pinch of mace

175g (6oz) chopped walnuts

1 egg

75ml (3fl oz) Armagnac

1. Preheat the oven to 170°C/325°F/gas mark 3 and lightly oil a 900g (2lb) terrine dish or loaf tin.

2. Place all the minced meat in a large bowl and add some seasoning, then the juniper berries, garlic and mace. Mix with your hands to combine evenly.

3. Add the walnuts, egg and Armagnac, mix well and place in the oiled container. Press the mixture down and give the container a few taps on the work surface to remove any air pockets.

4. Cover the dish with its lid, or tightly wrap the loaf tin with baking parchment and foil. Place the container in a roasting tin and pour enough hot water around it to reach halfway up the sides. Cook in the oven for 1–1½ hours, until a metal skewer inserted in the middle comes out piping hot.

5. When ready, if you've used a loaf tin, place a weight on top of the foil to compress the pâté, then set aside to cool. Once cold, place in the fridge overnight.

6. Serve in slices with a small leaf salad and some cornichons. The first slice is always the most difficult to remove and then it is far easier to ease out.

Serves 10–12

Takes 3 hours, plus overnight setting

Ask your butcher to mince the belly of pork for you, or do it yourself by roughly chopping it and then blitzing in a food processor. If you'd like a strongly flavoured pâté, replace the lamb's livers with the same weight of pig's liver.

Chicken & trotters in aspic

3 pig's trotters, cleaned and hair removed

2 celery sticks, chopped

2 carrots, peeled and chopped into thirds

2 onions, peeled and quartered

1 leek, white part only, sliced into large rounds

3 bay leaves

1 sprig of rosemary

1 star anise

handful of flat leaf parsley

20 black peppercorns

2 tsp salt

2 large chicken legs

1. Place the trotters in a pan of boiling water and simmer for 5 minutes. Drain, discarding the liquid.

2. Put the trotters into a stock pot along with all the other ingredients, except the chicken legs. Add 4 litres (7 pints) of water, bring to the boil, then simmer gently for 2 hours with the lid off. Skim the surface now and then to remove any scum or impurities.

3. Add the chicken legs and simmer very gently for 1 hour.

4. Strain through a colander, reserving the stock. Put the chicken legs, trotters and 2 pieces of carrot to one side and discard the rest of the solids.

5. Put the stock back on the stove and bring to a rolling boil. Reduce for 10 minutes.

6. Meanwhile, flake the chicken and trotter meat (there won't be much on the trotters), discarding the skin and bones. Slice the reserved carrot pieces into very fine rounds.

7. Taste the reduced stock and season it well as it will lose a little flavour when it chills in the next step.

8. Divide the meat and carrot between 8 ramekins and pour in enough stock to cover them. Chill in the fridge, making sure the dishes are level so that the aspic sets evenly.

9. To serve, run a knife around the edge of the aspic, invert each dish onto a plate and shake gently until the moulded meat and jelly come out. Serve with pickle and farmhouse white bread and butter.

Serves 8

Takes 4½ hours, plus overnight setting

The result in this case is soft, fragrant chicken meat set in a rich, meaty, delicious jelly. Like a good stock, the jelly becomes liquid again if heated, and isn't at all rubbery when set. Great as a starter or light lunch.

Layered terrine

4 pheasant breast fillets

6 wood pigeon breast fillets

4 wild duck breast fillets

sea salt

freshly ground black pepper

sunflower oil, for frying

24 rashers of long streaky bacon, rind removed

For the forcemeat

600g (1lb 5oz) minced pork with a good amount of fat

leaves from 2 sprigs of thyme, chopped

1 scant tsp fine salt

1 egg

6 dried apricots, finely chopped

6 tbsp thick chicken or trotter stock

For the chicken liver pâté

75g (2½oz) butter

300g (10½oz) very fresh chicken livers, trimmed

1 large banana shallot, peeled and finely chopped

1 garlic clove, crushed, peeled and finely chopped

50ml (2fl oz) brandy

100ml (3½fl oz) double cream

1. Put the game fillets on a board and season all over. Heat the oil in a large pan and, when very hot, sear the fillets in batches. You want to brown them without cooking. Set aside.

2. Put all the forcemeat ingredients in a bowl and mix well.

3. Line a 900g (2lb) terrine dish with the bacon, arranging it widthways, slightly overlapping, and overhanging the sides.

4. To make the pâté, put the butter in a large, hot frying pan. When it foams, add the chicken livers, seasoning with salt. Sauté until browned but not cooked, then remove from the pan. Lower the heat, add the shallot and garlic and cook gently without colouring until soft. Deglaze the pan with the brandy and heat for a few minutes to burn off the alcohol. Transfer to a blender, add the cream and chicken livers and whiz until smooth.

5. Pour the pâté into the lined dish. Take one-third of the forcemeat, flatten it into chunks and lay them on top of the pâté. Arrange half the game on top, then cover with forcemeat as before. Repeat these layers once more. Fold the overhanging bacon over the terrine and put the lid on: it should sit on the meat so that it will compact the layers as they expand. Bake in a preheated oven at 170°C/325°F/gas mark 3 for 2 hours, until a metal skewer inserted in the middle comes out piping hot.

6. Set aside to cool. Once cold, place in the fridge overnight. To turn out, run a knife around the edge of the terrine and invert onto a plate. Slice with your sharpest knife.

Serves 10

Takes 3 hours, plus overnight setting

Although the ingredient list is long, this terrine is a really simple starter to prepare and stunning to serve. Make the pâté just before you assemble the whole thing as it needs to set in the dish, not before. If you don't have a terrine dish, use a similar-sized loaf tin, wrap it tightly in foil and baking parchment and cook in a bain-marie. As soon as it comes out of the oven, put a board over it and place a heavy weight on top – this will have the same compacting effect as the terrine lid.

Smoked pig's cheek terrine

600g (1lb 5oz) smoked pig's cheek

250g (9oz) onions, peeled and chopped

1 garlic clove, crushed, peeled and chopped

2 celery sticks, chopped

25g (1oz) butter

350g (12oz) chicken or pig's liver, chopped

100ml (3½fl oz) milk

1 tsp salt

½ tsp freshly ground white pepper

½ tsp freshly ground black pepper

½ tsp freshly grated nutmeg

1 tbsp chopped flat leaf parsley

1 small egg, beaten

100g (3½oz) streaky bacon

1. Roughly chop the pig's cheek, including the skin, and place in a pan. Add just enough water to cover, then simmer with a lid on for 2 hours, or in a preheated oven at 180°C/350°F/gas mark 4.

2. Put the onions, garlic and celery in a frying pan with the butter and fry gently until soft. Add the liver and cook for 5 minutes, until browned on the outside.

3. Preheat the oven to 170°C/325°F/gas mark 3.

4. Place the pig's cheeks and 300ml (½ pint) of their cooking liquid in a food processor. Add the liver, milk, seasoning, nutmeg, parsley and egg and whiz until coarsely blended.

5. Lightly oil a 900g (2lb) terrine dish or loaf tin and add the pâté mixture. Tap the container a couple of times on the work surface to remove any air pockets. Lay the streaky bacon over the pâté, then cover with lid, or baking parchment and foil.

6. Place the terrine in a roasting tin and pour in enough hot water to come halfway up the sides. Cook in the oven for 1–1½ hours, until a metal skewer inserted in the middle comes out piping hot.

7. When ready, if you've used a loaf tin, place a weight on top of the foil to compress the pâté, then set aside to cool. Once cold, place in the fridge overnight. Slice and serve when ready.

Serves 10–12

Takes 4 hours, plus overnight setting

This is a very popular soft pâté bursting with rich, sweet and delicious smoky flavours. Classically, it is made with pig's liver, which delivers a strong, earthy flavour, but I prefer it made with chicken livers for a gentler, rounded-tasting pâté.

Ham & parsley terrine

2 ham hocks, about 2kg
(4lb 8oz)

1 pig's trotter, split in half

400ml (14fl oz) white wine

1 large bunch of flat leaf
parsley, leaves chopped
and stalks reserved

1 sprig of thyme

2 bay leaves

good pinch of salt

5 black peppercorns

1. Place the hocks and trotter in a saucepan, then add the wine and enough water to cover the meat. Cover with a lid and bring to the boil, occasionally skimming off any scum that comes to the surface. When boiling, add the parsley stalks, thyme, bay leaves, salt and peppercorns, then lower the heat and simmer gently for 2 hours.

2. Remove the ham hocks from the pan and set aside until cool enough to handle. Meanwhile, continue simmering the trotter, uncovered, until the stock is reduced by half.

3. Peel the skin and fat off the cooled ham hocks, discarding both. Pick the meat off the bones and shred by hand into a bowl.

4. Pass the contents of the trotter pan through a sieve, reserving the stock, then pass the stock through a sieve lined with muslin.

5. Lightly oil a 900g (2lb) terrine dish or loaf tin and add a layer of shredded ham about 5cm (2in) thick. Sprinkle with chopped parsley and a twist of black pepper. Repeat until the terrine is full, making sure the meat is firmly packed down and finishing with a generous layer of chopped parsley.

6. Carefully pour in the strained stock, which will be gelatinous thanks to the trotter. Gently tap the terrine on the work surface to remove any air pockets, then place in the fridge for at least 3 hours, but preferably overnight.

7. When ready, serve in slices with some mixed salad leaves and slices of fresh or toasted bread.

Serves 10–12

Takes 3 hours, plus overnight setting

Here is a traditional French terrine, using the sweet, juicy pink meat from ham hocks. In France the recipe is called jambon persillé.

Oxtail terrine

1 oxtail, cut into rounds

400ml (14fl oz) red wine

2 bay leaves

sea salt

freshly ground black pepper

1 tsp grain mustard

½ tsp English mustard powder

1 tsp Worcestershire sauce

4 celery sticks, diced

1. Place the oxtail in a saucepan with the wine, bay leaves and seasoning, then add just enough water to half-cover the meat. Bring to the boil, cover with a tight-fitting lid and simmer for 3 hours, checking every hour and adding more water if needed. When ready, the meat should easily part from the bone.

2. Remove the meat from the pan and, when cool enough to handle, pick the meat off the bones, discarding any fat or gristle. Chop roughly by hand and place in a bowl with both mustards, the Worcestershire sauce and seasoning. Mix well and place in a 900g (2lb) terrine dish or loaf tin.

3. Carefully skim the excess fat off the cooking liquid, then pass through a sieve lined with muslin. Return the liquid to the heat and reduce to about 400ml (14fl oz).

4. Meanwhile, place a layer of chopped celery on top of the filled terrine. Slowly pour in the reduced liquid until it just covers the celery, leave to cool then place in the fridge and leave to set overnight.

Serves 8

Takes 3½ hours, plus 1 hour cooling and overnight setting

Robust and packed with deep, rich flavours, this is a hearty terrine, ideal for serving at lunch with a selection of tossed salad leaves, tomato salad and toasted sourdough bread.

Chicken liver pâté

200g (7oz) butter

1 large onion, peeled and chopped

2 garlic cloves, crushed, peeled and chopped

450g (1lb) chicken livers

sea salt

freshly ground black pepper

50ml (2fl oz) sherry or brandy

For the clarified butter

100g (3½ oz) butter

2 sprigs of thyme

1. Heat the butter in a large frying pan, add the onion and garlic and sauté gently over a low heat. Meanwhile, trim the livers of any veins or white bits and roughly chop. Add to the pan and cook until the pieces are just browned. Season, pour in the sherry or brandy and mix well.

2. Place the mixture in a food processor and whiz until creamy smooth. Transfer to a 900g (2lb) terrine dish or individual ramekins.

3. Make the clarified butter by gently melting the butter and, when liquid, with a steady hand pour off all the oil and discard the watery residue.

4. Place the thyme sprigs in the clarified butter and heat for 1 minute to infuse the flavour. Place the sprigs on top of the pâté, then pour the butter all over the top. When set, it will completely seal the pâté, allowing it to be kept for 4 days. Place in the fridge to cool and set for 2 hours.

5. When ready, turn out of the terrine or ramekins, cut into slices and serve with toast or oatcakes.

Serves 6

Takes 30 minutes, plus 2 hours setting

Deliciously simple and economical, this dish lends itself to lots of flavours. Try adding crumbled Stilton, chopped prunes or any other items you fancy.

Duck rillettes

1 duck carcass and
2 duck legs

100g (3½oz) stoned
prunes

50g (2oz) sultanas,
soaked overnight in 50ml
(2fl oz) brandy

sprig of flat leaf parsley,
to garnish

For the stock
400ml (14fl oz) white
wine

200ml (7fl oz) water

3 garlic cloves, crushed,
peeled and chopped

½ tsp allspice

2 bay leaves

2 sprigs of thyme

sea salt

freshly ground black
pepper

1. Place the duck carcass and legs in a saucepan, add all the stock ingredients and bring to the boil. Reduce to a gentle simmer, cover with a tight-fitting lid and cook for 1½ hours, stirring frequently and adding a little wine if more liquid is needed.

2. When ready, the meat should be falling off the bones, so take the pan off the heat and leave to cool. Pick over the carcass and legs and place all the meat and skin in a food processor. Add the prunes and blitz until roughly chopped.

3. Remove the bay leaves and thyme from the stock. Add 200ml (7fl oz) of the liquid to the meat, then stir in the sultanas and brandy. Spoon the mixture into a terrine dish or wide-necked jar, flatten the top and garnish with a sprig of parsley. Set aside to cool, then refrigerate for at least 2 hours, but preferably overnight.

Serves 6

Takes 2½ hours, plus 1 hour cooling

Rillettes is a type of pâté cooked in the natural fat of the animal, which ducks are well known for, making this a tasty pâté. Buy a whole duck and ask your butcher to cut off the breasts and legs, and to chop the carcass into four pieces. Use the legs and the carcass for this dish.

Mixed game pâté

600g (1lb 5oz) minced game meat (e.g. a mixture of grouse, partridge, pheasant, quail, rabbit or venison)

400g (14oz) minced fatty pork (shoulder or belly)

1 orange

sea salt

freshly ground black pepper

1 garlic clove, crushed, peeled and minced

1 tsp chopped thyme leaves

30ml (1fl oz) brandy

30ml (1fl oz) port

1. Preheat the oven to 170°C/325°F/gas mark 3.

2. Place the minced game and fatty pork in a large bowl. Add the zest of half the orange, then add all the other ingredients. Mix well with your hands as this gives the most even result.

3. Lightly oil a 900g (2lb) terrine dish or loaf tin and put the meat mixture in it. Thinly slice the unzested half of the orange, remove the pips and arrange the slices on top of the meat. Cover the dish with its lid, or tightly wrap the loaf tin with baking parchment and foil.

4. Place the container in a roasting tin and pour enough hot water around it to reach halfway up the sides. Cook in the oven for 1¾ hours, until a metal skewer inserted in the middle comes out piping hot.

5. When ready, if you've used a loaf tin, place a weight on top of the foil to compress the pâté, then set aside to cool. Once cold, place in the fridge overnight. Turn out of the container, then slice and serve.

Serves 10

Takes 2 hours, plus overnight setting

If you live in the country and the shooting season is in full swing, this recipe is ideal for using up the variety of game that may be landing at your back door. Play around with the quantities of each meat until you have a pâté that suits your taste.

Spiced rabbit pâté

1 rabbit, cut into joints

200g (7oz) belly of pork

4 shallots, diced

2 garlic cloves, crushed
and peeled

good pinch of allspice

½ tsp curry powder

3 blades of mace

sea salt

freshly ground black
pepper

300ml (½ pint) white
wine

200g (7oz) chicken thighs

50g (2oz) butter

leaves from 1 bunch of
sage, chopped

1. Place the rabbit joints and pork in a large saucepan. Add the shallots, garlic, spices, seasoning and wine, then pour in enough water to come halfway up the ingredients. Bring to the boil, then cover and simmer for 1 hour, adding more water if needed.

2. Add the chicken thighs and simmer for a further hour: the meat should be falling off the bones. Set aside to cool, then pick all the rabbit and chicken meat from the bones. Do this carefully as rabbits have very small, almost needle-like bones that you do not want in your pâté. Peel the skin off the pork and discard it. Chop all the meat by hand if you want a coarse pâté; if you want it smoother, blitz in a food processor, but do leave some texture.

3. Return the saucepan and its contents to the heat and reduce the liquid to about 200ml (7 fl oz). Place the liquid and vegetables in a blender and whiz until smooth.

4. Add the liquid to the meat mixture, taste and adjust the seasoning. Place in a 900g (2lb) terrine dish, loaf tin or wide-necked jar and press down with the back of a spoon.

5. Make the clarified butter by gently melting the butter and, when liquid, with a steady hand pour off all the oil and discard the watery residue.

6. Heat the butter, add the sage and cook for 2 minutes. Pour over the pâté and set aside to cool. Place in the fridge for at least 2 hours, but preferably overnight. Serve with crusty bread or hot toast and a salad.

Serves 6

Takes 3 hours, plus overnight chilling

The spices used in this pâté really enhance the subtle flavours of the rabbit. It's a pleasure to eat at any time of the year.

Rabbit, pork & prune terrine

1kg (2lb 4oz) boned saddles and hindquarters of rabbit

leaves from 1 bunch of flat leaf parsley, chopped

4 carrots, peeled and cut into 5cm (2in) sticks

400g (14oz) minced pork

175g (6oz) rabbit livers, finely chopped

50g (2oz) breadcrumbs

1 egg

leaves from 3 sprigs of thyme

leaves from 1 bunch of tarragon, chopped

2 garlic cloves, crushed, peeled and chopped

30ml (1fl oz) brandy

sea salt

freshly ground black pepper

320g (11oz) streaky bacon, rind removed

125g (4½oz) stoned prunes

1. Preheat the oven to 170°C/325°F/gas mark 3.

2. Lay the saddles and hindquarters out flat on a board, skin side down. Sprinkle a line of chopped parsley down the length of each piece and place the carrots on top. Season, then roll the meat around the carrots and set aside.

3. Place the minced pork and rabbit livers in a bowl, add the breadcrumbs, egg, herbs, garlic, brandy and seasoning and mix well by hand to get an even result.

4. Using the back of a knife, flatten and stretch each rasher of bacon. Use all but 3 or 4 slices to line a 450g (1lb) terrine dish or loaf tin, overlapping the pieces slightly and leaving the ends overhanging the edge.

5. Place just under half the pork mixture in the prepared dish and arrange the prunes in a row along the middle. Place the stuffed rabbit rolls in a layer over and around the prunes, then spread the remaining pork mixture on top and pack down until level. Fold the overhanging bacon up and over the terrine, then arrange the remaining bacon to completely cover the top. Cover the dish with its lid, or tightly wrap the loaf tin with baking parchment and foil. Place in a roasting tin and pour enough hot water around it to reach halfway up the sides. Cook in the oven for 1½ hours, until a metal skewer inserted in the middle comes out piping hot.

6. Set the terrine aside to cool, placing a weight on top of the foil if you've used a loaf tin. Once cold, place in the fridge overnight.

Serves 12

Takes 2 hours 20 minutes, plus overnight setting

Terrines are great for serving at dinner parties as a glamorous entrée with a pretty leaf salad, good bread and chutney, but they also make a good lunchtime dish, and are perfect for picnics because they travel so well.

It's easy to vary this recipe, swapping the rabbit for any other game you happen to have, and perhaps using different dried fruits, such as sultanas, figs or apricots.

Casseroles, stews & pan cooking

Casseroles, stews & pan-cooking

Suitable cuts for casseroles, stews and braises

Beef
Shin
Tail
Flank
Chuck
Clod & sticking

Pork
Shoulder
Hand & spring
Neck
Belly

Lamb
Shoulder
Neck
Breast

Poultry and Game
Whole
Jointed
Leg
Thigh

Rules for stewing

1. Choose the right sort of cut. A piece of lean meat will make a poor casserole, so make sure you buy something robust with some marbling of fat. Don't be tempted to trim off excess fat before slow-cooking; it will render into the finished dish, giving body and flavour. If you're concerned about the effects on your waistline, have a salad for lunch the next day.

2. Keep the meat in fairly big chunks, around 5cm (2in) cubes, or else cook as a whole piece. This helps retain succulence, as smaller pieces will dry out much faster.

3. Brown the meat beforehand in a little oil, either at a high temperature in the oven or in a hot frying pan. Meat should be browned very quickly so that the inside remains pink while the outside develops a crust; it is the crust that really makes the flavour of the finished dish.

4. Slow cook in the oven rather than on the hob, as the meat cooks much more evenly. Use a deep baking dish that allows the meat to be spread out in an even, closely packed layer. Add some vegetables – always an onion or two – some herbs, a little stock and seasoning if required and cook at a very low temperature no more than 140°C/225°F/gas mark 1 until tender.

Slow-cooked Chinese spiced belly of pork

1.5kg (3lb 5oz) belly of pork, skin on, cut into 8 equal squares

3 tsp Chinese five-spice powder

6cm (2½in) piece of fresh root ginger, grated

2 star anise

100ml (3½fl oz) soy sauce

½ tsp fish sauce

4 garlic cloves, crushed, peeled and diced

5cm (2in) cinnamon stick, broken in half

150ml (¼ pint) vegetable stock

1 bunch of coriander, chopped

1 bunch of chives, chopped

1. Place the pork in a dish in a single layer. Add the five-spice, ginger, star anise, soy sauce, fish sauce, garlic, cinnamon stick and stock and turn to coat. Cover and place in the fridge for 24 hours, turning frequently.

2. Heat 100ml (3½fl oz) of water in a pan large enough to hold the pork in a single layer. Add the meat, skin side down, bring to the boil, then cover with a lid and cook over the lowest possible heat for 50 minutes.

3. Turn the pork and add enough water to come halfway up the meat. Cover again and cook very gently for another 50 minutes, adding a little more liquid if necessary.

4. Before serving, sprinkle with the chopped herbs and serve with stir-fried vegetables.

Serves 8

Takes 2 hours, plus overnight marinating

While belly of pork is delicious when its skin is crisp and crunchy, it's also fantastic when gelatinous and sticky – as it is in this recipe.

Faggots

250g (9oz) pig's liver

500g (1lb 2oz) coarsely minced shoulder of pork

250g (9oz) finely minced belly of pork

¼ tsp white pepper

½ tsp black pepper

1 tsp salt

3 garlic cloves, crushed, peeled and diced

8 sage leaves, finely chopped

leaves from 2 sprigs of thyme, finely chopped

8 sheets of caul fat

2 or 3 white onions, peeled and thinly sliced

lard, dripping or butter, for frying

about 500ml (18fl oz) beef stock

Faggots are an economical and savoury dish. Order the caul fat in advance from your butcher.

Serves 4

Takes 2 hours

1. Put all the ingredients except the caul fat, onions, lard and stock in a bowl and mix. Form into balls about 5cm (2in) in diameter, and wrap each in a sheet of caul fat.

2. Preheat the oven to 150°C/300°F/gas mark 2. Fry the onions in the fat until soft. Set aside and brown the faggots in the pan.

3. Place the faggots and onions in a baking dish, pour in stock to come halfway up the faggots. Cook in the oven for 1–1½ hours.

Pork knuckles cooked in a chilli broth

6 dried chillies, boiling water poured over and soaked for 2 hours

2 heads of garlic, cloves separated and peeled

1 tbsp cooking oil

2 knuckles of pork, whole or chopped

5cm (2in) piece of fresh root ginger, peeled and sliced

100ml (3½fl oz) rice vinegar

200ml (7fl oz) soy sauce

250g (9oz) muscovado sugar

pork or vegetable stock, to cover the knuckles

1 bunch of coriander, chopped

1. Preheat the oven to 180°C/350°F/gas mark 4.

2. Put the chillies, garlic and oil in an ovenproof pan and sauté until just golden. Add the pork knuckles and cook until brown all over.

3. Add the ginger, vinegar, soy sauce, sugar and enough stock to almost cover the knuckles. Bring to the boil, cover with a lid and transfer to the oven for 1 hour. Turn the hocks, reduce the heat to 170°C/325°F/gas mark 3 and cook for a further 2 hours, turning the hocks twice.

4. Before serving, use a metal spoon to skim off any excess fat floating on the surface of the stock. Add the chopped coriander and serve in bowls with steamed rice and cabbage.

Serves 2–4

Takes 3½ hours

Here's a truly rich and delicious way of cooking pork. Forget about crispy skin – this is all about gently cooking the hocks so that the skin breaks down to a soft, velvety texture. Of course, eating the skin is not to everybody's liking, so in that case, simply peel it back and eat just the tasty gems of tender hock meat underneath.

Borscht beef casserole — Valentine's beef

1 kg (2lb 4oz) shin, clod or sticking beef, cubed

2 tsp caraway seeds

2 tbsp olive oil

2 onions, peeled and diced

500g (1lb 2oz) raw beetroot, trimmed but unpeeled, diced

1 garlic clove, crushed, peeled and diced

25g (1oz) plain flour

850ml (1½ pints) beef stock

2 tsp tomato purée

sea salt

freshly ground black pepper

2 tsp dried mixed herbs

zest and juice of 1 orange

300ml (½ pint) soured cream

1 bunch of chives, chopped

1. Preheat the oven to 200°C/400°F/gas mark 6.

2. Place the beef and caraway seeds in a roasting tin with half the olive oil and toss to coat.

3. Place the onions, beetroot and garlic in another roasting tin, add the remaining oil and toss well.

4. Place both tins in the oven for 20–30 minutes, until browned, then remove and reduce the temperature to 150°C/300°F/gas mark 2.

5. Add the flour to the meat and mix well. Stir in the beef stock, then add the roasted vegetables, tomato purée, seasoning, mixed herbs and orange zest and juice. Stir well, adding a little more stock if needed to keep the meat submerged (this depends on the size of the roasting tin).

6. Cover with foil and cook in the oven for 3 hours, checking every hour and adding more stock if necessary. Serve topped with the soured cream and chopped chives.

Serves 6

Takes 4 hours

The colour of this casserole is just amazing — shades of mahogany and deepest red. When working on this recipe in February, I decided to serve it to friends who came to supper on the 14th, so I named it Valentine's beef. Forget the red roses — just serve this dish to warm the heart of anyone who tastes it. Mashed potatoes make the ideal accompaniment.

Slow-braised ox cheek in stout

3 ox cheeks (about
1.5kg/3lb 5oz in total)

1 litre (1¾ pints) Guinness
or dark stout

1 tbsp olive oil

2 red onions, peeled and
cut into wedges

2 garlic cloves, crushed,
peeled and diced

25g (1oz) flour

100ml (3½fl oz) beef stock

1 red chilli, chopped

2 tsp tomato purée

1 bay leaf

1 tsp Worcestershire sauce

sea salt

freshly ground black
pepper

400g (14oz) small carrots

400g (14oz) potatoes

1. Trim the cheeks of any sinew or fat, then cut into quarters. Place in a glass bowl with the stout and marinate in the fridge for 24 hours.

2. Preheat the oven to 170°C/325°F/gas mark 3.

3. Remove the cheeks from the marinade, reserving the beer, and pat dry with kitchen paper. Place in an ovenproof pan with the oil and fry until brown. Set the cheeks aside and fry the onions and garlic for 4 minutes.

4. Take the pan off the heat and stir in the flour. Slowly pour in the marinade liquid and stock, return to the heat and bring to a simmer. Add the chilli, tomato purée, bay leaf, Worcestershire sauce, seasoning and finally the cheeks. Depending on the size of your pan, you might need to add more liquid, as the beef and vegetables should be covered, so top up with water if necessary.

5. Cover the pan with a cartouche (circle of baking parchment or greaseproof paper), put a lid over it and gently cook in the oven for 4¼ hours. Check the pan from time to time, giving it a stir and adding more liquid if needed.

6. When the beef has cooked, peel and cut the carrots and potatoes into equal-sized pieces about 5cm (2in), unless you are using baby carrots as shown in the photograph. Stir them into the pan and cover again with a cartouche and the lid. Return to the oven for a further 45 minutes. Serve in bowls with creamy mashed peas (see page 178).

Serves 8–10

Takes 5½ hours, plus overnight marinating

You might need to order the ox cheeks from your butcher, but it's worth doing so because I'm sure you will enjoy the unctuous richness of this dish. Do not try to rush it, as the cheek is a well-worked muscle and needs long, gentle cooking.

Blanquette of veal

850g (1lb 14oz) veal leg meat (from heel out of back leg above knee), sliced into rounds

1 onion, peeled and studded with 2 cloves

2 carrots, peeled and cut into big chunks

1 leek, cut into big chunks

1 celery stick, cut into big chunks

1 fresh bouquet garni (parsley, thyme and bay leaf tied together)

2 litres (3½ pints) veal or chicken stock

24 baby onions, peeled

250g (9oz) button mushrooms

freshly ground white pepper

sea salt

300ml (½ pint) double cream

3 egg yolks, beaten

1 bunch of parsley, chopped

1. Trim the veal of any excess fat or sinew and place in a medium to large pan with the studded onion, carrots, leek, celery and bouquet garni. Add the stock (there should be enough to cover everything) and bring to the boil. Skim the top of the liquid carefully, then reduce the heat and simmer for 1 hour.

2. Add the baby onions and mushrooms and simmer for a further 30 minutes. Remove from the heat and set aside for 20 minutes.

3. Discard the studded onion, vegetable chunks and bouquet garni. Using a slotted spoon, transfer the meat, baby onions and mushrooms to an ovenproof serving dish, cover and keep warm.

4. Return the pan of stock to the heat and boil until it has reduced to about 600ml (1 pint). Add seasoning and all but a tablespoon of the cream, then bring to the boil and simmer for 10 minutes, until the mixture has thickened slightly and become a sauce. Remove from the heat.

5. Whisk the remaining cream with the egg yolks, then whisk into the sauce off the heat. Place the sauce on a very low heat and warm until just thick enough to coat the back of a spoon. Do not boil or the eggs will scramble and give the sauce a gritty appearance.

6. Return the veal and reserved vegetables to the sauce along with the chopped parsley. Mix gently and serve with long-grain rice and spinach.

Serves 6

Takes 2¾ hours

This is a classic white casserole, where the meat is cooked so gently in butter that it does not brown. The vegetables are cut into large chunks as these are easier to extract later.

Veal kidneys in a rich mustard sauce

4 veal kidneys

1 tbsp olive oil

20g (¾oz) butter

1 shallot, diced

100ml (3½fl oz) white wine

100ml (3½fl oz) chicken stock

2½ tbsp grain mustard

sea salt

freshly ground black pepper

1. Trim the kidneys of any fat or skin, cut in half and remove the central sinewy bits.

2. Heat the olive oil in a frying pan, add the butter and, when foaming, add the kidneys. Cook for 2–3 minutes, then turn and cook for another 2–3 minutes. Remove from the pan and keep warm.

3. Drain all but 1 tablespoon of fat from the pan, add the shallot and sauté for 2 minutes, until soft.

4. Pour in the wine and stock and boil rapidly until reduced by half. Add the mustard and stir thoroughly.

5. To serve, slice the kidneys thinly, sprinkle with salt and pepper, then place on hot toast with the sauce spooned over.

Serves 4

Takes 20 minutes

Veal kidneys are superb and need very little cooking. Ideally, they should be pink in the middle, but if that is not to your liking, cook for a little longer, taking care not to overcook them or they will be tough.

Classic osso buco with gremolata

4 veal shins, sliced with the bone in, 5cm (2in) thick

50g (2oz) plain flour, seasoned

2 tbsp olive oil

2 onions, peeled and diced

2 garlic cloves, crushed, peeled and diced

1 carrot, peeled and diced

2 celery sticks, diced

300ml (½ pint) white wine

2 large tomatoes, chopped

400ml (14fl oz) veal, chicken or vegetable stock

1 bay leaf

sea salt

freshly ground black pepper

For the gremolata

zest of 1 lemon

2 garlic cloves, crushed, peeled and diced

1 bunch of parsley, finely chopped

1. Preheat the oven to 170°C/325°F/gas mark 3.

2. Dredge the shins in the seasoned flour, coating them all over. Heat the olive oil in a large, flameproof casserole dish, then brown the shins in it, one side at a time. Transfer to a plate and set aside.

3. Add the onions, garlic, carrot and celery to the casserole dish and sauté gently until soft. Sprinkle in any leftover seasoned flour and mix well. Remove from the heat, slowly stir in the wine, then return to the heat and simmer until you have a rich sauce.

4. Return the shins to the pan and add the tomatoes, stock, bay leaf and seasoning. The liquid should just cover the meat – if not, add a little extra stock if needed. Bring to a gentle simmer, then cover and cook in the oven for 3 hours.

5. Just before serving, mix all the gremolata, ingredients together. Spoon the osso buco onto deep plates and top each serving with a spoonful of gremolata, offering the rest at the table.

Serves 4

Takes 4¼ hours

As we care about animal welfare at The Ginger Pig, we make this dish with veau sous la mère *(veal under the mother), which means the calf has lived in a field with its mother and been fed naturally on her milk. The favoured breeds are Limousin and Belgian Blue as they put weight on quickly, and the calves are usually slaughtered at five or six months old (otherwise they are known as bullocks). The meat yielded from these animals is pink and very similar to lamb.*

If you do not want to eat veal, this dish can also be made with beef shin, but it delivers a totally different flavour and a darker result. Although it's delicious, I call it 'poor man's osso buco'. Serve with creamy mashed potatoes to mop up all the tasty juices, or try it with the classic risotto on page 88.

If you ever have any leftover gremolata from your osso buco, serve it tossed through a little pasta with a dash of olive oil for a light and zesty lunch dish.

Risotto Milanese

1 litre (1¾ pints) chicken stock

75g (2½oz) butter

1 tbsp olive oil

2 onions, peeled and finely diced

425g (15oz) Arborio rice

good pinch of saffron

125ml (4fl oz) dry vermouth

125g (4½oz) Parmesan cheese, freshly grated

sea salt

freshly ground black pepper

1. Place the stock in a pan and bring to a gentle simmer.

2. Melt 50g (2oz) of the butter in a large frying pan, add the olive oil, then gently sauté the onions for 5 minutes.

3. Pour the rice into the pan and stir well to coat with the oil. Add just enough hot stock to cover the rice, stir well and simmer gently, stirring frequently. When most of the stock has been absorbed, add the same amount again, along with the saffron, and continue simmering and stirring until it has been absorbed.

4. Continue adding stock in this way until it has all been used; this will take about 15 minutes.

5. Finally, add the vermouth, most of the Parmesan, reserving a little for finishing off, the remaining butter and some seasoning. Mix well and serve topped with a scattering of Parmesan.

Serves 4

Takes 40 minutes

If you want a dish to complement the rich osso buco on page 86, serve this classic risotto from northern Italy. It is beautifully flavoured, and also wonderful served on its own, topped with just a handful of peppery rocket leaves.

Malay lamb

1 tbsp vegetable oil

2 lemongrass stalks, finely sliced

4 garlic cloves, crushed, peeled and diced

1 hot red chilli, finely chopped

5cm (2in) piece of fresh root ginger, peeled and chopped

2 onions, peeled and finely sliced

3 lamb neck fillets, sliced into 2.5cm (1in) rounds

2 tbsp curry powder

500ml (18fl oz) lamb stock

freshly ground black pepper

1 bunch of coriander, chopped

1 lime, cut into wedges

200ml (7fl oz) natural yoghurt

1. Heat the oil in a large saucepan, add the lemongrass, garlic, chilli, ginger and onions and cook on a low to medium heat for 15 minutes, until soft.

2. Add the lamb and cook until sealed. Mix in the curry powder, stir in the stock, season, then cover and cook gently for 3 hours, stirring frequently. When cooked, the sauce should coat the back of a spoon; if not, just increase the heat and reduce the liquid.

3. Stir the coriander through the dish before serving with lime wedges and yoghurt.

Serves 4

Takes 3¾ hours

Full of rich, spicy flavour, this dish is also economical because it can be made with any cut of meat.

The slow cooking renders even the cheapest cut meltingly tender, so simply adjust the cooking time to suit. Mutton, if available, is a great alternative to lamb, and is what would normally be used in a Malayan kitchen.

Scotch broth

350g (12oz) mutton neck, cut into pieces

1 large onion, peeled and diced

1 large turnip, peeled and diced

1 large carrot, peeled and diced

350g (12oz) potatoes, peeled and diced

75g (2½oz) pearl barley

sea salt

freshly ground black pepper

1 bunch of parsley, stalks reserved, leaves chopped

1. Put the meat in a pan, add 1.2 litres (2 pints) of water and bring to the boil. Skim off any scum, then cover and simmer for 2 hours.

2. Add the vegetables, pearl barley and seasoning. Tie the parsley stalks together and tie the end of string to the saucepan handle. Simmer for a further hour.

3. Before serving, discard the parsley stalks and stir the chopped leaves into the soup. Check the seasoning and serve.

Serves 4

Takes 3½ hours

Here's a delicious and hearty soup that is a marriage of subtle flavours.

Spent hen or yard cockerel casserole

2.5–3kg (5lb 8oz–6lb 8oz) broiler hen or cockerel, cut into 12 pieces

2 tbsp olive oil

500g (1lb 2oz) flat or field mushrooms, sliced

3 red onions, peeled and cut into wedges

200g (7oz) smoked bacon, chopped

3 garlic cloves, crushed, peeled and diced

25g (1oz) plain flour

300ml (½ pint) red wine

450ml (¾ pint) chicken stock

1 tbsp grain mustard

2 bay leaves

leaves from 1 bunch of thyme

sea salt

freshly ground black pepper

For the scone topping

300g (10½oz) self-raising flour

pinch of salt

100g (3½oz) shredded suet

140g (5oz) Montgomery or mature Cheddar cheese, grated

250ml (9fl oz) milk

1. Preheat the oven to 180°C/350°F/gas mark 4.

2. Heat half the oil in a flameproof casserole dish and fry the chicken in batches, setting them aside once they have browned. Add the remaining oil to the pan and fry the mushrooms, onions, bacon and garlic for 3 minutes on a medium heat.

3. Take the pan off the heat, sprinkle in the flour and mix with the oil. Slowly add the wine and stock, blending with the flour mixture, then return to the heat and gently bring to a simmer, stirring. Add the mustard, herbs and seasoning. Place the 4 carcass pieces at the bottom of the casserole dish, then add the remaining chicken pieces. Place a lid on the dish and cook in the oven – 1 hour for a senior fowl, and 30 minutes for a younger bird until the chicken pieces are cooked through.

4. Meanwhile, make the topping. Place the flour, salt, suet and cheese in a large bowl and mix until evenly blended. Pour in the milk, mixing until a dough forms. Lightly flour a work surface and roll out the dough to a thickness of 1.5cm (¾in). Using a 6cm (2½in) pastry cutter or tumbler, stamp out 12 rounds, then brush the top of them with milk.

5. Remove the casserole dish from the oven and transfer the chicken and sauce to a large ovenproof baking dish (about 30 x 22 x 10cm/ 12 x 9 x 4in). If there is too much sauce to fit, keep it warm and serve at the table in a jug. Arrange the dough rounds on top of the chicken mixture, then return to the oven for 30 minutes, until the scones are cooked.

Serves 6–8

Takes 2 hours 20 minutes

A smallholder often has birds that are no longer producing eggs, or a cockerel that is no longer productive, so it's time for the pot. As these are older birds, they need longer cooking than young ones, but they will have a richer flavour and denser texture. If you do not have a senior chicken to hand, you can still make this dish with a young bird, but reduce the cooking times as directed. Ask your butcher to joint the bird as follows: two lower legs, two thighs, breast cut into four and remaining carcass cut into four.

Bag-poached Bresse chicken with Madeira sauce

1 poulet de Bresse, about
2kg (4lb 8oz)

1 small black truffle, thinly
sliced

300ml (½ pint) chicken
stock

100ml (3½fl oz) Madeira

sea salt

freshly ground black
pepper

2 shallots, peeled and
diced

1 tsp olive oil

200ml (7fl oz) double
cream

1. Remove the wishbone from the bird. To do this, cut around the outside of it with a small knife, then bend it back and lift out. Cut off the wings.

2. Carefully wriggle your fingers under the skin covering the breast and legs to make a space, then place the truffle slices between the skin and flesh. Tie the legs together to keep the bird in a good shape. Weigh the bird and calculate the cooking time, allowing 25 minutes per 500g (1lb 2oz) at a very gentle poach.

3. Place the chicken in a strong plastic bag, then add the stock, Madeira and some seasoning. Tie a knot in the bag, and for extra security tie with string too.

4. Place the bag in a large saucepan of barely simmering water. Cover and cook for 1¾ hours, checking every 15 minutes and turning the chicken to ensure even cooking.

5. Meanwhile, sauté the shallots in the oil until just soft. Add the chicken feet, neck, wings, wishbone and giblets, cover with water and simmer gently for 1 hour. Strain the stock, then boil the liquid to reduce by half. Add the cream and simmer until thick, about 5 minutes.

6. When the chicken is cooked through, transfer it from the bag to a board and pour the cooking juices into a jug. Carve the chicken and serve it on a bed of sautéed mixed vegetables. Just before serving, pour some of the cooking juices over it followed by the rich cream sauce.

Serves 4–6

Takes 1 hour 40 minutes

This is a traditional French dish that calls for the chicken to be cooked in a pig's bladder, but I have substituted a strong plastic bag, which works just as well. The idea is to cook sous vide *(in a vacuum) so that all the flavour is locked in. The result is a very delicate and balanced dish.*

Poulet de Bresse is a high-quality bird sold complete, so get your butcher to draw it for you, but keep the neck, giblets and feet to make the stock.

Poulet de Bresse

Poulet de Bresse is considered to be the Rolls-Royce of chickens. Originating from the Rhône-Alpes region of France, they are reared to exacting standards on small farms, and are protected by law through their AOC (Appellation d'origine controlée) status, which they have held since 1957. In fact, this breed of chicken was the first livestock to receive such protection and honour.

Poulet de Bresse is favoured for its gamey depth of flavour, the fine texture of its meat and the even layer of fat that serves to keep the flesh moist during cooking. Chicken this good needs to be cooked simply as it would be a sin to disguise its superior flavour.

The Ginger Pig has been working hard to produce its own 100-day-old chickens with the Botterill family of Lings Farm on the Belvoir Estate in Leicestershire. Our chickens are a cross between a Cornish game cockerel and Sussex (Dorking) hen, and we believe they compete favourably with any other famous and recognized chicken breeds that our friends in France may be producing.

Chicken & vegetable broth

6 chicken legs

2 litres (3½ pints) chicken or vegetable stock

2 tbsp olive oil

1 large onion, peeled and chopped

2 garlic cloves, crushed, peeled and diced

2 leeks, chopped

3 carrots, peeled and chopped

25g (1oz) flour

300g (10½oz) potatoes, scrubbed and chopped

sea salt

freshly ground black pepper

3 corn cobs

1 bunch of parsley, chopped

1. Place the chicken legs and stock in a saucepan, bring to the boil and simmer for 25 minutes until the chicken is cooked through. Lift out the chicken legs and, when cool enough to handle, remove and discard the skin. Flake off the meat and roughly chop.

2. Heat the oil in a saucepan, add the onion, garlic, leeks and carrots and sauté gently for 8 minutes without browning.

3. Remove the pan from the heat, sprinkle in the flour and mix well. Slowly add the stock, stirring as you do so, then return the pan to the heat and bring to a simmer. Add the potatoes, chicken and seasoning and simmer for 15 minutes.

4. Cut the corn kernels off the cobs, add to the soup and cook for 8 minutes until tender. Finally, stir in the parsley and serve.

Serves 6

Takes 1½ hours

A hearty soup that is good enough to serve as a main meal with lots of warm bread.

Turkey & mango curry

1 garlic clove, crushed, peeled and diced

2 onions, peeled and chopped

2 hot green chillies, chopped

1 lemongrass stalk, chopped

5cm (2in) piece of fresh root ginger, peeled and diced

2 tsp vegetable oil

1.3kg (3lb) cooked turkey meat, roughly shredded

2 tsp ground cumin

2 tsp ground coriander

400ml (14fl oz) coconut cream

500ml (18fl oz) turkey or chicken stock

1 large mango, peeled and stoned

sea salt

freshly ground black pepper

1 bunch of coriander, chopped

1. Put the garlic, onions, chillies, lemongrass and ginger in a large pan with the oil and sweat for 5 minutes. Add the turkey meat, cumin and ground coriander and mix well.

2. Pour in the coconut cream, add 300ml (½ pint) of the stock and bring to a gentle boil for 5 minutes. Add the remaining stock and simmer for 10 minutes.

3. Chop the mango flesh into small pieces and add to the pan along with some seasoning and cook for a further 2 minutes. Just before serving, stir in the coriander.

Serves 6

Takes 30 minutes

Although it's not exactly British farmhouse fare, I've included this dish because I think it's time to introduce some global flavours to the farmhouse table. All the ingredients are available in the UK, and lamb, chicken or beef can be used instead of turkey if you wish.

Roasts

Roasting meat

When I roast meat on the farm, what I'm really trying to taste is the quality of the meat, so I tend to cook it very simply, with little else added. If the meat you buy comes from happy, slow-grown animals and has a good covering of fat, it will roast very well if given a strong blast of heat at the beginning, followed by a longer time on a low heat.

The Sunday roast is a cornerstone at Grange Farm, a generous celebration of the best meat it is possible to produce (or buy), with a stock made from the bones to set you up for the week ahead. It is reward and sustenance of the finest because roasting brings out the very best in meat: the fat renders, lending succulence and flavour, and the surface develops a beautifully browned crust that is deeply savoury with just a hint of sweetness.

Among the traditional recipes in this chapter, you will find some from further afield, plus a few that are suitable for small households, but can be multiplied up for larger gatherings.

Roasting table

	Temperature			Cooking time		
	°C	°F	Gas	Mins (kg)	Mins (lb)	Extra time
Beef						
first 20 mins	220	425	7			
reduce to	170	325	3	30	15	
Veal	180	350	4	55	25	20
Lamb	190	375	5	55	20	
Pork	200	400	6	65	25	
Ham	40	20				
Chicken	180	350	4	40	20	20
Duck	190	375	5	45	20	
Goose	190	375	5	55	25	
Turkey						
under 6kg (13lb)	200	400	6	30	14	
over 6kg (13lb)	180	350	4	35	15	
Grouse	190	375	5	25		
Guinea fowl	190	375	5	35–40		
Mallard	190	375	5	40		
Partridge	190	375	5	30		
Pheasant	190	375	5	35–40		
Pigeon	190	375	5	20		
Quail	190	375	5	20		
Teal	190	375	5	20		

Note: All the poultry timings are for unstuffed birds. The temperatures above are for fan ovens; if using a conventional oven, increase the heat by 10–20°C/50–70°F or one gas mark, or as your oven manufacturer recommends.

Pot-roasting

When I cook meat, the thing that interests me most is the quality and flavour of the cut. There's no adornment, no fuss and no ketchup on my bacon sandwich. Although there are few greater dishes than rare roast beef, on the farm we are also very keen on pot-roasting. A pot roast will make the most of an economical cut and give it maximum flavour. However, I urge you to make the two simple pot-roasts below using the very best cuts you can afford, simply to see what top-notch meat can do.

The meat must be cooked in a lidded pot, but don't be tempted to add water because it will simply boil and take all the flavour itself. Instead, sit the meat on a few vegetables and give it a brief blast at a high temperature: this will allow the fat to render, which, along with the vegetables, will provide all the flavour you need. Good-quality shoulder or brisket cooked like this will result in a pot half-filled with a wonderfully intense sauce.

One final point: most of us are accustomed to a little (often too much) salt in our food, but try making one of the recipes below with exceptional meat and leaving the salt out – the result will amaze you.

Pot-roast beef

1. Preheat the oven to 180°C/350°F/gas mark 4. Peel and cut a few carrots, parsnips and some swede into large chunks and place them in a large, lidded casserole dish along with a couple of peeled, halved onions.

2. Place a whole beef brisket on top, cover with a lid and place in the oven for 20 minutes. After that, lower the heat to 140°C/275°F/gas mark 1.

3. Busy yourself elsewhere for 3 hours, then return to tender beef, soft vegetables rich with flavour and meaty juice.

Pot-roast pork

1. Ask your butcher for both of the boned-out rib-eye joints (you should give him a little warning as this is not a common cut).

2. Preheat the oven to 200°C/400°F/gas mark 6. On the flat side of one joint, lay a row of bruised sage leaves along with a handful of prunes or apricots. Place the other joint on top, forming a sandwich, then tie together with string.

3. Sit the tied joint on a bed of peeled and chopped onions and carrots in a casserole dish and cover with a lid. Place in the oven for 20 minutes, then lower the temperature to 170°C/325°F/gas mark 3 and leave to simmer gently, with the lid on, for 2 hours.

Pot-roast pork tip: This cut of meat is taken from the fore of the pig's ribcage, giving you two marbled pieces of meat with an essential seam of fat, but no skin or bone. To serve, simply pull the meat apart with two forks and enjoy with potatoes – mashed, roasted or boiled.

Glazed & roasted spare ribs

4 pork spare ribs, cut from the shoulder

For the glaze

1 tbsp honey

zest and juice of 1 lemon

2 tbsp soy sauce

2 garlic cloves, crushed, peeled and diced

½ tsp chilli flakes

½ tsp ground ginger

50g (2oz) muscovado sugar

1 tbsp tomato purée

1 tbsp Worcestershire sauce

1 tbsp vinegar

1 tbsp Dijon mustard

sea salt

freshly ground black pepper

1. Preheat the oven to 180°C/350°F/gas mark 4.

2. Put all the glaze ingredients in a small saucepan and bring to a simmer. Heat gently for 5 minutes. Smear the glaze all over the ribs.

3. Place in a lightly oiled roasting tin and roast for 30 minutes. Turn the ribs, basting them with the cooking juices, and roast for a further 20 minutes. They should be browned, sizzling and tender.

Serves 2

Takes 1¼ hours

Shoulder ribs are bigger and meatier than the lower ones, and I recommend you choose them rather than any other ribs for this dish.

Stuffed & rolled shoulder of pork

2.5kg (5lb 8oz) boned
shoulder of pork
sea salt
freshly ground black
pepper
8 large carrots, peeled and
left whole
8 banana shallots or small
onions, peeled
25g (1oz) flour
1 tsp Dijon mustard
250ml (9fl oz) white wine

For the stuffing
1 tbsp olive oil
2 garlic cloves, crushed,
peeled and diced
2 onions, peeled and diced
100g (3½oz) chicken
livers, chopped
200g (7oz) minced pork
75g (2½oz) toasted pine
nuts
100g (3½oz) stoned
prunes, chopped
100g (3½oz) grated apple
leaves from 1 bunch of
sage, chopped
75ml (3fl oz) red wine

1. Preheat the oven to 200°C/400°F/gas mark 6.

2. First make the stuffing. Heat the olive oil in a pan, add the garlic and onions and sauté until soft. Add the livers, mince, pine nuts, prunes, apple and sage, pour in the red wine and mix well. Bring just to the boil, then transfer to a bowl and set aside until cold.

3. Open out the pork, skin side down, sprinkle with seasoning and vigorously massage into the meat. Spread the cold stuffing evenly down the middle of the pork, then wrap the meat around it and tie firmly with string.

4. Arrange the carrots and shallots in a single layer in the bottom of a roasting tin. Sit the meat on top and place in the oven for 25 minutes. Reduce the heat to 170°C/325°F/gas mark 3 and cook for a further 3 hours.

5. Transfer the pork and vegetables to a carving plate, cover with foil and allow to rest for 15 minutes. Meanwhile, skim the excess fat from the roasting tin, then stir the flour and mustard into the juices. Slowly add the white wine and mix until smooth, then place on the heat and bring to a simmer, constantly stirring so that it does not catch on the bottom. Check the seasoning and adjust the consistency, if necessary, with a little vegetable water.

6. Remove the string from the pork, break away the crackling, then slice the meat and serve with the carrots and shallots.

Serves 10–12
Takes 4 hours, plus cooking
Shoulder of pork comes from a well-worked muscle, so it needs a long cooking time. The result, though, is well worth the wait, as you will have a beautifully succulent and tasty joint that looks wonderfully appetizing.

Pulled spicy pork

2kg (4lb 8oz) boned shoulder of pork (roughly half a whole shoulder)

For the spicy rub
2 tsp smoked paprika
2 tsp onion granules or flakes
2 tsp garlic salt
1–2 tsp chilli flakes
1 tsp sea salt
1 tsp ground cumin
2 tsp English mustard powder
1 tsp freshly ground black pepper
4 tbsp red wine vinegar
4 tbsp brown sugar

1. Place all the rub ingredients in a large bowl and mix well. Add the pork, rub the spicy mixture all over it, then cover and marinate in the fridge for 24 hours, turning and basting occasionally.

2. Preheat the oven to 170°C/325°F/gas mark 3. Place the marinated pork in a small roasting tin, spoon over some of the marinade and cover with foil. Place in the oven for 2 hours. Reduce the heat to 150°C/300°F/gas mark 2, turn and baste the pork, cover with the foil again and cook for a further 2 hours.

3. Remove the foil and drain the cooking juices into a saucepan. Increase the heat to 170°/325°F/gas mark 3, return the meat to the oven, uncovered, and brown for 20 minutes. When cooked, cover with foil and allow to rest for 15 minutes.

4. Meanwhile, skim off and discard the excess fat from the cooking juices, then place the pan over a low heat to warm them through.

5. Once the pork has rested, peel off the skin and tear the meat into shreds using 2 forks. It should be so well cooked that it falls apart easily. Pour the warm juices over the meat and serve in ciabatta rolls or on top of a crunchy salad consisting of beansprouts, iceberg lettuce, chopped carrot, cucumber and red peppers all tossed in lime juice.

Serves 10
Takes 5½ hours, plus overnight marinating
While this may not be the neatest-looking dish, it is certainly one of the most delicious ways to use a pork shoulder. It's a great roast to serve at a gathering.

Roasted wing rib with Yorkshire pudding & best gravy

2kg (4lb 8oz) rib of beef on the bone
1 tbsp plain flour
1 tsp English mustard powder
sea salt
freshly ground black pepper

For the Yorkshire pudding
125g (4½oz) plain flour
2 eggs
300ml (½ pint) milk
2 tbsp beef dripping

For the gravy
1 tbsp flour
1 tsp soy sauce
50ml (2fl oz) red wine
250ml (9fl oz) beef stock

1. Preheat the oven to 220°C/425°F/gas mark 7. Weigh the meat and calculate its cooking time (30 minutes per 1 kg/2lb 4oz for rare, 40 minutes per 1kg/2lb 4oz for medium, plus 20 minutes).

2. Mix together the flour, mustard powder and seasoning and rub all over the beef. Place on a rack in a roasting tin and roast for 15 minutes, then reduce the temperature to 170°C/325°F/gas mark 3 and cook for the remainder of the cooking time. When done, cover the meat with foil and set aside to rest for 15 minutes.

3. If you have a second oven, use it now to make the Yorkshire pudding. Preheat the oven to 200°C/400°F/gas mark 6. Mix together the flour, eggs, milk and some seasoning in a blender until smooth. Set aside to rest for 30 minutes.

4. Melt the dripping in a shallow baking tin and brush it around the sides. Heat in the oven for 8 minutes so that it is almost smoking. Carefully pour the batter into the tin and cook in the top of the oven for 20–25 minutes, until golden, puffed up and crisp. Serve at once.

5. Meanwhile, to make the gravy, spoon off the excess fat from the roasting tin (keep it to use in other dishes). Mix the flour into the juices, then blend in the soy sauce and wine. Slowly add the stock, stirring to prevent lumps forming. Place over a medium heat and bring to a simmer, stirring constantly and scraping up all the roasting bits. Add any cooking juices from the resting beef, then taste, season and serve.

Serves 6–8
Takes about 1½ hours for rare (2 hours if you are not lucky enough to have a double oven)
Wing rib is great roasted on the bone, but do ask the butcher to chine the joint for you. Chining involves sawing through the length of the backbone so that it's easy to remove before carving. This is a classy cut of meat, so cook it at least slightly rare – well done would be sacrilege!

Tom's veal paupiettes

300g (10½oz) minced veal

300g (10½oz) minced pork

1 small red onion, peeled and chopped

1 garlic clove, crushed, peeled and diced

1 bunch of flat leaf parsley, chopped

sea salt

freshly ground black pepper

85g (3oz) Gorgonzola cheese

4 veal escalopes (about 500g/1lb 2oz total weight)

175g (6oz) lardo or Gloucester Old Spot streaky bacon

2 cherry tomatoes, cut in half

100ml (3½ fl oz) white wine

100ml (3½ fl oz) double cream

1. Preheat the oven to 180°C/350°F/gas mark 4.

2. Put the minced veal and pork in a large bowl, add the onion, garlic, parsley and seasoning and mix thoroughly by hand to get a really even blend.

3. Divide the mixture into 4 equal pieces, then roll into balls. Push your finger into the centre of each ball, stuff with a quarter of the Gorgonzola, then seal the hole with the meat.

4. Cut a quarter off each escalope, sit a meatball on each quarter, then drape a three-quarter piece over each ball like a blanket and pat around it with your hands. These covered balls are the paupiettes.

5. Cut the lardo or bacon into strips – you will need 3 strips per paupiette. Wrap a strip around the circumference of each paupiette (like putting a ribbon around a cake), then place 2 strips over the top in a cross.

6. Carefully tie string around the paupiettes to hold them together. Sit half a cherry tomato in the centre of each cross, then place the parcels in a baking tin and roast in the oven for 20 minutes.

7. When cooked, transfer the paupiettes to a plate and keep warm. Add the wine to the roasting tin, bring to the boil, then stir in the cream. Simmer until the sauce thickens and serve it with the paupiettes.

Serves 4

Takes 1½ hours

These little veal parcels might sound fiddly to make, but are actually quite easy, and perfect for serving at a dinner party as all the preparation is done in advance.

Beef Wellington with red wine & green peppercorn sauce

1 .25kg (2lb 12oz) beef fillet, cut from the thick end or middle

1 tbsp beef dripping or olive oil

3 tbsp grain mustard

1 egg, beaten

1 bunch of watercress, to serve

For the puff pastry

225g (½lb) plain flour, preferably strong

140g (5oz) chilled butter

pinch of salt

2 tsp white wine vinegar

1 egg beaten

For the chicken liver pâté

75g (2½oz) butter

1 small onion, peeled and chopped

1 garlic clove, crushed, peeled and diced

225g (½lb) chicken livers, trimmed of any veins or white bits

sea salt

freshly ground black pepper

30ml (1fl oz) sherry or brandy

For the sauce

175ml (6fl oz) red wine

175ml (6fl oz) double cream

3 tsp green peppercorns

(See pages 114–16)

Serves 4

Takes 7 hours, plus overnight chilling and 3 hours to cook

Here is a classic dish: tender pink beef fillet spread with chicken liver pâté and mustard, encased in crisp, golden pastry and served with a rich, peppery sauce. It is perfect for a celebration meal as it can be prepared in advance. In fact, the pastry and pâté should be made the day before and thoroughly chilled so that they will not adversely affect the beef and it remains pink when cooked.

To make the pastry

1. Sift the flour into a large bowl. Melt 15g (½oz) of the butter and mix with the salt, vinegar and 75ml (3fl oz) of ice-cold water. Add to the flour and mix to a smooth dough. Cover in clingfilm and place in the fridge for 1 hour.

2. Place the remaining butter between 2 sheets of clingfilm and roll out to the thickness of your finger. Roll out the pastry to a rectangle just over twice the size of the butter. Place the butter in the middle of the pastry and fold the sides over it. Roll out the pastry again to a rectangle the same size as it was before the butter was added. Fold into thirds, roll out once more, turn 90 degrees and fold in thirds again. Cover in clingfilm and place in the fridge for 1 hour.

3. Repeat the rolling and folding process 4 more times, adding a light dusting of flour each time, then wrapping and chilling after each repetition. (In total, the process should be performed 5 times.) Wrap the finished pastry in greaseproof paper and rest in the fridge overnight.

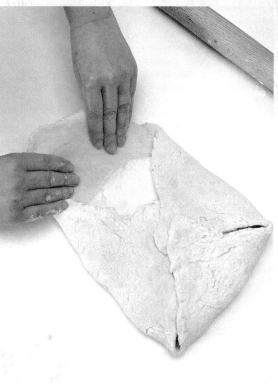
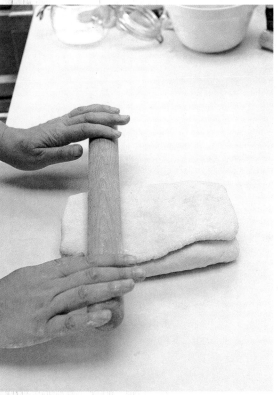

To make the pâté

1. Heat the butter in a large frying pan, add the onion and garlic and gently sauté over a low heat. Roughly chop the livers, add to the pan and cook until they are all just browned on the outside. Season, pour in the sherry or brandy and stir well.

2. Place the mixture in a food processor and whiz until creamy smooth. Transfer to a bowl, set aside to cool, then cover the pâté and place in the fridge until you are ready to use it.

To assemble the Wellington

1. Preheat the oven to 230°C/450°F/gas mark 8. Heat the dripping in a large roasting tin on the hob for 5 minutes. Meanwhile, trim the beef of any silvery skin and fatty or gristly bits. When hot, place the beef in the hot oil and quickly brown all over to seal it, which will take about 5 minutes. Place in the oven and cook for 15 minutes. Transfer to a plate to cool, reserving any juices in the tin.

2. Roll out one-third of the pastry until slightly longer and wider than the fillet. Place the pastry on a lightly oiled baking sheet, prick with a fork and bake for 20 minutes. Transfer to a wire rack to cool.

3. Place the baked sheet of pastry back on the baking sheet. Mix the pâté with the grain mustard and spread the mixture all over the cooled fillet. Place the beef on the baked pastry and brush around the edges with beaten egg.

4. Roll out the remaining pastry until it is large enough to blanket the fillet and the pastry base. Place it over the beef and gently shape around it, pressing the pastry edges together with your fingers or crimping them with a fork. Reroll the offcuts of pastry and cut into long ribbons. Place the pastry parcel and ribbons in the fridge to rest for 12 minutes.

5. Brush the pastry all over with the beaten egg and make 4 slits along the top so the steam can escape (a snip with scissors gives the best result). Place the ribbons in a zigzag pattern across the Wellington and brush them with egg. Bake in the middle of the oven for 25 minutes, until crisp and golden.

To make the sauce

1. Heat the red wine and any cooking juices from the fillet in a frying pan until reduced by half. Lower the heat, add the cream and peppercorns and simmer until the sauce is thick enough to coat the back of a spoon.

To serve

1. Slice the beef Wellington into 4 equal pieces, garnish with the watercress and serve the sauce on the side.

Lamb chump roast with quince

400g (14oz) chump
of lamb

1 quince

25g (1oz) soft butter

sea salt

freshly ground black
pepper

100ml (3½fl oz) red wine

2 tsp quince jelly or
redcurrant jelly

1. Preheat the oven to 200°C/400°F/gas
mark 6.

2. Place the lamb chump in a roasting tin.
Slice the quince lengthways, coat with the
butter and sit alongside the joint.

3. Season the lamb and roast in the oven: 15
minutes for pink, 20 minutes for medium
and 25–30 minutes for well done.

4. When the lamb is cooked, transfer it to a
carving plate, cover with foil and rest it for
8 minutes.

5. Put the red wine and jelly in a small
saucepan or a microwaveable bowl, heat for
30 seconds and blend until smooth. Carve
the lamb and serve with the roasted quince
slices and red wine sauce.

Serves 2

Takes 30-45 minutes

*Chump is a neat little cut that comes
from above the leg. It is great value
and makes a perfect quick roast for
two people.*

How to choose a chicken

Buying a chicken can be surprisingly complicated because labelling is not entirely straightforward. Cheapest birds can be 10 times less expensive than one at the top of the range, a huge difference.

In the UK there is no official body that regulates exactly what a free range chicken is. Allowing the birds outside is a basic requirement, but this can be for as little as one hour a day. If you want a flavoursome bird that has been reared in humane conditions, make sure the label says it's free range, organic or RSPCA Freedom Food.

We could also learn a lot from the French. Around 30 years ago the French Ministry of Agriculture developed a production programme for farmers raising free range chickens. This laid down rules about breed, feed, living conditions and the age of the birds before slaughter. The ministry granted farmers who met their standards the *label rouge* (red label), which guaranteed that each chicken bearing it was from a slow-growing breed (one with a lifespan about twice that of a factory chicken), had been reared in the open air in groups of limited numbers and had been fed only a natural, cereal-based diet.

The French then went on to produce a category of chicken – poulet de Bresse – of even more exceptional quality. So good was this breed that it gained protected AOC status in 1957. For more about poulet de Bresse, and our own 100-day-old chickens, see page 95.

Excellent roast chicken

100g (3½oz) soft butter

2kg (4lb 8oz) black-leg chicken

juice of 1 lemon

sea salt

freshly ground black pepper

1 head of garlic, cut in half horizontally

2 sprigs of thyme

200ml (7fl oz) white wine

1. Preheat the oven to 200°C/400°F/gas mark 6.

2. Use a little of the butter to lightly grease a roasting tin. Put the chicken in the tin, then smear all over with the remaining butter. Pour the lemon juice all over the bird, placing the squeezed lemon halves alongside it, then sprinkle with seasoning. Add the garlic, thyme and wine to the tin.

3. Using one or more sheets of foil, make a tent and place it over the chicken without allowing it to touch the bird. Seal it tightly all around the edges of the tin.

4. Place in the oven for 20 minutes, then reduce the temperature to 170°C/325°F/gas mark 3 and cook for a further 1 hour 20 minutes, until cooked through.

5. Increase the heat to 180°C/350°F/gas mark 4, remove the foil tent and baste the bird with the cooking juices. Return to the oven for 10 minutes so that the skin crisps up.

6. Transfer the chicken and garlic to a carving plate, cover with foil to keep warm and leave to rest for 10 minutes.

7. Strain the juices from the roasting tin, then bring to the boil, whisking, and reduce by a third. Carve the chicken and serve with the roasted garlic and a spoonful of the rich, buttery juices.

Serves 4

Takes 2¼ hours

The only way to ensure excellent roast chicken is to use a bird of fantastic quality. For this reason, I recommend you buy a free range black-leg chicken produced in France. You won't be disappointed.

Stuffing & flavouring chicken

Much of the cooking on our farm centres on tasting the quality of the meat, so I can say with confidence that a good chicken will do all the hard work for you in terms of supplying flavour. That's not to say, though, that adding a little something is a bad idea.

Aromatics
An onion, lemon or head of garlic cut in half and placed inside the cavity of a bird will moisten the meat from the inside and gently flavour it as it steams. Add a few bay leaves, some thyme or a bunch of tarragon and, with very little effort, you've got a delicately scented roast chicken.

Stuffing
Filling the cavity of a chicken with a stuffing of seasoned minced pork, breadcrumbs and a few herbs and flavourings not only helps to add flavour and keep the chicken moist, but also makes the meat go a little further.

You'll need about 450g (1lb) of stuffing for a chicken. Start with 220g (½lb) of minced pork and 115g (4oz) fresh breadcrumbs. Add a finely chopped onion, a minced garlic clove and a reasonable amount of salt and pepper. To this you can add whatever takes your fancy: perhaps mince in the chicken liver and add some finely chopped apricots, dates or grated apple; or add plenty of whatever herbs you have to hand and some grated lemon zest; or add fennel seeds and oregano for an Italian twist; or replace half the minced pork with cooking chorizo or black pudding for a richer stuffing.

How to stuff a bird
At the neck end, you will find a flap of skin. Carefully push your fingers underneath this, gently working the skin away from the breast. Push about two-thirds of your stuffing mixture into the space you've created, then tuck the flap of skin back in or 'pin' it with a cocktail stick. At the other end of the bird, just spoon the remaining mixture inside the body cavity. Remember to weigh the bird *after* it has been stuffed to calculate the correct roasting time.

How to add flavour under the skin
If you're not stuffing a bird, the easiest way to add extra flavour is to loosen the breast skin as described above, then to push a flavoured butter into the space. Simply add your favourite chopped herbs, aromatics and seasoning to the butter and it will impart their flavour as well as basting the flesh. Please note that this process is neither necessary nor advisable with high-quality birds, as the skin contains enough fat to keep the flesh moist, and it would be a shame to hide the flavour of such wonderful meat with gratuitous accompaniments.

If you are using a bird with less natural fat and flavour, a seasoned butter mixed with some of the items listed below is very good.

Fresh herbs: chives, lemon thyme, oregano, parsley, tarragon, thyme
Cured meats: finely chopped pancetta or streaky bacon, crumbled chorizo or smoked Toulouse sausage, lardo
Aromatics: celery salt, fennel seeds, garlic, lemon zest, paprika, sundried tomatoes (finely chopped)

Pancetta-wrapped chicken

4 boneless chicken fillets

100g (3½oz) goats' cheese

8 sage leaves

freshly ground black pepper

12 slices of pancetta

1. Preheat the oven to 180°C/350°F/gas mark 4.

2. Using a small knife, make an incision in the side of each chicken fillet. Fill each of these 'pockets' with 25g (1oz) of the cheese.

3. Place 2 sage leaves on top of each fillet, sprinkle with pepper and wrap 3 slices of pancetta around each one, securing the ends with a cocktail stick.

4. Lightly oil a roasting tin, sit the chicken in it and place in the oven for 20 minutes. Check and turn to ensure even cooking, then cook for a further 10 minutes and serve.

Serves 4

Takes 45 minutes

Simple and fast, yet very tasty, this good-looking dish turns out a treat every time. To make it totally your own, try making your own pancetta (see page 31).

Spiced chicken wings

2kg (4lb 8oz) chicken wings

zest and juice of 2 limes

For the marinade

4 tbsp sesame oil

100ml (3½fl oz) light soy sauce

4 garlic cloves, crushed, peeled and chopped

1 tsp chilli powder

1 tsp ground cumin

1 tsp hot paprika

5 spring onions, chopped

freshly ground black pepper

1. Put all the marinade ingredients into a large bowl and mix together. Add the chicken wings and toss until totally coated in the mixture. Cover and place in the fridge overnight.

2. Remove the wings from the fridge 1 hour before cooking. Preheat the oven to 180°C/350°F/gas mark 4. Place the chicken in a single layer in a large roasting tin and cook for 30 minutes.

3. Reduce the oven temperature to 170°C/325°F/gas mark 3 and cook for a further 25 minutes until cooked through.

4. Add the lime zest and juice to the cooked wings, toss well and serve with all the sticky bits scraped from the bottom of the tin.

Serves 6–8

Takes 1 hour, plus overnight marinating

I think it's essential to eat these wings with your fingers to ensure that every morsel of sticky, crunchy chicken is stripped from each bone.

Spanish pot-roast chicken

3kg (6lb 8oz) good-quality chicken

1 tbsp olive oil

1 tbsp sweet paprika

sea salt

freshly ground black pepper

For the bed of vegetables

3 onions, peeled and cut into quarters

3 carrots, peeled and cut into quarters

3 large tomatoes, cut into quarters

2 red chillies, cut into quarters

2 heads of garlic, cut in half horizontally

3 red peppers, deseeded and cut into chunks

2 bay leaves

2 sprigs of thyme

2 tbsp balsamic vinegar

400ml (14fl oz) white wine

300g (10½oz) black olives, stoned (optional)

1. Preheat the oven to 180°C/350°F/gas mark 4.

2. Put all the ingredients for the bed of vegetables into a large lidded casserole dish. Mix well.

3. Rub the chicken all over with the olive oil. Sprinkle with the paprika and seasoning and rub these into the chicken too.

4. Place the chicken in the dish on top of the vegetables and cover with a tight-fitting lid. Place in the oven for 1½ hours, then remove the lid and cook for a further 20 minutes to crisp up the skin. Serve with rice or pasta.

Serves 6

Takes 2 hours

Pot-roasting keeps a chicken beautifully moist and allows it to steam gently in its own juices. The bed of vegetables it sits on also delivers fantastic flavour to this lovely dish.

Festive stuffed turkey

Serves 12

Takes about 6½ hours

7kg (15lb 4oz) free range turkey with giblets

18 rashers of streaky bacon, rind removed

For the stuffing

140g (5oz) fresh breadcrumbs

1kg (2lb 4oz) pork sausagemeat

zest and juice of 3 lemons

4 garlic cloves, crushed, peeled and finely diced

2 red onions, peeled and grated

200g (7oz) cooked chestnuts, peeled and chopped

leaves from 6 sprigs of rosemary, chopped

sea salt and black pepper

1 egg, beaten with 200ml (7fl oz) cold water

For the gravy

1 onion

1 leek

2 bay leaves

2 celery sticks, cut in half

6 black peppercorns

50g (2oz) plain flour

100ml (3½fl oz) white wine

On Christmas Eve

1. Place the giblets, onion, leek, bay leaves, celery and peppercorns in a large saucepan, add 2 litres (3½ pints) of water, bring to the boil and simmer for 1 hour. Strain the liquid, discarding the solids and you should be left with about 1 litre (1¾ pints) of stock. Cool the stock, then refrigerate and keep for the gravy.

2. Meanwhile, combine all the stuffing ingredients in a bowl and mix well before stirring in the egg and water mixture. Stuff the turkey, placing two-thirds in the body cavity and the remainder under the skin at the neck end (see page 120). Weigh the stuffed turkey and calculate the cooking time, allowing 20 minutes per 500g (1lb 2oz). Write this down so as not to forget.

3. Use a skewer or wooden cocktail sticks to keep the flap of neck skin closed and the stuffing in place. Sit the turkey on a trivet in a large roasting tin and place the bacon rashers over the breast. Cover with a tent of foil (see page 119) and store in the fridge or larder overnight.

On Christmas Day

1. Remove the turkey from the fridge at least 2 hours before starting to cook so it can come up to room temperature. Preheat the oven to 220°C/425°F/gas mark 7.

2. With a note of your calculated cooking time to hand, place the prepared turkey in the oven and roast for 40 minutes until cooked through. Reduce the temperature to 170°C/325°F/gas mark 3 and continue to cook as calculated. For the final 30 minutes of cooking remove the foil and bacon and increase the temperature to 180°C/350°F/gas mark 4 to brown the skin.

3. Transfer the turkey to a carving plate, replace the crisp bacon over the breast and cover with foil. Leave to rest in a warm place for 30 minutes.

To make the gravy

1. Skim off the excess fat from the turkey roasting tin, sprinkle in the flour and mix with a whisk.

2. Slowly add the stock and wine, whisking as you do so, then place the tin over the heat and bring to the boil. Simmer for a few minutes to cook the flour, then add any juices that may have run out of the turkey.

3. Check the seasoning, adjusting it as necessary, then serve the gravy alongside the carved turkey.

How to choose a turkey

There's only one place we go for our turkeys, and that is to the Botterill family – Gerald and Ann, their son Richard and his wife Jo – who farm poultry on the Belvoir Estate on the Lincolnshire/Leicestershire borders. Spending time with them in the tiny hamlet of Croxton Kerrial is a real pleasure, and gives the all-too-rare feeling of being in the company of people who are truly knowledgeable and passionate about what they do. The Botterills have been fiercely committed to raising free range turkeys, geese and chickens for over 70 years, and take every care to ensure the best possible animal husbandry.

They rear broad-breasted bronze turkeys, which grow slowly to full maturity at a minimum of six months – a good two months after many commercial birds are slaughtered. The Botterills also grow a natural cereal and vegetable diet for the birds – no growth hormones for them – and the birds are truly free range, reared outdoors in the farm's grassy fields. The birds are dry-plucked and hung for up to 14 days after slaughter, which gives the flesh a rich, deep flavour and helps with succulence too.

Three-bird celebration roast

Serves 10

Takes 5 hours

Here we have an idea from Tudor times – a pheasant inside a chicken inside a goose. Be sure to order your birds in advance and get them tunnel-boned. Also ask the butcher to skin the chicken and pheasant.

5kg (11lb) goose, tunnel-boned

1.3kg (3lb) chicken, tunnel-boned and skinned

1 pheasant, tunnel-boned and skinned

25g (1oz) flour, for the gravy

For the stock

bird bones from butcher

2 carrots

2 celery sticks, cut in half

2 onions, peeled

1 bouquet garni

For the stuffing

1kg (2lb 4oz) pork sausagemeat

3 shallots, peeled and diced

2 garlic cloves, peeled, crushed and diced

4 apples, peeled and grated

zest and juice of 2 oranges

1 tbsp chopped sage leaves

1 tbsp chopped parsley

sea salt

freshly ground black pepper

1. First make the stock. Place the bones in a pan and add the carrots, celery, onions and bouquet garni, cover with water and simmer for 1½ hours. Strain discarding the solids, then simmer the stock again to reduce to about 750ml (1¼ pints).

2. Meanwhile, put all the stuffing ingredients in a bowl, add seasoning and mix thoroughly by hand.

3. Fill the pheasant with a small amount of the stuffing and place inside the chicken. Carefully insert a layer of stuffing between the pheasant and chicken. Place these two birds inside the goose, then insert the remaining stuffing between the chicken and goose, working it to recreate the shape of the outer bird.

4. Secure each end of the goose with a couple of skewers to keep the stuffing inside.

5. Preheat the oven to 180°C/350°F/gas mark 4. Place the three-bird roast in a lightly oiled roasting tin, cover with a foil tent (see page 119) and cook for 3 hours and 20 minutes, checking and basting a couple of times. Remove the foil and roast for a further 40 minutes so that the skin can crisp up.

6. When cooked through, transfer the roast to a warm serving plate, cover and keep warm for at least 25 minutes before carving.

7. Meanwhile, make the gravy. Sprinkle the flour into the roasting tin and blend until smooth. Place over the heat and slowly pour in the stock, stirring constantly until boiling and just thickened. Season and serve hot with the three-bird roast.

Note: When carving, cut from the middle outwards so that everyone gets a slice containing the three different meats.

Lardo roast leg of venison & beetroot with red wine sauce

1.8kg (4lb) boned haunch of venison (ask your butcher for the bone)

200g (7oz) lardo or thinly sliced streaky bacon

400g (14oz) raw beetroot, topped, tailed and washed

200g (7oz) quinces, poached, cut into wedges and cored

1 tbsp olive oil

For the gravy

300ml (½ pint) red wine

200g (7oz) quinces, poached

4 tbsp quince jelly

sea salt

freshly ground black pepper

1. Preheat the oven to 220°C/425°F/gas mark 7.

2. If your butcher has not already done so, wrap the venison in lardo or streaky bacon and tie with string every 5cm (2in).

3. Cut the beetroot into even sized wedges. Toss in the olive oil with the quinces and place in a roasting tin with the bone from the venison. Sit the joint on top and roast in the oven for 35 minutes. Reduce the temperature to 170°C/325°F/gas mark 3 and cook for a further 30 minutes for rare venison, and 40 minutes for medium-rare.

4. Transfer the joint and beetroot to a carving board, discarding the bone. Cover with foil and leave in a warm place for 20 minutes.

5. Meanwhile, make the gravy. Place the roasting tin on the hob, add all the gravy ingredients and simmer for 8 minutes, scraping up all the crusty bits from the bottom of the tin. Pour in any juices released by the rested meat, then reduce to a glossy sauce. Check the seasoning and serve with the carved venison and roasted beetroot.

Serves 6–8

Takes 1¾ hours

Ask your butcher to bone the leg and remove the silver-coloured skin that encases the muscle. If your butcher is an artisan, also ask him to wrap the joint in lardo, which is paper-thin sheets of cured pork back fat (see page 35 to make your own). If this is not possible, good-quality streaky bacon is an excellent alternative. Venison is a very lean meat, so it needs this extra fat to keep it moist while cooking.

Indian roast game birds

4 small game birds,
e.g. pigeon, partridge,
pheasant
1 tbsp oil

For the marinade
6 cloves
1½ tsp ground cinnamon
2 tsp ground coriander
generous grating of fresh
nutmeg
1 tsp turmeric
2 tsp ground cumin
8 cardamom pods
2 tsp cayenne pepper
2 tsp sea salt
5cm (2in) piece of fresh
root ginger, peeled and
roughly chopped
5 garlic cloves, crushed,
peeled and roughly
chopped
1 onion, peeled and
roughly chopped
200ml (7 fl oz) natural
yoghurt
zest and juice of 1 lemon

1. First make the marinade. Put all the spices and salt in a blender and whiz together until all finely ground. Add the ginger, garlic and onion and whiz again until you have a paste. Finally, blend in the yoghurt, lemon zest and juice.

2. Skin the birds and cut in half along the breastbone and then the spine. Cut these pieces in half and score 3 slashes in the flesh of each piece. Place in the marinade and stir to coat thoroughly. Cover and place in the fridge overnight.

3. Remove the chilled game from the fridge at least 1 hour before starting to cook so it can come up to room temperature. Preheat the oven to 200°C/400°F/gas mark 6 and heat the oil in a large roasting tin.

4. Arrange the game in a single layer in the tin and place at the top of the oven. Cook for 8–10 minutes, then turn and cook for a further 8–10 minutes. Serve with spiced rice, a tomato, onion and coriander salad, and naan breads.

Serves 4–6
Takes 1 hour plus overnight marinating

These spices add razzle and sparkle to this dish and if you are lucky and the autumn weather is kind it all adds to the authenticity of an Indian summer or on a cold winter's day delivers lovely complex flavours to what is usually cooked very simply. Even before cooking and marinating (as shown opposite) the birds themselves are exotic and beautiful, transporting you to a warmer, spice-laden climate.

Savoury baking, pies & puddings

Sourdough

There is something almost magical about the ancient method of making a natural starter in order to make bread. Simply mix together flour and water, following the directions opposite, and watch the mixture gradually come to life: pinprick-sized bubbles start to appear and slowly multiply, until you have a frothy batter. How does that happen? It's just carbon dioxide forming in the batter – simple but amazing.

Another surprise is that you can keep a starter going for literally years. In fact, it's worth doing just that because the older the starter, the better the results. Sourdough bread is a complex living thing, and you will get a lot of variety in the beginning, but don't give up too early. As time goes on, everything starts to settle down and you will get a more reliable loaf. Never again will you take a baker's skill for granted.

The speed that your starter takes to get going can vary a lot, depending on temperature, location and season. These differences can also affect the end result, and that, I believe, is what makes sourdough bread so fascinating. Try it yourself and I'm sure you'll be hooked.

Sourdough starter

200g (7oz) strong bread flour
200ml (7fl oz) bottled mineral water

1. Mix the flour and water in a large Kilner jar or something similar. Cover and leave in a warm place for 24 hours, until tiny bubbles start to erupt on the surface.

2. At this point, discard half the mix and add the listed ingredients again. Mix well, cover and leave for a further 24 hours.

3. Repeat this process a further 3 times and the starter is now ready to use.

Takes 5 days
Making a starter is a slow process, but very gratifying. Each day the activity in the jar should increase, with more and more bubbles on the surface of the mixture, and a distinct sour note will develop, which is exactly what you want.

Sourdough bread

500g (1lb 2oz) strong bread flour
250ml (9fl oz) sourdough starter (see above)
200ml (7fl oz) warm water
2 tsp salt

1. Place the flour, starter and water in a bowl and stir well. The mixture will be a little wet and sticky, but that is normal. Leave for 10 minutes, then sprinkle in the salt and knead for 5 minutes using an electric mixer fitted with a dough hook.

2. Line a wicker bread basket or ovenproof dish with a tea towel, generously sprinkle with flour and place the shaped dough within it. Cover with another tea towel and put in a warm place to prove (rise) for 10–20 hours, until almost doubled in size.

3. Preheat the oven to 230°C/450°F/gas mark 8. Place a heatproof dish filled with hot water at the bottom of the oven – this will help to create a good crust on the bread. Put the dough on a floured baking sheet and bake for 20 minutes. Reduce the heat to 200°C/400°F/gas mark 6 and bake for a further 20 minutes. The bread should sound hollow when tapped on the bottom; if it doesn't, bake for longer and test again.

Makes 1 loaf
Takes 1 hour, plus 10-20 hours to prove
Sourdough cannot be rushed – and why would you want to when you have painstakingly created your own starter? The bread will take longer to prove than an ordinary yeast loaf, so if you're impatient, make the dough before you go to bed and leave it to prove overnight. The wait won't seem so long if you're asleep!

Farmhouse loaf

775g (1lb 11oz) strong white bread flour

15g (½oz) fresh yeast, or 1 heaped tsp dried yeast

2 tsp salt

1. Lightly grease a 900g (2lb) loaf tin with butter. Put the flour into a large mixing bowl, crumble in the fresh yeast and rub in so that it is evenly distributed. Alternatively, add the dried yeast and stir in thoroughly. Add the salt once the yeast has been combined.

2. Make a well in the centre of the flour, then pour in 530ml (18½fl oz) cold water if using fresh yeast, or tepid water if using dried yeast. Using the fingertips of one hand, gradually mix the flour from the sides of the bowl into the water until you have a sticky dough.

3. Turn the dough onto a floured work surface and knead until it becomes elastic and slightly shiny. This will take several minutes. Return the dough to the bowl, cover with a clean tea towel and leave somewhere warm until it has doubled in size (up to 1 hour).

4. Lift the dough from the bowl, being careful not to knock out too much air, and lay it on a floured work surface. Using your fingertips, gradually work the dough into a large rectangle about the same length as your loaf tin and 3 times its width.

5. Fold the outer thirds of the dough into the middle to make it roughly the same size as the loaf tin and place it inside. Cover again with the tea towel and leave to double in size while the oven heats up to 220°C/425°F/gas mark 7.

6. Once the dough has proved, bake it for 25–30 minutes, until the base of the loaf sounds hollow when tapped. Set aside in the tin for 10 minutes, then transfer to a wire rack to cool.

Makes 1 large loaf

Takes 1 hour, plus 1½ hours to prove

Nothing beats the taste and smell of freshly made bread.
This farmhouse loaf provides the perfect base for a tasty sandwich with some mature cheddar and tangy pickle.

Soda bread

Bicarbonate of soda rather than yeast is used as the raising agent in the recipe below: it's quicker to use and produces a slightly denser loaf with a tighter texture. Traditionally, soda bread is made with buttermilk, but I have always found ordinary milk just as good. The loaf is a quick solution when you have run out of bread and there's no time to go to the shops – something that often happens on the farm when we are busy with the stock. All the ingredients are store-cupboard staples, so it's easy knock up a fresh loaf of soda bread to go with soup or good cheeses and pickles. You can also add sugar and dried fruit to the dough for a lovely teatime loaf. We toast slices on the Aga and top them with lots of melting butter. What could be nicer with a good cup of Yorkshire tea?

Ginger Pig soda bread

400g (14oz) wholemeal flour

1 tsp bicarbonate of soda

dash of salt

2 tsp cream of tartar

400ml (14fl oz) full-fat milk

2 tbsp olive oil

1. Preheat the oven to 180°C/350°F/gas mark 4.

2. Combine all the dry ingredients in a bowl, then add the milk and half the olive oil. Using your hands, quickly mix together until you have a smooth dough.

3. Place the dough on a floured surface and knead for 5 minutes, until smooth and soft.

4. Shape into a ball, flatten with your hand and cut a cross on the top. Transfer to a floured baking sheet and bake for 30–35 minutes. Serve hot.

Serves 6–8

Takes 50 minutes

With this recipe on hand and a few staple ingredients in the cupboard, you need never fear running out of bread. The loaf does not keep as well as yeasted bread, but that's rarely a problem because it's eaten so quickly.

Shortcrust pastry

The basic ingredients for shortcrust are flour, fat and water, but egg(s) can be added for greater richness. Soft, plain wheat flour gives the best texture; bread flour is too high in gluten, producing a tough end result. Always combine it with butter or lard, preferably at room temperature so that they can be easily incorporated without overworking the dough. The aim is to achieve a light, crumbly texture. When mixing shortcrust ingredients, it is important to incorporate as much air as possible. For this reason, flour should always be sifted, and the fat worked in gently, lifting your fingers high out of the bowl to trap lots of air in the crumb.

Baking an empty pastry case before adding the filling helps to prevent it becoming soggy. The technique is called blind baking, and the first step is to line the pastry case with a sheet of crumpled baking parchment (the crumpling makes it easier to fit). Fill it with uncooked rice or dried pulses (or special ceramic beans, if you have them) and bake in the middle of an oven preheated to 200°c, 400°F, gas 6 for 15 minutes. Reduce the temperature to 170°C, 325°F, gas mark 3, remove the beans and paper, then bake for a further 10 minutes, until the pastry is dry and lightly golden.

Basic quiche with two fillings

For the basic custard

6 eggs

350ml (12 fl oz) double
cream

250ml (9fl oz) milk

freshly ground black
pepper

½ tsp salt (less if using
bacon or lots of cheese)

Cheese and bacon filling

350g (12oz) lardons or
bacon trimmings

1 large onion, peeled and
finely sliced

200g (7oz) strong, firm
cheese, such as Cheddar
or Lancashire, grated

*Roasted vegetable and
feta filling*

1 red pepper, deseeded
and roughly chopped

1 green pepper, deseeded
and roughly chopped

1 red onion, peeled and
roughly chopped

6 garlic cloves, peeled

3 tbsp olive oil

150g (5½oz) feta, cut into
1cm (½in) chunks

For the pastry

250g (9oz) plain flour

125g (4½oz) soft butter

1 egg

1 tsp salt and ½ tsp sugar

1. First make the pastry. Tip the flour onto a work surface, make a well in the middle and place the butter, egg, salt and sugar in it. Mix the ingredients in the well, then draw in the flour around the sides, taking care not to overwork the mixture. Add 40ml (1½fl oz) water, knead a few times to ensure the dough is smooth, adding a little more water if needed, then kneading again. Cover with clingfilm and place in the fridge for 1 hour.

2. Butter a 33 x 26cm (13 x 10in) baking dish, or two 20cm (8in) tart tins. Roll out the chilled pastry and use to line your prepared dish/tins. Prick the base with a fork, then place in the fridge for 10 minutes.

3. Meanwhile, preheat the oven to 170°C/ 325°F/gas mark 3. Make the basic custard by whisking together the eggs, cream, milk and seasoning.

4. Remove the pastry case/s from the fridge and blind bake as described on page 140. If making the cheese and bacon filling, sauté the lardons in a dry frying pan until the fat runs. Add the onions and cook gently until soft. Remove the cases from the oven and scatter the mixture across the base, pour in the egg mix and top with the cheese.

5. If making the vegetable filling, toss the peppers, onion and garlic in the olive oil. Season and roast for 30 minutes, stirring halfway through. When soft, use the back of a spoon to crush the garlic and mix it through the vegetables. Scatter them across the pastry base, sprinkle with the feta, then pour in the egg mix .

6. Bake the large quiche for 40 minutes or the 2 smaller ones for 20–30 minutes, until set.

Serves 6–8

Takes about 2 hours, plus 1 hour
to chill

The quiche has been done a huge disservice by mass-production, which turns out bland and flabby articles. With a proper shortcrust pastry case and an egg-rich filling, the quiche is a fantastic dish. It should be served just warm, when it will have enough stability to be neatly sliced.

You can add almost whatever you please to the basic custard – smoked salmon and chopped asparagus; slow-cooked onions and rosemary; lots of fresh green herbs and garden peas – the combinations are endless. Here we give a couple of our favourite fillings.

Quiche with mustard and cheese crust

1 tbsp olive oil

400g (14oz) smoked bacon, chopped

125ml (4fl oz) double cream

2 eggs

sea salt

freshly ground black pepper

50g (2oz) Parmesan or Cheddar cheese, grated

For the pastry

250g (9oz) plain flour

175g (6oz) chilled butter, diced

1 tsp English mustard powder

50g (2oz) Parmesan or Cheddar cheese, grated

2 egg yolks, beaten

1. First make the pastry. Put the flour and butter into a bowl and rub together with your fingertips until the mixture resembles breadcrumbs. Mix in the mustard and cheese, then pour in the egg yolks and mix with a round-bladed knife until a dough forms. Knead lightly on a floured surface until smooth, then cover in clingfilm and place in the fridge for 30 minutes.

2. Preheat the oven to 200°C/400°F/gas mark 6.

3. Roll out the pastry on a lightly floured surface and use to line a 30cm (12in) loose-bottomed tart tin. Make sure there are no cracks in the pastry, then prick the base with a fork.

4. Chill the pastry case for 10 minutes, then blind bake as described on page 140 for 20 minutes. After the temperature is reduced, bake for a further 20 minutes.

5. Meanwhile, heat the olive oil in a frying pan and fry the bacon until just cooked. Whisk together the cream, eggs and seasoning and pour into the pastry case. Add the bacon, sprinkle with the cheese and bake for 40 minutes. The filling should be soft but set in the centre.

Serves 6

Takes 2 hours, plus 40 minutes to chill

Deliciously flavoured with cheese, the rich yet crisp pastry used here also includes a bit of mustard for a slight kick. With its classic egg and bacon filling, the quiche makes a perfect meal with steamed new potatoes and fresh salad leaves.

Mutton and black pudding pie

3kg (6lb 8oz) shoulder of mutton, boned and cubed

1 tbsp olive oil

2 onions, peeled and chopped

25g (1oz) flour

500ml (18fl oz) red wine

sea salt

freshly ground black pepper

1 bay leaf

300g (10½oz) black pudding, roughly chopped

1 egg, beaten (for brushing the pastry)

For the pastry

650g (1lb 7oz) plain flour

250g (9oz) chilled lard, diced

2 eggs, beaten

pinch of salt

1. Preheat the oven to 200°C/400°F/gas mark 6. Place the mutton in a large ovenproof pie dish with the oil, toss well, then roast for 35 minutes, until browned. Add the onions and roast for a further 10 minutes. Reduce the temperature to 170°C/325°F/gas mark 3. Sprinkle the flour over the mutton and stir well. Pour in the wine, then add the seasoning and bay leaf, mixing well. If the meat is not covered with the liquid, top it up with water. Cover with a cartouche (circle of baking parchment or greaseproof paper) and foil and place in the oven for 3 hours. Stir in the black pudding and set aside to cool slightly.

2. Meanwhile, make the pastry. Put the flour and lard in a bowl and rub together until evenly blended. Add the eggs, salt and 100ml (3½fl oz) chilled water and mix until you have a smooth dough. Cover in clingfilm and place in the fridge for 25 minutes. Preheat the oven to 190°C/375°F/gas mark 5.

3. Lightly flour a work surface and roll out the pastry until large enough to cover the pie dish with some overhang. Cut strips of pastry as wide as the lip of the dish and brush on one side with beaten egg. Lay them, egg side down, all around the lip, then brush with beaten egg again.

4. Working quickly, cover with the remaining pastry, pressing the edges together. Trim off the excess pastry, then crimp around the edges. Brush the remaining beaten egg all over the pie, cut a cross in the middle of the top and bake for 45 minutes.

Serves 6–8

Takes 4¾ hours

This recipe is a speciality that Les, our chief pie-maker, researched and produced. It is a real man's pie, with thick, crispy pastry and a hearty filling full of earthy flavours in a rich sauce. It's so good that Les cooked it for the Two Hairy Bikers *crew, who came to the farm to film him making it.*

Wensleydale and onion tart

2 onions, peeled and sliced

1 tbsp olive oil

2 eggs

275ml (9½fl oz) double cream

sea salt

freshly ground black pepper

1 bunch of chives, chopped

250g (9oz) Wensleydale cheese, grated

For the pastry

250g (9oz) plain flour

75g (2½oz) chilled butter, diced

50g (2oz) chilled lard, diced

2 egg yolks, beaten

1. First make the pastry. Put the flour into a bowl, add the butter and lard and rub together with your fingertips until the mixture resembles breadcrumbs. Using a round-bladed knife and a cutting motion, mix in the egg yolks until a dough forms. Knead gently until smooth. Lightly flour a work surface and roll out the pastry to roughly the size of a teaplate. Cover in clingfilm and place in the fridge for 10 minutes.

2. Preheat the oven to 180°C/350°F/gas mark 4. Lightly butter a 23cm (9in) loose-bottomed tart tin.

3. Roll out the chilled pastry again and use to line the tin. Prick the base with a fork, then blind bake as described on page 140. Set aside and reduce the oven temperature to 170°C/325°F/gas mark 3.

4. Place the onions and oil in a pan and fry gently for 10 minutes, until lightly golden, then scatter into the cooked pastry case.

5. Mix together the eggs, cream, seasoning and chives, add the cheese and carefully pour into the pastry case. Bake for 35 minutes, until set and golden.

Serves 4

Takes 2 hours

Our friends in Hawes, North Yorkshire, make fantastic Wensleydale cheese. Being firm believers in local produce, we use it in this tart, which is much loved by everyone in our Yorkshire fold. Alter the cheese as you wish to suit your locality or palate.

Chicken & chorizo sausage pie

2kg (4lb 8oz) chicken

4 chorizo sausages

50g (2oz) butter

50g (2oz) plain flour

freshly ground black pepper

pinch of salt

4 sprigs of flat leaf parsley, chopped

1 egg, beaten (for brushing the pastry)

For the pastry

650g (1lb 7oz) plain flour

250g (9oz) chilled lard, diced

2 eggs, beaten

pinch of salt

1. Preheat the oven to 190°C/375°F/gas mark 5. Place the chicken and sausages in a lidded casserole dish. Cover with water, place a sheet a sheet of baking parchment over the dish, then put the lid on . Place in the oven for 1½ hours.

2. Transfer all the meat to a bowl and set aside until cool enough to handle. Discard the chicken skin, then strip the meat off the bones. Roughly chop both the chicken and chorizo, return to the bowl and mix.

3. Skim the fat off the stock in the casserole dish. Melt the butter in a saucepan, add the flour and mix to a smooth paste. Slowly pour in 850ml (1½ pints) of the stock, stirring constantly until it thickens and boils. Pour it over the meat mixture, add the seasoning and parsley and mix well. Place in a large pie dish about 10cm (4in) deep. Set aside.

4. To make the pastry, put the flour and lard in a bowl and rub together until evenly blended. Add the eggs, salt and 75ml (3fl oz) of chilled water and mix until you have a smooth dough.

5. Preheat the oven to 200°C/400°F/gas mark 6. Lightly flour a work surface and roll out the pastry until large enough to cover the pie dish with some overhang. Cut strips as wide as the lip of the dish and brush on one side with beaten egg. Lay them, brushed side down, all around the lip, then brush with egg again. Cover the dish with the remaining pastry, trim off the excess, then crimp the edges together. Brush egg all over the pie, cut a cross in the middle and bake for 20 minutes, then reduce the temperature to 170°C/325°F/gas mark 3 and bake for a further 30 minutes.

Serves 6–8

Takes 3½ hours

Here's a delicious pie full of tender chicken and spicy chorizo under a shortcrust lid. It's perfect for a family meal or casual lunch with friends.

Hot-water crust

As the name suggests, hot-water crust is a crispy pastry that uses hot water rather than cold to help form the dough. It also differs from other pastries in using hot lard rather than butter for the fat content, but we like to be different and use a mixture of both for extra flavour and a good texture. The result is a thick, sticky pastry that bakes to a smooth, shiny and firm finish, just as you see in pork pies. While most pastries need time to rest and cool before use, hot-water crust must be used immediately, otherwise it dries and cracks and becomes impossible to shape.

Being robust and easy to mould, hot-water crust is particularly suitable for making hand-raised meat and game pies. In this case, the pastry is rolled out in the usual way, but a mould, such as a large tin or jam jar, is placed in the middle, then the pastry is raised up around it and patted into shape. After chilling, the mould is carefully lifted out and the pastry case is filled with a meat mixture. A pastry lid is added to cover the filling, a small hole is pierced in the top and the pie is then baked. The filling shrinks slightly as the pie cooks, so a rich jelly is poured through the hole to fill any gaps between the meat and the pastry. Once set, the pie will freeze well or it will keep for several days in the fridge, but it is better eaten fresh.

Ginger Pig pork pies

For the filling

100g (3½ oz) butter, melted

25g (1oz) lard, melted

1kg (2lb 4oz) fatty minced pork

1tsp freshly ground nutmeg

1tsp freshly ground white pepper

1½ tsp salt

1 egg, beaten (for brushing the pastry)

2tsp flat-leaf parsley, chopped

For the pastry

700g (1lb 9oz) plain flour

50g (2oz) icing sugar

pinch of salt

200g (7oz) lard

For the jelly

2 pig's trotters, cleaned

4 peppercorns

2 bay leaves

1. Place the trotters in a saucepan of cold water and bring to the boil. Remove the trotters and discard the liquid. Return them to the pan, cover with 3 litres (5¼ pints) fresh water, add the peppercorns and bay leaves and cover tightly. Bring to a simmer and cook for 4 hours, ensuring that the trotters are immersed and adding a little more water if necessary. Strain the liquid through muslin, cover and chill until set. If runny, heat to reduce; if extremely firm, reheat with a little water or stock to loosen.

2. Preheat the oven to 170°C/325°F/gas mark 3. Brush four 12 x 6cm (5 x 2½in) pie tins with the melted lard. Dust with flour.

3. Put the pork in a bowl with the nutmeg, pepper, parsley and salt. Mix well, then set aside. To make the pastry, mix the flour, sugar and salt in a bowl. Melt the butter and lard with 200ml (7fl oz) of water until almost boiling. Pour this liquid over the dry ingredients and mix quickly to make a smooth, glossy dough.

4. Divide the dough into 8 pieces, 4 at 185g (6½oz) and 4 at 115g (4oz). Cover with clingfilm and a clean tea towel to stop them from cooling and setting hard. Roll out the larger pieces of dough and use to line the pie tins, pressing lightly to fit. Divide the filling between the tins, then brush the pastry rim with beaten egg. Roll out each small piece of pastry and make a 1cm (½in) hole in the centre. Place on top of the pies and crimp the edges together. Brush with the egg and bake for 1 hour. Set aside to cool in the tins.

5. Heat up the jelly, then slowly pour through a small funnel into each pie hole. Allow to set for 2 hours before serving.

Makes 4 pies

Takes 6 hours, plus overnight setting

Here's our recipe for a traditional pork pie. It's a classic and we are known for it, though our recipe has never been published before. The jelly, which is made the night before should be firm but not rubbery.

Puff pastry

The origins of puff pastry are unclear. It was certainly known in ancient Greece and during medieval times, but it is the nineteenth-century pastry cook Richard Feuillet who is credited with popularizing it since then.

Making puff pastry requires time and patience because the dough is layered with butter, then folded and rolled several times to create multiple layers that puff up when baked. The process for doing this is explained and illustrated on pages 116–17 and 154–155, and the end result is delectable and well worth the effort. However, do note the following tips:

• Chilling puff pastry is very important because without it you won't get such defined layering. Also, if warm pastry goes into the oven, it is more likely to become gooey than to rise, so keep any pastry you're not actually working with covered in clingfilm in the fridge.

• Handle the pastry carefully, as bending or squashing the layers means it won't rise properly.

• Have the oven nice and hot. The layers rise when the butter boils, creating steam that lifts the dough.

• Make extra to freeze and you've got a speedy meal in the bank. Puff pastry keeps for up to three months if well covered in clingfilm, and can make a quick pie lid for leftovers, or an open tart base simply scattered with roasted vegetables, bacon and cheese.

Sausage rolls with Stilton

550g (1lb 4oz) minced pork

175g (6oz) pork fat, minced

100g (3½oz) breadcrumbs

2 tsp dried mixed herbs

1 tsp chopped sage

150g (5½oz) Stilton cheese, crumbled

sea salt

freshly ground black pepper

1 egg, beaten (for brushing the pastry)

For the pastry

600g (1lb 5oz) very strong white flour, preferably '00'

450g (1lb) chilled butter

pinch of salt

2 tbsp white wine vinegar

1. To make the pastry, sift the flour into a large bowl. Melt 50g (2oz) of the butter and mix with the salt, vinegar and 230ml (8fl oz) of ice-cold water. Add this liquid to the flour and mix to a smooth dough. Cover in clingfilm and place in the fridge for 1 hour.

2. The following process is illustrated overleaf. Place the remaining butter between 2 sheets of clingfilm and roll it out to the thickness of your finger. On a lightly floured work surface, roll out the chilled pastry to a rectangle just over twice the size of the butter. Place the butter in the middle and fold the sides of the pastry over it. Roll out again to a rectangle the same size as it was before the butter was added, then fold in thirds. Roll out once more, give it a quarter turn and fold in thirds again. Cover in clingfilm and chill for 1 hour. Repeat the rolling and folding 4 more times, adding a light dusting of flour each time, then wrapping and chilling as before. Leave to rest in the fridge overnight.

3. Combine the pork and fat in a bowl. Add the breadcrumbs, herbs, cheese, seasoning and 125ml (4fl oz) of water. Mix with your hands until evenly blended. Chill overnight.

4. Preheat the oven to 180°C/350°F/gas mark 4. Roll the pastry out to about 40 x 30cm (16 x 12in) and cut it into 3 lengthways strips about 10cm (4in) wide. Work the sausagemeat into a long roll as thick as your thumb and place along a strip of pastry. Brush the exposed pastry with egg, then roll over and crimp the edges. Repeat twice more, then cut each length into 4 equal pieces. Brush with egg, place on a baking sheet and bake for 50 minutes.

Makes 12

Takes 7 hours to make the pastry, plus overnight chilling and 1½ hours to cook

Perfect for parties and picnics, sausage rolls are popular with everyone. With the addition of tangy Stilton, they are even better, so make lots!

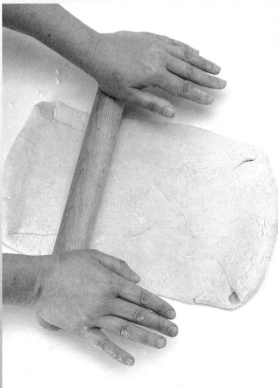

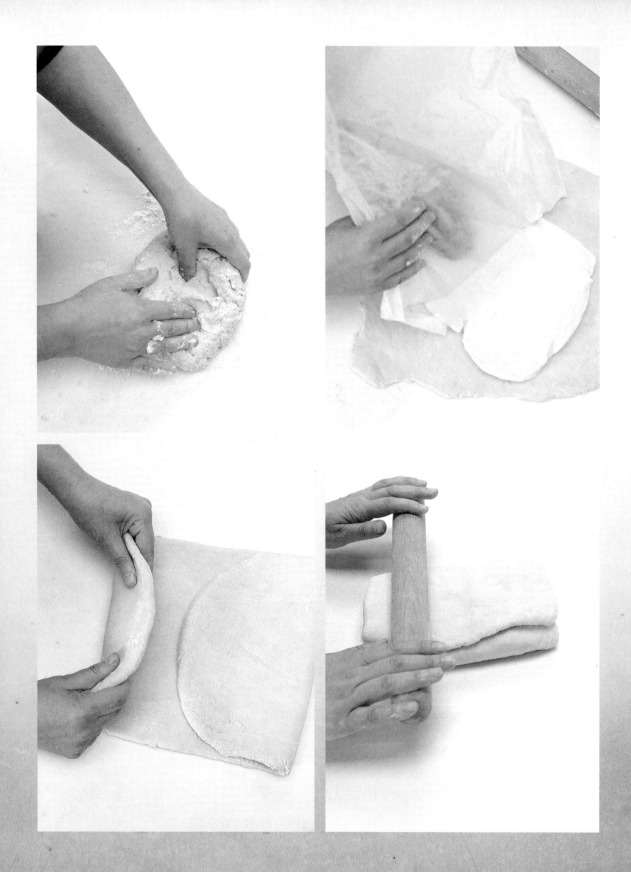

Sausage rolls with smoked bacon & chilli

1 quantity chilled puff
pastry (see page 153)
1 egg, beaten (for brushing
the pastry)

For the filling
200g (7oz) smoked,
rindless streaky bacon
500g (1lb 2oz) minced
fatty pork
100g (3½oz) breadcrumbs
1 tsp sweet, smoked
paprika
½ tsp chilli powder
1 tbsp sweet chilli sauce
sea salt and freshly ground
black pepper

1. Chop the bacon as finely as you can; you
might find this quicker if you start with
scissors and then use a sharp knife.

2. Mix the bacon with all the other filling
ingredients, seasoning liberally with pepper,
but adding just a little salt as the bacon is
already quite salty.

3. Make the sausage rolls as described in step
4 on page 153.

Makes 12
Takes 1½ hours
*Made with slightly salty, smoked
streaky bacon, minced pork and
just a touch of spice and sweet chilli
sauce to pep them up.*

Sausage rolls with spicy lamb

1 quantity chilled puff
pastry (see page 153)
1 egg, beaten (for brushing
the pastry)

For the filling
700g (1lb 9oz) minced
fatty lamb
100g (3½oz) breadcrumbs
2 tsp cumin
2 garlic cloves, crushed,
peeled and finely minced
1 tbsp finely chopped flat
leaf parsley
1 tsp harissa paste

1. Put all the filling ingredients into a large
bowl, season generously and mix until well
combined.

2. Make the sausage rolls as described
in step 4 on page 153.

Makes 12
Takes 1½ hours
*A nod to northern Africa with
our lamb merguez sausagemeat
encased in butter-rich puff pastry.
Serve with a minty yoghurt for
perfect picnic fodder.*

Black pudding & sausagemeat palmiers

500g (1lb 2oz) minced pork

½ tsp fine sea salt

½ tsp freshly ground black pepper

4 sage leaves, finely chopped

1 bunch of parsley, finely chopped

½ tsp dried thyme

50g (2oz) breadcrumbs, dried on a tray in a low oven for 20 minutes

½ quantity chilled puff pastry (see page 153)

125g (4½oz) black pudding, casing removed

1 egg, beaten (for brushing the pastry)

1. Mix the pork with the seasoning, herbs and breadcrumbs, then stir the mixture well for 2 minutes to get a good texture.

2. On a lightly floured surface, roll the pastry into a rectangle the thickness of a £1 coin.

3. Roll the sausagemeat mixture into a similar-sized rectangle and place on top of the pastry.

4. About 2.5cm (1in) away from the edge of one long side, crumble the black pudding onto the sausagemeat in a strip about 1cm (½in) wide.

5. Starting at the edge with the black pudding, roll up the rectangle fairly tightly. Cover in flour-dusted clingfilm and chill for 45 minutes, or until you're ready to use it (the roll will keep for 2 days in the fridge).

6. Preheat the oven to 200°C/400°F/gas mark 6. Slice the chilled roll into 5mm (¼in) rounds and lay them flat on a baking sheet, leaving a 2.5cm (1in) gap between them to allow for expansion. Brush with a little beaten egg and bake until crisp and golden – about 10 minutes.

Makes 50

Takes 25 minutes, plus 45 minutes to chill

Traditionally shaped like palm leaves (hence their name), palmiers are usually made as sweet biscuits. Here, though, I've given them a savoury twist, and they're really delicious.

Sue's Cornish pasties

1 large potato, peeled and diced

1 large carrot, peeled and diced

1 large onion, peeled and diced

200g (7oz) beef fillet tail, diced

sea salt

freshly ground black pepper

dash of Worcestershire sauce

½ quantity chilled puff pastry (see page 153)

1 egg, beaten (for brushing the pastry)

1. Preheat the oven to 200°C/400°F/gas mark 6.

2. Place the potato, carrot and onion in a saucepan, cover with water and bring to the boil. Simmer for 2 minutes, then drain and set aside to cool. When cool, add the beef, seasoning and Worcestershire sauce and stir together.

3. Divide the pastry into 4 equal pieces. Place on a lightly floured surface and roll each piece into a rough circle about 20cm (8in) wide. Using an upturned round teaplate, cut a regular circle from each piece.

4. Spoon the beef mixture into the centre of each pastry circle. Brush beaten egg around the filling, then carefully bring the edges of the pastry together and crimp tightly with floured fingers. Brush beaten egg all over each pasty and place on a baking sheet. Bake for 15 minutes, then lower the temperature to 180°C/350°F/gas mark 4 and bake for a further 30 minutes.

Makes 4

Takes 1½ hours, plus 30 minutes to chill

Sue has been working as my housekeeper for many years and last year when we became really busy she extended her days to help in the bakery and undertook making the Cornish pasties. Tail end of beef fillet is not the right shape for use as steak, but it is ideal for making these superior pasties, and relatively cheap too. Enjoy the pasties hot or cold – they are delicious either way.

Classic steamed suet pudding

Filling of your choice
(see pages 161-162)

For the pastry
350g (12oz) plain flour
175g (6oz) beef suet
pinch of salt
25g (1oz) lard

1. To make the pastry, combine the flour, suet and salt in a bowl. Add 100–150ml (3½–5fl oz) of cold water and mix until a smooth dough forms.

2. Grease a 900g (2lb) pudding basin, preferably metal, with lard. On a lightly floured surface, roll the pastry into a circle large enough to line the basin and slightly overhang the sides. Fold the circle in half, then into thirds. Unfold and cut away one-third. Carefully lift the pastry into the basin, working it into the base and sides, and brushing the overlap with water to make a good seal. Roll out the discarded third of pastry to fit the top of the basin.

3. Fill the lined basin with your chosen filling. Add some liquid as specified opposite.

4. Brush the pastry edge with water, sit the pastry circle on top and press together to seal. Fold in the overhang after adding the circle lid.

5. Cover the top of the pudding with a double sheet of baking parchment and foil, both of them pleated in the middle to allow for expansion as the pudding cooks. Tie in place with string and make a loop across the top as a handle.

6. Sit the basin on a trivet in a saucepan and pour in enough boiling water to come halfway up the sides. Cover with a tight-fitting lid and simmer gently for 4½ hours, checking the water level frequently.

7. To serve, remove the foil and parchment, run a sharp knife around the edge of the pudding, then invert onto a plate.

Serves 4
Takes 5 hours

A steamed savoury pudding is real comfort food on a cold winter's day, and fairly thrifty too because the long, slow cooking tenderizes even the cheapest cut of meat.

Suet puddings are best made in a metal basin because it reaches a higher temperature than glass or earthenware and allows the pastry to take on a light golden colour, which makes the pudding look even more appetizing.

Pea & ham filling

650g (1lb 7oz) raw bacon or ham, cubed

15g (½oz) flour

200g (7oz) freshly shelled or frozen peas

1 onion, peeled and diced

1 bunch of flat leaf parsley, chopped

1 tsp grain mustard

100ml (3½fl oz) double cream

1 bay leaf

freshly ground black pepper

1. Place the bacon in a bowl, add the flour and toss to coat.

2. Add all the other ingredients and mix well. Spoon the mixture into the pastry-lined pudding basin.

3. Add enough water to come about 2.5cm (1in) from the top. Continue as described opposite.

Serves 4

Takes 20 minutes

Ask your butcher if he has any offcuts of bacon or ham that you can use for this dish. Alternatively, use a small slipper cut (corner piece) of ham.

Mutton & carrot filling

750g (1lb 10oz) shoulder or neck of mutton, cubed

15g (½oz) flour

2 carrots, peeled and diced

1 onion, peeled and diced

1 garlic clove, crushed, peeled and diced

leaves from 1 large sprig of thyme, chopped

1 bay leaf

sea salt

freshly ground black pepper

100ml (3½fl oz) red wine, or very good beef stock

1. Place the mutton in a bowl, add the flour and toss to coat.

2. Add the vegetables, garlic, herbs and seasoning and mix well. Spoon the mixture into the pastry-lined pudding basin.

3. Pour in the wine and top up with enough water to come about 2.5cm (1in) from the top. Continue as described opposite.

Serves 4

Takes 25 minutes

The intense flavour of mutton is perfect for this pudding. For this filling, and the two steak versions overleaf, stock can be used instead of wine, but do try to use a full-bodied, jellied stock. Apart from adding lots of flavour, it reduces the amount of salt required and does away with the need for gravy browning. If you don't have a good stock already, see the recipe on page 277.

Steak & smoked oyster filling

650g (1lb 7oz) braising beef, skirt, chuck or brisket, cubed

15g (½oz) flour

2 cans of smoked oysters (about 175g/6oz in total)

1 onion, peeled and diced

1 garlic clove, crushed, peeled and diced

1 bunch of flat leaf parsley, chopped

1 bay leaf

sea salt and black pepper

150ml (¼ pint) red wine

1. Place the beef in a bowl, add the flour and toss to coat.

2. Add the smoked oysters in their oil, the onion, garlic, herbs and seasoning and mix well. Spoon the mixture into the pastry-lined pudding basin.

3. Pour in the wine and top up with enough water to come about 2.5cm (1in) from the top. Continue as described on page 160.

Serves 4

Takes 20 minutes

The oysters add a delicious depth of flavour to this filling. If you would rather not add red wine, you can use good beef stock instead.

Steak & kidney filling

650g (1lb 7oz) braising beef, skirt, chuck or brisket, cubed

200g (7oz) kidneys, cored and cubed

15g (½oz) flour

1 onion, peeled and diced

1 garlic clove, crushed, peeled and diced

1 bunch of flat leaf parsley, chopped

1 bay leaf

½ tsp Worcestershire sauce

1 tsp soy sauce

sea salt and black pepper

150ml (¼ pint) red wine

1. Place all the meat in a bowl, add the flour and toss to coat.

2. Add the onion, garlic, herbs, sauces and seasoning and mix well. Spoon the mixture into a pastry-lined pudding basin.

3. Pour in the wine and top up with enough water to come about 2.5cm (1in) from the top. Continue as described on page 160.

Serves 4

Takes 25 minutes

If you're not fond of kidneys, use mushrooms instead. If you would rather not add red wine, you can use good beef stock instead.

Vegetables

How does your garden grow?

Our patch of North Yorkshire can sometimes be wild, wet and windy, but it's amazing what our head gardener, Lesley, achieves. Her knowhow and green fingers produce a wide variety of vegetables and salad crops, including potatoes, red and green cabbages, onions, courgettes, beetroot, carrots, tomatoes and lettuces, plus rhubarb and lots of fresh herbs. Some of the produce goes into the tasty chutneys and pickles that are sold in Ginger Pig shops; the rest is generally used up on the farm.

If you want to try growing your own, it's really important to work out what kind of soil you have. Clay is claggy, wet and poor-draining; chalk is stony and coarse, so drains well; sand is gritty and free-draining; and peat is dark and spongy, so it retains moisture. If you're very lucky, you may have loamy soil, which is excellent for growing. It has an even, well-structured and almost smooth texture, which is easy to work, retains moisture and warms up quickly in spring. Remember, whatever type of soil you have, the quality can always be improved by adding coarse sand or organic matter to improve drainage, or fertilizer to improve the nutrient content.

Our soil is clay over limestone, so the ground retains moisture but is quick to drain, which keeps both plants and pigs happy. While clay isn't the easiest soil to work, it's relatively supple in the autumn, and that's when we sow for the year ahead.

Potatoes

There are many varieties of potato – far more than you see in the shops – so why not experiment and grow a few unusual types alongside your favourites? Here are some tips.

• Always buy seed potatoes from garden centres and specialist retailers to ensure a disease-free crop.
• To chit seed potatoes (i.e. get them to sprout before planting), leave them somewhere light, airy and cool until small, sturdy shoots form. Shoots formed in the dark are too fragile.
• Plant maincrop potatoes from around mid-March, when ground-freezing frosts are over, until the beginning of June.
• Always plant with the shoots facing upwards about 30cm (12in) apart in a little trench about 10cm (4in) deep and cover loosely with soil – don't pat it down. As the shoots appear, keep earthing them up, adding extra soil so that just the very tip shows.
• As the flowers begin to die off, cut the plant down and wait a week or so before harvesting; this allows the skin to toughen a bit, which makes for easier lifting and storage.

Accord
New potato; small, oval, waxy and firm; easy to grow and high-yielding. Steam or boil.

Anya
A cross between Pink Fir Apple and Desiree: long, oval and knobbly; waxy with nutty flavour. Fairly easy to grow and high-yielding. Steam or boil.

Charlotte
New potato, white and waxy but with plenty of 'give'; easy to grow, moderate yields. Steam or boil; also good for roasting if parboiled in the skin, lightly bashed and roasted in dripping and olive oil.

Desiree
Maincrop red-skinned potato, neither floury nor waxy; holds its shape. High-yielding and drought resistant. Use for roasting and chipping.

Dunbar Rover
Maincrop white heritage variety; floury texture. Moderate yield, if grown successfully. Steam or boil and butter.

Jersey Royal
New potato, grown exclusively in Jersey; white, sweet and nutty. Needs little adornment: simply steam and butter.

King Edward
Maincrop white potato; floury texture; easy to grow, moderate yields. Use for mashing, roasting and extra crispy chips.

Maris Piper
Maincrop; light-skinned, easy to grow, good yields. Very versatile: use for chipping, mashing, roasting and baking.

Nicola
Maincrop; long, yellowish and waxy, but with a bit of 'give'. Moderately resistant to disease. Boil or use in salads.

Pink Fir Apple
Maincrop salad variety; sweet, smallish, knobbly potato; a little waxy. Fairly easy to grow, but tricky to harvest and store. Use for boiling or steaming.

Rooster
Maincrop red-skinned, floury potato. Needs careful seed handling. Use for roasting, chipping and mashing.

Sante
Early maincrop variety; dry and firm-textured; grows well in all soils and very disease-resistant; good all-rounder for cooking.

Saxon
New potato, with pale skin and creamy-coloured flesh; firm rather than floury. Easy to grow; stores well; good all-rounder.

Garden minestrone soup

2 tbsp olive oil

1 onion, peeled and diced

1 garlic clove, crushed, peeled and diced

2 celery sticks, diced

1 leek, diced

2 carrots, peeled and diced

1 courgette, diced

about 850ml (1½ pints) chicken stock

400g (14oz) can chopped tomatoes

100g (3½oz) raw spaghetti

100g (3½oz) canned haricot beans

sea salt and black pepper

½ head of cabbage, shredded

1 bunch of parsley, chopped

50g (2oz) Parmesan cheese, freshly grated

1. Put the oil and all the diced ingredients in a large saucepan and cook over a medium heat for 8 minutes without browning.

2. Add the stock and canned tomatoes, bring to the boil and simmer for 10 minutes.

3. Break the spaghetti into pieces and add to the pan, then stir in the haricot beans and simmer for 12 minutes. Season and stir again.

4. Finally, add the cabbage and parsley, simmer for 2 minutes, then serve with Parmesan sprinkled on the top.

Serves 4–6
Takes 45 minutes
This great Italian soup is now a firm favourite around the world, and inevitably there are many variations of it. For example, some people add diced bacon at the start of the cooking process, others add chilli, but I have given you our classic version.

Parsnip soup

4 shallots, peeled and chopped

700g (1lb 9oz) parsnips, peeled and chopped

2 tsp ground cumin

25g (1oz) butter

1.2 litres (2 pints) duck stock

100ml (3½fl oz) double cream

1. Gently sauté the shallots, parsnips and cumin in the butter for 10 minutes, but do not allow them to brown.

2. Add the stock and season, bring to the boil and simmer for 20 minutes.

3. Using a hand-held blender, whiz the soup until smooth. Return to the pan, add the cream and reheat. Serve with a sprinkling of chopped parsley if you wish.

Serves 4
Takes 45 minutes
The sweet flavour and almost creamy texture of parsnips makes them fantastic for soup. Here the cumin adds a gentle spiciness, while the duck stock adds richness and depth.

Spiced butternut soup

900g (2lb) butternut squash

25g (1oz) butter

2 tbsp olive oil

1 onion, peeled and diced

1 garlic clove, crushed, peeled and diced

75g (2½oz) cashew nuts, chopped

2 tsp curry powder

sea salt

freshly ground black pepper

1 litre (1¾ pints) vegetable or chicken stock

1. Wash the squash, cut it in half and scoop out all the seeds. Roughly chop into 5cm (2in) pieces.

2. Heat the butter and olive oil in a large pan, add the onion and sauté gently for 5 minutes without browning.

3. Add the garlic, cashew nuts, curry powder and seasoning. Cook for a further 2 minutes.

4. Add all the squash and stock, bring to the boil and simmer for 25 minutes. Using a hand-held blender, whiz the soup until smooth. Serve with a sprinkling of chopped coriander if you wish.

Serves 4

Takes 40 minutes

We also call this 'sunshine soup' because of its amazing colour. There is no need to peel the **squash** *because the skin is relatively thin and softens during cooking. Also, like many vegetables, the skin contains most of the vitamins, so keeping it makes a more nutritious soup.*

Cauliflower cheese

1 large cauliflower

50g (2oz) butter

50g (2oz) flour

600ml (1 pint) milk

sea salt

freshly ground white pepper

1 tsp English mustard powder

140g (5oz) Montgomery Cheddar cheese or Beaufort cheese, grated

1. Trim the cauliflower, cut into florets and steam for 5 minutes.

2. Melt the butter in a saucepan, add the flour and mix until smooth. Stir over a low heat for 2 minutes. Take off the heat and slowly whisk in the milk, seasoning and mustard until smooth.

3. Return to the heat and bring to the boil, stirring constantly, so that it does not catch. Boil for 1 minute, then add half the cheese and mix off the heat.

4. Preheat the grill. Add the steamed cauliflower to the sauce, stir to coat, then place in an ovenproof dish. Sprinkle with the remaining cheese and place under the hot grill for 5 minutes, until golden.

Serves 4

Takes 30 minutes

As a supper dish or a vegetable accompaniment to a roast, you can't go wrong with cauliflower cheese. It's important to steam rather than boil the cauliflower because it absorbs less water and won't dilute the cheese sauce. While the cheese traditionally used is mature Cheddar, you might like to try Beaufort, which is an excellent hard cheese from the Savoie region of France.

Beetroot tops with anchovies

1 tbsp olive oil

1 garlic clove, crushed, peeled and diced

1 red chilli, chopped

3 preserved anchovy fillets, chopped

100g (3½oz) breadcrumbs

500g (1lb 2oz) beetroot tops, roughly chopped

1. Heat the oil in a large pan, add the garlic, chilli, anchovies and breadcrumbs and cook until just golden. Transfer to a plate.

2. Add a little more oil to the pan, place the beetroot tops in it and toss well. Sauté until wilted, about 5 minutes.

3. Add the reserved breadcrumb mixture to the pan, stir well and serve at once.

Serves 4

Takes 15 minutes

Once you've tried this tasty way of cooking beetroot tops, never again will you throw them away.

Roasted beetroot & carrots

3 tbsp olive oil

4 raw beetroot, trimmed but not peeled

4 carrots, peeled and cut into chunks

1 sprig of thyme

sea salt

freshly ground black pepper

1. Preheat the oven to 190°C/375°F/gas mark 5.

2. Cut the beetroot into wedges. Place in a roasting tin with all the other ingredients and toss well. Roast for 40 minutes, turning halfway through the cooking time. Serve straight away.

Serves 4

Takes 45 minutes

Roasting beetroot intensifies its flavour, and the beautiful velvety texture marries well with carrots. While great with roasts, this dish can very easily be turned into a starter or salad. Cook as directed, then place on a bed of mixed salad leaves and crumble creamy goats' cheese over the top.

Potato gnocchi with mushrooms & spinach

750g (1lb 10oz) floury
potatoes (see page 167)
175g (6oz) semolina flour
1 egg
pinch of freshly grated
nutmeg

For the vegetables
1 tbsp olive oil
300g (10½oz)
mushrooms, sliced
1 garlic clove, crushed,
peeled and diced
200g (7oz) young leaf
spinach
4 tbsp crème fraîche
100g (3½oz) mature
Cheddar cheese, grated

1. Cook the potatoes in salted boiling water for 20 minutes, until soft. Drain and mash. Add the semolina flour, egg and nutmeg and mix together until it forms a smooth ball.

2. Lightly dust a work surface with semolina flour. Divide the potato mixture into 4 equal pieces and roll each piece into a sausage shape just over 2.5cm (1in) in diameter. Cut them into 2.5cm (1in) lengths, then mark each little 'pillow' with a fork on each side.

3. Heat a large pan of salted water and, when boiling, add the gnocchi in small batches – do not overcrowd the pan. Cook for 2 minutes and they will rise to the top. Remove with a slotted spoon and place on a clean tea towel to drain.

4. Preheat the oven to 180°C/350°F/gas mark 4.

5. Put the oil and mushrooms in a pan and sauté for 5 minutes. Add the garlic and cook for a further 2 minutes.

6. Combine the gnocchi, spinach and mushrooms with the crème fraîche and half the cheese. Place in an ovenproof dish, top with the remaining cheese and bake in the top of the oven for 15–20 minutes.

Serves 4
Takes 1½ hours
There is something very rewarding about making your own gnocchi: it's relaxing and makes a very economical family supper.
The spinach does not need additional cooking – instead it wilts in the heat of the finished dish.

Creamed potatoes
with fresh horseradish sauce

800g (1lb 12oz) Nadine or Saxon potatoes, peeled
175ml (6fl oz) milk
50g (2oz) butter
sea salt
freshly ground white pepper
8cm (3in) piece of fresh horseradish, peeled and finely grated

1. Cut the potatoes into similar-sized pieces and place in a pan of water. Bring to the boil, then simmer for 20 minutes. When soft to the point of a knife, drain and return them to the pan. Shake over a low heat to release any excess moisture.

2. Pass the potatoes through a ricer, then return them to the pan. Add the milk, butter, seasoning and horseradish and mix well using a hand masher.

Serves 4
Takes 35 minutes
Here's the ideal accompaniment to a beef casserole, such as Slow-braised ox cheek cooked in stout (see page 82). Mashed potato can carry lots of different flavours, so why not try it with other variations, such as mustard powder, fried onions, chopped parsley, grated cheese or fried bacon?

Celeriac gratin

1 kg (2lb 4oz) celeriac, peeled and cut into 5cm (2in) cubes
200g (7oz) smoked bacon lardons
50g (2oz) butter
50g (2oz) flour
400ml (14fl oz) milk
sea salt
freshly ground white pepper
200g (7oz) Cheddar cheese, grated

1. Put the celeriac into a pan of salted water, boil for 5 minutes, then drain.

2. In another pan, fry the bacon lardons for about 5 minutes, until golden, and set aside.

3. Preheat the grill. Melt the butter in the bacon pan, add the flour and mix to a paste. Slowly add the milk off the heat, stirring until blended. Return to the heat and bring to the boil, stirring constantly until thick. Remove from the heat, add the celeriac, bacon, seasoning and half the cheese. Mix well, then place in an ovenproof baking dish and sprinkle with the remaining cheese.

4. Place under the grill for 8–10 minutes, until bubbling and golden.

Serves 4 as a main course, or 8 as an accompaniment
Takes 45 minutes
While celeriac is related to celery and has a similar flavour, it is totally different in appearance and texture – a knobbly ball rather than stringy sticks. In fact, celeriac is a a versatile vegetable because the stalks can be used as celery and the leaves as parsley.

Purple Peruvian potato pea crush

400g (14oz) Purple
Peruvian potatoes,
unpeeled

400g (14oz) freshly
shelled or frozen peas

50g (2oz) butter

2 tbsp olive oil

sea salt

freshly ground black
pepper

1. Put the potatoes in a saucepan of salted water, bring to the boil and simmer for 20 minutes. Lift out of the pan with a slotted spoon, then add the peas and simmer for 3–4 minutes.

2. Roughly chop the potatoes, drain the peas and return both to the saucepan. Crush lightly with a masher, then stir in the butter, oil and seasoning.

Serves 4

Takes 35 minutes

You're in for a surprise if you've never seen the potatoes used in this recipe. The tubers are purple all the way through and make a colourful addition to any table.

Creamy mashed peas

200g (7oz) new potatoes

400g (14oz) freshly
shelled peas

100g (3½oz) bacon bits

50g (2oz) butter

1 tbsp crème fraîche

1 bunch of mint, chopped

sea salt

freshly ground black
pepper

1. Boil the potatoes in salted water until tender – about 15 minutes. Add the peas and cook for a further 3 minutes. Using a slotted spoon, set aside 2 spoonfuls of the peas.

2. Put the bacon into a small pan with half the butter and cook for 5 minutes, until just golden.

3. Meanwhile, drain the potatoes and peas, then return to their pan and toss over a low heat to remove excess moisture.

4. Take off the heat and mash until smooth. Add the reserved peas, plus the bacon, remaining butter, crème fraîche, mint and seasoning. Mix well over a low heat and serve piping hot.

Serves 4

Takes 30 minutes

Potatoes, peas and bacon are three ingredients that really complement each other. Try this dish with roast spring lamb.

Shredded ham & pea pot

2 smoked pork hocks

175g (6oz) freshly shelled peas

leaves from 1 large bunch of flat leaf parsley, chopped

85g (3oz) Parmesan cheese, freshly grated

sea salt

freshly ground black pepper

4 tbsp mascarpone

100ml (3½fl oz) double cream

1. Place the hocks in a large pan, cover with cold water and bring to the boil. Cover and simmer for 2 hours, until the meat is tender.

2. Transfer the hocks to a plate and set aside. Reserve 125ml (4fl oz) of the stock and freeze the remainder to use another time.

3. When the hocks are cool enough to handle, remove and discard the skin along with any excess fat. Pick all the meat off the bones, roughly chop it and place in a bowl.

4. Heat the reserved stock with the peas and cook for 3 minutes. Add to the ham, then stir in the parsley, Parmesan, seasoning, mascarpone and cream until evenly combined. Serve immediately.

Serves 6–8

Takes 2½ hours

The pork hocks used here have wonderfully sweet, melting meat, and their smoky flavour combines perfectly with the other ingredients. The finished dish makes a tasty sauce for pasta or jacket potatoes.

Vegetable stir-fry

5cm (2 in) piece of fresh root ginger, peeled and diced

1 green chilli, chopped

2 garlic cloves, crushed, peeled and diced

1 onion, peeled and finely sliced

300g (10½oz) carrots, peeled and cut into sticks

½ head of green cabbage, shredded

4 spring onions, sliced

1 bunch of coriander, chopped

200g (7oz) dried noodles

1 tbsp sesame oil

1 tbsp vegetable oil

3 tbsp soy sauce

juice of 1 lime

Serves 4

Takes 20 minutes

If you are a keen gardener, this stir-fry is for you.

Do vary the ingredients according to availability and your personal likes. If you want to make this dish more substantial, add some strips of flash-fried chicken or beef.

1. It's best to prepare all the ingredients before starting to cook as you need to work fast with a stir-fry. Make sure you keep them in separate piles.

2. Cook the noodles according to the packet instructions (usually in boiling water for about 5 minutes). Drain well and toss in the sesame oil.

3. Meanwhile, heat the vegetable oil in a wok and add the ginger, chilli, garlic, onion and carrots. Stir-fry for 4 minutes, moving the vegetables constantly. Add the cabbage and spring onions and stir-fry for 1 minute. Add the coriander, cooked noodles, soy sauce and lime juice and toss well. Serve immediately.

Broad bean & chorizo risotto

1 tbsp olive oil

100g (3½oz) smoked bacon, diced

2 shallots, peeled and diced

2 garlic cloves, crushed, peeled and chopped

400g (14oz) chorizo sausages

300g (10½oz) Carnaroli rice

1 litre (1¾ pints) hot chicken stock

300g (10½oz) freshly shelled broad beans

75g (2½oz) Parmesan cheese, freshly grated

sea salt

freshly ground black pepper

75g (2½oz) Parmesan cheese, grated

1. Put the oil, bacon, shallots, garlic and whole chorizo sausages into a pan and cook gently for 8 minutes, stirring now and again.

2. Add the rice and stir to coat with the cooking juices.

3. Add just enough chicken stock to cover the rice, stir well, then simmer gently, stirring frequently. As the liquid is absorbed, add more stock, allowing each addition to be absorbed before adding the next.

4. Just before adding the last of the stock, stir in the broad beans and cook for 4 minutes.

5. Remove the sausages and slice thinly. Return them to the pan, season, then add the Parmesan and mix well.

Serves 4

Takes 40 minutes

I like to use Carnaroli rice in this dish as it has a high starch content, which helps to deliver a creamier risotto. We make our own chorizo sausages on the farm in Yorkshire, but you can get them from almost any supermarket these days.

Tomatoes

On the farm we've been known to grow over 40 different varieties of tomato, giving us lots to use in the kitchen, especially in our chutneys (see pages 230–34).

Good tomatoes need very little done to them: they can either be eaten straight from the plant a blissful experience on a sunny morning – or sliced, dotted with buffalo mozzarella, torn basil and maybe a sprinkling of finely sliced red onion, then dressed and seasoned.

When the summer is in full swing and a glut is upon you, it is really worth making your own passata (see below) to use later in the year because it adds fantastic flavour to so many dishes.

Passata

1.5kg (3lb 5oz) ripe tomatoes

5 garlic cloves, crushed, peeled and diced

3 tbsp olive oil

sea salt

freshly ground black pepper

1. Put all the ingredients in a large saucepan. Place over a low to medium heat, cover and simmer very gently, stirring from time to time, until the tomatoes break down and the mixture becomes very juicy. At this point, increase the heat and simmer for 1¼ hours, stirring frequently.

2. Pass the tomato mixture through a mouli or sieve to remove the skins and seeds. Return the pulp to a large saucepan and simmer with the lid off for a further 1 hour until the sauce becomes rich and thick.

3. Pour into sterilized bottles or jars (see page 222) and seal tightly. Label and date each one, then store in a cool, dark place until needed.

Makes 1 litre (1¾ pints)

Takes 3 hours

Making passata is a terrific way of using up a glut of tomatoes, and it's such a useful ingredient for sauces, casseroles, pizza toppings and soups. It can be stored for up to eight months in a cool, dark larder.

Tomato & green bean salad

200g (7oz) French beans, trimmed and chopped

200g (7oz) runner beans, trimmed and chopped

200g (7oz) freshly shelled broad beans

200g (7oz) freshly shelled peas

300g (10½oz) variously coloured fresh tomatoes, chopped

8 spring onions, sliced

leaves from 1 large bunch of mint, chopped

3 tbsp olive oil

juice of 1 lemon

sea salt

freshly ground black pepper

1 tsp black onion seeds

1. Cook all the beans and peas in a large pan of boiling water for 4 minutes. Drain and plunge into iced water until cold, then drain again.

2. Place the cold beans and peas in a large bowl, add the tomatoes, spring onions, mint, olive oil, lemon juice and seasoning and toss well. Sprinkle with the onion seeds and serve.

Serves 8

Takes 35 minutes

A vibrant and delicious salad packed with summer flavours, this is great for serving at barbecues. Try adding crumbled feta for a different twist.

Bulgur wheat salad

200g (7oz) bulgur wheat

6 vine tomatoes, diced

1 red onion, peeled and diced

1 large bunch of flat leaf parsley, chopped

2 tbsp olive oil

juice of 2 lemons

sea salt

freshly ground black pepper

1. Put the bulgur wheat in a pan of boiling water, then simmer for 15 minutes. Drain and set aside to cool.

2. Place all the other ingredients in a bowl and mix well.

3. When the bulgur is cool, add it to the bowl and mix again. Check the seasoning and serve.

Serves 4

Takes 40 minutes

This fresh-tasting but simple salad needs an abundance of chopped parsley. In fact, it should be so green that you can hardly see the bulgur. It's a great addition to summer barbecues.

Bread salad

200g (7oz) stale sourdough or rustic-style bread, cut into cubes

6 vine tomatoes, cored and sliced into thin wedges

1 small red onion, peeled and diced

1 tbsp small capers

6 preserved anchovies, diced

1 cucumber, peeled, deseeded and cut into chunks

juice of 1 lemon

5 tbsp olive oil

1 tbsp red wine vinegar

sea salt

freshly ground black pepper

1 bunch of flat-leaf parsley, chopped

1. Place the bread in a single layer in the bottom of a large bowl. Add the tomatoes, then sprinkle with the onion, capers, anchovies and cucumber.

2. Pour over the lemon juice, olive oil and vinegar, add seasoning and finish with the chopped parsley.

3. Cover and leave the salad to sit for 3–4 hours. Just before serving, toss well to mix all those wonderful flavours.

Serves 4–6

Takes 30 minutes, plus 3-4 hours to marinate

Also known as panzanella, this Tuscan salad is served throughout Italy and all along the French Mediterranean coast. It is a delicious lunchtime dish, bursting with flavours that will bring a ray of sunshine to your summer table.

Food from the wild

The lure of the wild

There's enormous satisfaction to be had from gathering elements of a meal from the wild, and even more when you find enough to turn into jelly or jam, or use to flavour alcohol. You can enjoy these products for a long time after the growing season is over and glory in your farsightedness. Similarly, game is plentiful during the late summer and autumn, and while you might not be able to shoot your own, game is available from many butchers and offers loads of flavour for relatively little expense, especially when bought late in the season.

Hedgerows provide a marvellous introduction to foraging because they're often full of nuts, berries and seeds. Inevitably, the edible delights are numerous – sloes, cob nuts, wild pears, elderflowers and berries, rosehips, nettles, dandelions – the list goes on and on.

So why not find yourself a large, twisting and unruly hedge, wear long sleeves to protect your arms from thorns, and start picking. And, of course, foraging needn't be restricted to country lanes and fields, In fact, it is becoming increasingly popular in towns and cities.

Tips for successful foraging

• Be prepared. Wear a long-sleeved jumper or jacket and thick gloves, lest you be stung by nettles and pricked by thorns. A pair of scissors and a small penknife can be a great help where fingers alone might struggle or, even worse, crush your spoils. But at the same time:

• Be opportunist. Keep a carrier bag at the ready so you can take advantage if you happen to spy perfectly ripe brambles or elderflower in full bloom.

• Be respectful – and legal. Don't trespass on private land. If, for example, you spot a crop of wild gooseberries that appears to be going begging, politely ask the landowners if you may pick some, and offer to bake them a pie in return.

• Don't be greedy. It's selfish to pick everything in sight, so make sure you leave plenty for fellow foragers and, most importantly, for the birds and other wildlife.

• Don't eat anything you cannot confidently identify. The results can be anything from unpleasant to deadly.

Mushrooms

Although they can prove elusive, wild mushrooms are definitely worth a foraging trip or two because of their wonderful flavour and also because they tend to be rather expensive in markets and shops. First, though, you must get at least one good handbook about mushrooms, with clear pictures so you can identify what is edible and what is not, and that helps you to distinguish similar-looking mushrooms, some of which are unsafe to eat.

We've yet to find any particularly valuable or exotic mushrooms around the farm, thanks to the ground being constantly fertilized by livestock, but we do come across delicious puffball and oyster mushrooms, and are occasionally surprised with a bumper crop of button mushrooms. In 2009 the Alma field, home to some of our belted Galloway cattle, contained so many button mushrooms, many as big as a hand, that we had to carry them back to the farm by wheelbarrow.

Basic mushroom-foraging kit

• Paring knife, to cut the mushrooms at the stem rather than pull them out of the ground.

• Basket or some paper bags, never plastic, as the mushrooms will sweat and quickly spoil.

• Two handbooks – one for making the first identification, and the second for cross-checking it.

• Long cane or walking stick, which can be handy for gently moving plants to see if there's anything below them.

• Brush – a decent-sized pastry brush is ideal – for gently removing dirt and debris, which can damage the spores of the mushroom.

Mushroom & bacon suet-crust pudding

250g (9oz) smoked bacon pieces

1 onion, peeled and diced

2 garlic cloves, crushed, peeled and diced

400g (14oz) mushrooms, chopped

1 bunch of flat leaf parsley, chopped

1 tbsp flour

sea salt (optional if using salty bacon)

freshly ground black pepper

200ml (7fl oz) stock or red wine

For the pastry

300g (10½oz) plain flour

160g (5¾oz) shredded suet

1. First make the pastry. Rub the flour and suet together in a bowl. Add a little cold water and mix with a round-bladed knife. Gradually add more water until a dough forms, then knead lightly until smooth.

2. Butter a 1.2 litre (2 pint) pudding basin. Cut off two-thirds of the dough and, on a lightly floured work surface, roll it into a circle large enough to line the basin and slightly overhang the sides (for the lining technique, see page 160). Roll out the remaining pastry to fit the top of the basin.

3. Place the bacon, onion, garlic, mushrooms, parsley, flour and seasoning (if using) in a bowl and mix well. Spoon the mixture into the prepared basin and press the mixture down firmly. Add the stock or wine.

4. Brush the pastry edge with water, sit the pastry circle on top and press together to seal.

5. Cover the top of the pudding with a double sheet of baking parchment and foil, both of them pleated in the middle to allow for expansion as the pudding cooks. Tie in place with string and make a loop across the top as a handle.

6. Sit the basin on a trivet in a saucepan and pour in enough boiling water to come halfway up the sides. Cover with a tight-fitting lid and simmer gently for 2¼ hours, checking the water level frequently.

7. To serve, remove the foil and parchment, run a sharp knife around the edge of the pudding, then invert onto a plate.

Serves 4

Takes 3¼ hours

This savoury pudding is the perfect winter warmer. Don't be surprised if the basin seems too full when you add the filling – the mushrooms will shrink as the pudding steams.

Mushroom stroganoff

400g (14oz) rump steak

vegetable oil, for frying

sea salt

freshly ground black
pepper

60g (2¼oz) butter

2 onions, peeled and sliced

3 garlic cloves, crushed,
peeled and finely diced

250g (9oz) wild field
mushrooms or Portobello
mushrooms, cut into 1cm
(½in) slices

2 tbsp brandy

6 tbsp crème fraîche

handful of flat leaf parsley,
roughly chopped

1. Rub the steak with a little oil and lightly season with salt and pepper. Heat a large frying pan over a high heat, and fry the steak until medium rare, about 3–5 minutes on each side, depending on thickness. Transfer to a plate, leave to rest for 5 minutes, then cut into strips 1.5cm (¾in) wide.

2. Put 30g (1oz) of the butter in the steak pan and gently fry the onions and garlic until soft with just a little colour. Transfer to a bowl.

3. Add the remaining butter to the pan, increase the heat and sauté the mushrooms until nicely browned and nutty. Return the onions to the pan, lower the heat and stir.

4. Pour in the brandy, stir until absorbed, then add the crème fraîche. Return the beef to the pan, add the parsley and let everything cook gently for 2 minutes. Season to taste and serve with boiled rice.

Serves 3–4

Takes 40 minutes

The secret of a good stroganoff is plenty of onions, lots of garlic, a little brandy and a good dollop of crème fraîche. For a vegetarian version, you can omit the beef and double the quantity of mushrooms.

Mushroom pancakes

50g (2oz) butter

500g (1lb 2oz) field mushrooms, sliced

1 onion, peeled and chopped

2 garlic cloves, crushed, peeled and chopped

sea salt

freshly ground black pepper

50ml (2fl oz) white wine

100ml (3½fl oz) double cream

1 bunch of chives, chopped

1 bunch of flat leaf parsley, chopped

100g (3½oz) soft goats' cheese, crumbled

For the batter

100g (3½oz) plain flour

pinch of salt

2 eggs

250ml (9fl oz) milk

1 tbsp vegetable oil, plus extra for frying

1. First make the batter. Sift the flour and salt into a large jug and make a well in the centre. Add the eggs and a little of the milk, then mix with a wooden spoon, gradually drawing in the flour until the mixture is smooth. Add the remaining milk and the oil and beat well. Cover and chill for 30 minutes.

2. Heat a pancake pan, brush lightly with oil and pour in small amount of the batter. Quickly swish it around the pan to spread it evenly over the base, then cook for 1 minute. Run a palette knife around the edge of the pancake, flip it over and cook for another minute. Slide the pancake onto a plate, cover and keep warm. Repeat this step until you have 12 pancakes. Be sure to interleave the finished pancakes with greaseproof paper to stop them sticking together.

3. Meanwhile, make the filling. Heat the butter in a large frying pan, add the mushrooms and onion and fry gently for 10 minutes, stirring frequently. Add the garlic, seasoning, wine and cream and cook very gently for 10 minutes. Finally, stir in the chives, parsley and cheese.

4. Divide the mushroom mixture equally between the pancakes, placing it across the middle of each one. Roll up and serve at once.

Serves 4

Takes 40 minutes, plus 30 minutes to rest

During the autumn, when wild mushrooms are abundant, try making this simple yet delicious supper dish. All you need to go with it is a green salad and perhaps some crusty bread.

Wild mushroom tagliatelle with tarragon

250g (9oz) good-quality dried tagliatelle or fettuccine

2 tbsp olive oil

sea salt

25g (1oz) butter

2 garlic cloves, crushed, peeled and diced

300g (10½oz) fresh wild mushrooms

30g (1¼oz) dried porcini mushrooms, rehydrated in a little hot water, then drained and liquid reserved

sea salt

freshly ground black pepper

100ml (3½fl oz) double cream

handful of tarragon, chopped

75g (2½oz) Parmesan cheese, freshly grated

1. Cook the pasta in a large pan of boiling salted water according to the packet instructions.

2. Meanwhile, put the oil and butter in a large, deep frying pan and gently sauté the garlic until soft but not brown.

3. Add all the mushrooms, a good pinch of salt and some pepper. Turn the heat up just a little and sauté the mushrooms until soft.

4. Pour in the mushroom stock (being careful not to tip in any sediment), add the cream and simmer for 2 minutes. Stir in the tarragon and season to taste.

5. Drain the pasta, add to the mushroom pan and mix well. Stir in the Parmesan and serve immediately.

Serves 4

Takes 30 minutes

Here's a simple pasta dish that makes the most of wild mushrooms. Feel free to use fresh pasta if you wish, but good-quality dried pasta is more than adequate.

Wild herbs

There are literally hundreds of edible leaves ripe for foraging in the UK, from magical-sounding plants such as mugwort and hogweed to the common-or-garden nettle. Below are a few basic tips, plus some information about the leaves you're most likely to find and recognize. But do take care that you use reputable sources to identify what you have foraged before you eat it. Never eat anything unless you are sure what it is and that you know it is safe to eat it.

Tips for successful herb foraging

• Be careful where you pick. Avoid places that have been sprayed with pesticides.

• Don't pick from roadsides as you'll consume more vehicle fumes than nutrients.

• Pick carefully so as not to bruise the leaves. A pair of kitchen scissors comes in very handy.

• Wear gloves, especially if you're picking nettles.

• Rinse herbs thoroughly before use, particularly if the leaves in question are going to be used raw in a salad or pesto (see page 202).

• As always, do not eat anything you cannot confidently identify.

Sorrel
Pleasantly sour, lemony-flavoured sorrel leaves make a good soup in their own right, but also lift iron-rich soups, such as watercress or spinach. The leaves also make a good salad ingredient when their acidic taste is complemented by a sweet or mustardy dressing.

Wild garlic
Chances are that you'll smell wild garlic, or ramsons, before you see it. It has the heady aroma of freshly chopped spring onions and can be found carpeting woodland floors across the UK during the spring. The long, green leaves rather than the bulbs are eaten, and they make a great addition to almost any savoury dish, either chopped and added at the last minute as you would chives or spring onions, or stir-fried, added to soups or made into a pesto (an excellent way of storing this fleeting spring ingredient).

Nettle
Childhood foe, kitchen friend, nettles taste like a deeper and sweeter version of spinach. Just ensure that you pick and rinse them carefully – gloves and tongs come in very useful – but the 'sting' disappears once the nettles are cooked. They can be used in lots of different ways: wilt them in butter with plenty of cracked pepper for a simple side dish; chop and stir them into stews and braises; use them in soups; or even dot them over a pizza base with a little garlic butter, some mozzarella and tiny cubes of cooked potato.

Dandelion
When the leaves are young and tender – before the flower has formed – dandelion leaves make a good addition to salads and soups. Larger leaves tend to be slightly bitter, but make a delicious side dish if gently fried in a little butter with garlic and bacon.

Baked eggs with wild garlic

1 slice of good white bread
or brioche

Dijon mustard

1 rasher of bacon, cubed

1 tbsp wild garlic, shredded

1 egg

2 tbsp double cream

freshly ground black
pepper

1 tsp grated mature hard
cheese, such as Cheddar,
Lancashire, Parmesan,
Gruyère or Comté

1. Preheat the oven to 180°C/350°F/gas
mark 4. Butter a large ramekin.

2. Lightly toast the bread, then cut a circle
from it that will fit in the bottom of the dish.
Spread the toast with a lick of mustard, then
place in the ramekin.

3. Heat a small frying pan and fry the bacon
until crisp. Add to the ramekin, sprinkle
with the wild garlic, then crack the egg on
top. Spoon over the cream, add a few twists
of pepper and sprinkle with the cheese.

4. Bake in the oven for 10–12 minutes, until
just firm.

Serves 1

Takes 20 minutes

*More than the sum of its
ingredients, this recipe makes
a satisfying breakfast, lunch or
supper dish. As the bacon and
cheese are both salty, no extra salt
is needed, but do offer some extra
toast for dipping because the dish
is luxuriously creamy. When wild
garlic is unavailable, replace with
finely chopped chives.*

Cheese & rosemary wafers

leaves from 2 sprigs of
rosemary, chopped

250g (9oz) hard cheese,
coarsely grated

1. Preheat the oven to 180°C/350°F/gas
mark 6 and line 2 baking sheets with baking
parchment.

2. Combine the rosemary with the cheese
and mix well.

3. Using a teaspoon, place little piles of the
cheese mixture on the parchment, spacing
them at least 2.5cm (1in) apart, as they
spread while cooking.

4. Bake for 8–10 minutes, until golden, then
set aside to cool for 5 minutes. Carefully
peel off the paper and serve the wafers with
drinks.

Makes 25

Takes 35 minutes

*Perfect to eat with any of your
hedgerow spirits (see pages 212-
18), these savoury morsels can be
made a day in advance, but must be
stored in an airtight container.
Use your favourite hard cheese,
such as Parmesan or Cheddar.*

Pesto

From the Latin word *pestare*, meaning 'to pound', pesto is a mixture of pounded ingredients, the classic ones being basil leaves, garlic and pine nuts, which are then combined with Parmesan cheese and olive oil to make a marvellously fragrant and delicious sauce. Home-made pesto knocks spots off anything you can buy in a jar because it retains the essence of each ingredient. It's far removed from the uniform purée sold in supermarkets.

Pesto can be made with a variety of other ingredients, such as rocket, parsley or watercress in place of basil, and hazelnuts, walnuts or pistachios instead of pine nuts. You can also omit the Parmesan if you wish, or substitute another type of cheese. Experiment with different flavours and ingredients, but don't be tempted to add too many. Whatever you choose, the method is basically the same. Using a large chopping board and a mezzaluna or big kitchen knife, start by chopping the garlic, then add the nuts, chopping them in batches. Gradually add small handfuls of whatever leaf you are using, chopping each addition. (Adding them last gives them less time to lose their colour.) Finally, work in the cheese (if using), then transfer the mixture to a bowl and top with a little light olive oil.

The rule with pesto is to be generous with the leaves and scant with the seasoning. In fact, if you're making pesto for pasta, gnocchi or potatoes, the salt added to their cooking water should be all the seasoning you need. Just add two tablespoons of it to the finished pesto.

Pesto-making tips

• Wash the leaves thoroughly and pat them dry on kitchen paper so that you don't introduce additional moisture.

• Toast the nuts, but don't overdo it or they will become too dry to produce a creamy texture. A few minutes of being shaken in a medium-hot pan is all they need.

• Store fresh pesto in the fridge, wiping the inside of the jar clean with kitchen paper (right down to the level of the pesto), then top with a layer of oil and seal tightly. This will ensure the content is airtight and it should keep for about a week.

• If you're making a large batch of pesto and intend to freeze it, don't add any cheese. It should be added later, once the pesto has defrosted.

Game

On Eastmoor and Blandsby farms, where we rear our cattle and pigs, there is a small population of wild game birds – pheasants, partridge, wood pigeons and wild duck – though in numbers barely enough to supply our own shops. We take birds from a few other local farms, but try to avoid buying from bigger shoots as their birds are bred in captivity, often with large doses of antibiotics, before being released in order to be shot. For me, the whole point of game is that it has lived a decent life in the wild so that the meat is full of flavour, not full of drugs.If possible, ask your butcher for the source of his game so you know what you're eating.

Pheasant risotto

2 pheasants, plucked and cleaned

2 tbsp olive oil

1 onion, peeled and diced

2 garlic cloves, crushed, peeled and diced

1 celery stick, diced

50g (2oz) smoked bacon, chopped

250g (9oz) Arborio rice

50g (2oz) butter

100g (3½oz) wild mushrooms, torn or sliced

sea salt

freshly ground black pepper

1 bunch of flat leaf parsley, chopped

50g (2oz) Parmesan cheese, freshly grated

1. Place the pheasants in a large saucepan, add 2 litres (3½ pints) of water and bring to the boil. Cover and simmer for 40 minutes, then transfer the birds to a plate and leave to cool for 1 hour. Reserve the stock.

2. Peel all the skin off the birds, then strip the meat off the bones, carefully removing the needle-like tendons from the legs. Discard the skin and bones, then roughly chop the meat.

3. Heat 1.4 litres (2½ pints) of the stock until warm. Meanwhile, heat the olive oil in medium-sized saucepan and gently cook the onion, garlic, celery and bacon for 5 minutes. Add the rice and stir to coat with the oil. Add a ladleful of the stock and stir until the rice has absorbed it. Continue adding stock until it has all been used.

4. Melt a little of the butter in a frying pan, add the mushrooms and pheasant meat, season and cook for 2 minutes.

5. When the rice is cooked, add the mushroom mixture, parsley, remaining butter and the Parmesan. Mix well, check the seasoning and serve.

Serves 6

Takes 2 hours, plus 1 hour to cool

When the game season opens in late summer/early autumn, there is great excitement about cooking and eating the first birds that become available. It is traditional to roast and serve them with game chips, bread sauce, watercress and a rich gravy, but as the season moves on, we begin to crave new ways of preparing them. This recipe is a favourite and never fails to deliver a comforting meal. Poaching the pheasant keeps the meat moist and tender, and also provides a tasty stock for cooking the rice.

Seasonal availability of game

This chart shows the dates between which it is permissible to shoot game in England (E), Scotland (S), Wales (W) and Northern Ireland (NI). The shooting seasons listed here determine the availability of fresh game. At all other times, any game sold has been farmed, frozen or imported.

Feathered game

Grouse: Aug 12–Dec 10 (E, S, W); Aug 12–Nov 30 (NI)

Black grouse: Aug 20–Dec 10 (E, S, W); not available in NI

Goose and Duck (inland): Sept 1–Jan 31 (E, S, W); Sept 1–Jan 31 (NI)

Goose and Duck (below high-water mark): Sept 1–Feb 20 (E, S, W); Sept 1–Jan 31 (NI)

Partridge: Sept 1–Feb 1 (E, S, W); Sept 1–Jan 31 (NI)

Pheasant: Oct 1–Feb 1 (E, S, W); Oct 1–Jan 31 (NI)

Woodcock: Oct 1–Jan 31 (E, W, NI); Sept 1–Jan 31 (S)

Furred game

Hare: no close season, but best during the winter months

Rabbit: should not be shot in summer breeding season

Red stags: Aug 1–April 30 (E, W, NI); July 1–Oct 20 (S)

Red hinds: Nov 1–Feb 28/29 (E, W, NI); Oct 21–Feb 15 (S)

Red deer is a native UK species and the most prolific breed. Its meat is considered the best thanks to its life in the wild and its diet of moorland herbs and heathers.

Roe bucks: April 1–Oct 31 (E, W, NI); April 1–Oct 20 (S)

Roe does: Nov 1–Feb 28/29 (E, W, NI); Oct 21–Mar 31 (S)

Reintroduced to the UK after being hunted to extinction in the seventeenth century.

Fallow bucks: Aug 1–April 30 (E, W, NI); Aug 1–April 30 (S)

Fallow does: Nov 1–Feb 28/29 (E, W, NI); Oct 21–Feb 15 (S)

Introduced by the Normans in the eleventh century, fallow deer are very widespread. There are several different types, which can be recognized by their coat colour.

Muntjac: no statutory close season (E, W, NI); Oct 21–Feb 15 (S)

Small and stocky, the muntjac was introduced to the UK in the early twentieth century and breeds all year round.

Rabbit ragù

1 rabbit, skinned, drawn and jointed

1 carrot, peeled and chopped

1 onion, peeled and chopped

2 celery sticks, chopped

1 leek, chopped

4 garlic cloves, crushed, peeled and diced

4 tomatoes, chopped

sea salt

freshly ground black pepper

200ml (7fl oz) red wine

leaves from 1 bunch of sage, chopped

1. Preheat the oven to 170°C/325°F/gas mark 3.

2. Place the rabbit in a casserole dish along with all the vegetables. Add the seasoning, wine and 500ml (18fl oz) of water, then cover with a tight-fitting lid and place in the oven for 5 hours.

3. Set aside and allow to cool. When cool enough to handle, carefully pick out all the rabbit bones. (This is a slow process because some of the bones are pin thin.)

4. Now use your hands to squeeze and break up the vegetables and meat. Adjust the consistency, if necessary, with a little extra wine. Check the seasoning and add the sage. Serve with pasta and sprinkle with grated Parmesan.

Serves 6

Takes 6 hours

Ragù is the Italian word for 'sauce'. and rabbit makes a rich and gutsy one. It requires long, slow cooking, but the end result is worth the wait.

Rabbit paupiettes with mushroom sauce

12 prunes, stoned

1 bunch of flat leaf parsley, chopped

2 sprigs of thyme

175g (6oz) minced pork

sea salt

freshly ground black pepper

1 egg

100g (3½oz) fresh breadcrumbs

4 rabbit legs, skinned and boned

8 rashers of streaky bacon

For the mushroom sauce

1 tbsp olive oil

25g (1oz) butter

1 shallot, peeled and chopped

100g (3½oz) field mushrooms, sliced

125ml (4fl oz) double cream

50ml (2fl oz) white wine

1. Preheat the oven to 180°C/350°F/gas mark 4. Lightly oil a roasting tin.

2. Chop 8 of the prunes and place in a bowl with the parsley, thyme, pork mince, seasoning, egg and breadcrumbs. Mix well, preferably with your hands.

3. Divide the mixture into 4 equal pieces and roll them into balls. Place 1 ball in the centre of each rabbit leg, wrap the meat around it and turn the parcel over so that the seam is underneath.

4. Place 2 strips of bacon around each parcel in the shape of a cross, folding the ends underneath. Top with a prune, then secure with 4 roasting bands around each parcel, or tie with string.

5. Put the paupiettes in the prepared tin and place in the oven for 30 minutes. Reduce the temperature to 150°C/300°F/gas mark 2 and cook for a further 15 minutes.

6. Meanwhile, make the sauce. Heat the oil and butter in a pan over a medium heat. Add the shallot and mushrooms and cook for 5 minutes, turning constantly until soft.

7. Add the cream and wine, bring to a simmer and cook for a futher 5 minutes, until the sauce coats the back of the spoon.

8. Add any roasting juices from the paupeittes and serve together.

Serves 2

Takes 1½ hours

Although a little fiddly to make, these parcels are worth the effort. To bone the rabbit legs, cut along the length of each one with a very sharp pointed knife, then ease the blade under the meat, working it away from the bones.

The mushroom sauce is delicious with the rabbit, and can also be tossed through pasta.

Edible flowers

It may come as a surprise that flowers can be used as much for flavour as garnish, but that is certainly the case, and there are lots to choose from. Here are listed some of the commonest edible species, plus a few ideas for using them. You could well find you already have some of them growing in your garden or window-box.

Rose

There a hundreds of rose varieties, but if you want the best flavour, use only those that have a strong, heady scent. Use as a garnish in Asian or Middle Eastern dishes. Less fragrant flowers can be sugared first. Lightly whisk an egg white with 2 tablespoons of water until a few bubbles form. Using a pastry brush, paint the separated rose petals with the mixture, then coat with caster sugar. Shake off the excess, then place on a baking sheet lined with parchment and dry for a few hours in a very low oven with the door slightly ajar. Rose petals can also be used to make rose water; simply steep a handful of fragrant petals in boiling water and leave to infuse overnight. Strain, bottle and use as a skin tonic, or strain and simmer with sugar for a syrup to use in cocktails or desserts.

Lavender

The beautiful bluey-mauve flowers of lavender can be seen growing as prodigiously in city gardens and parks as they do in the countryside. Lavender should be used quite sparingly in cooking as it has a strong flavour. Crush the flowers in a mortar and use as a rub for lamb or duck. Alternatively, infuse with cream for making custards, crème brûlée or panna cotta, or place a few flower heads in a jar of caster sugar to make scented sugar for baking.

Nasturtium

Both the flowers and leaves of nasturtium are edible, and have a peppery flavour similar to that of watercress. The orange or red flowers make a vibrant garnish, and the leaves can be used to make pesto (see page 202) – delicious with pasta or rubbed over chicken, pork or lamb for the final 20 minutes of roasting.

Chive blossom

The pretty purple flowers of the chive plant make a great garnish, adding colour and giving a milder taste of the herb itself. Add a few flower heads to a potato or tomato salad, stir through cream-based pasta dishes, or use to garnish creamy goats' cheese dressed with olive oil and black pepper.

Courgette flower

The flowers of the male courgette plant do not grow into courgettes, so can be used to make a wonderful starter. Stuff them with a mixture of ricotta, herbs and Parmesan, dust with flour, then dip into a light batter and deep-fry.

Elderflower

The season for elderflowers is brief, and varies slightly from year to year, depending on the weather. Keep your eyes peeled in mid- to late spring and try to pick the flowers on a sunny morning. Any later in the day and the sunshine could have take them past their best. However, if you come across a good-looking, fragrant crop on your way home in the evening, it's a good idea to take advantage of your find. The flowers can be used to make delicious cordial, jelly or sorbet, and even a lightly alcoholic 'champagne' (see page 217).

Lamb, lavender & herb sausages

125g (4½oz) fresh breadcrumbs

flowers from 1–2 lavender stalks (1 heaped tsp)

1 tsp fine salt

5 sage leaves, finely chopped

small handful of flat leaf parsley, finely chopped

15 chive stems, finely chopped

1kg (2lb 4oz) minced fatty lamb

1 garlic clove, crushed, peeled and finely minced

zest of 1 lemon

½ tsp freshly ground black pepper

1 tsp runny honey

8 pieces of lamb or pork caul fat (1 piece per sausage)

1. Preheat the oven to 140°C/275°F/gas mark 1. Spread the breadcrumbs over a baking tray and bake for 10–15 minutes, until they have dried a little but not coloured.

2. Put the lavender flowers in a mortar, add the salt and use the pestle to crush to a paste.

3. Combine the paste and breadcumbs in a large bowl with all the remaining ingredients, apart from the caul fat, and mix well.

4. Divide the lamb mixture into 8 equal pieces, then shape each one into a log by rolling it between your hands.

5. Carefully lay a piece of caul fat on a clean surface, place a lamb log towards the bottom edge and gently roll up, tucking the ends of the fat in as you go. Repeat to make 7 more sausages.

6. To cook the sausages, grill or barbecue them on a medium heat for 10–15 minutes, turning regularly, until cooked through. Serve with minty yoghurt and flatbreads.

Serves 4–5

Takes 1¼ hours

Here's an opportunity to try your hand at making sausages without the palaver of using traditional sausage casing. You simply roll the meat in caul fat, which you can order from your butcher, and it bastes the sausages as they cook. The lavender in the recipe lends a delicate floral, citrusy note that works well with the fresh herbs.

Duck, pear & nasturtium salad

4 confit duck legs (use 3 if they are particularly large, or see recipe introduction)

100g (3½oz) green leaves, such as watercress, baby chard or spinach

2 firm, but not hard, pears, thinly sliced

2 heads of chicory, leaves separated

light olive oil, for drizzling

12 nasturtium flowers, carefully rinsed and dried

1 handful of shelled walnuts, lightly toasted in a dry frying pan

For the dressing

1 heaped tsp Dijon mustard

1 tsp runny honey or maple syrup

juice of ½ lemon

50ml (2fl oz) olive oil

sea salt

freshly ground black pepper

1. Preheat the oven to 200°C/400°F/gas mark 6. Place the duck legs in a roasting tin and roast for 20 minutes. Set aside to cool in the tin.

2. Meanwhile, make the dressing. Put the mustard, honey and lemon juice into a small bowl, mix well, then whisk in the oil until emulsified. Taste and adjust as necessary, then add seasoning.

3. Place the leaves and pears in a bowl. Pour the dressing over them and mix well.

4. Arrange the chicory leaves on serving plates, drizzle with olive oil and sprinkle with salt. Top with the dressed pears and salad.

5. Remove the duck meat from the bones, tear into pieces and divide equally between the plates. Garnish with the nasturtiums and walnuts, then serve.

Serves 2

Takes 40 minutes

You can make this salad with fresh duck legs if you haven't made confit (see page 52) or can't find it. Simply season and roast them at 170°C/325°F/gas mark 3 for 1¼ hours, until golden and tender.

Hedgerow gin

450g (1lb) wild fruit
(e.g. damsons, sloes,
bullaces, brambles,
blackcurrants,
or a mixture)
220g (½lb) caster sugar
1 litre (1¾ pints) gin

1. Prick the fruit several times with a fork or the point of a sharp knife. Some say freezing fruit is a snappier way of piercing the skin, but I urge you not to do this. It could leave you with a dullard drink come Christmas.

2. Put the pricked fruit into a 1.4 litre (2½ pint) Kilner jar. Add the sugar and gin, then seal tightly and give it a good shake. Label and date, then store in a cool, dark place until Christmas (at least 3 months), inverting the jar 4 times every 2–3 days to ensure the sugar dissolves.

3. Taste the gin around Christmas-time. If it's too sharp or has too strong a taste of alcohol, add a little more sugar, then seal, store and invert as before for another few weeks. When ready, strain through a muslin-lined sieve and return the spirit to the empty gin bottle. Label, date and enjoy.

Makes 1 litre (1¾ pints)
Takes 30 minutes, plus at least
3 months to mature
Making hedgerow gin is far from an exact science because the fruit used will vary in flavour, acidity and juiciness. If you find your jar is not quite full when you have added the suggested amount of gin, simply top it up. Remember, a wasted space is an empty glass.

Wild versus cultivated

Almost all of the fresh produce in our gardens, greengrocers, markets and supermarkets has been cultivated and hybridized, meaning that the better characteristics of a particular fruit or vegetable have been accentuated by cross-breeding plants with particularly positive attributes. For example, the wild form of blackberries, known as brambles, are small, have a low flesh-to-seed ratio and tend to be quite tart. Cultivated blackberries, on the other hand, are larger, juicier and usually quite sweet. While blackberries are well suited to being used in puddings, tarts and sauces, wild brambles make fantastic jellies because the pectin in the seeds helps with setting. The berries are also great for flavouring gin or vodka because their tart flavour counteracts the sugar needed to soften the alcohol. Note: all wild produce should be carefully washed and dried before use.

Sloe gin or vodka

500g (1lb 2oz) sloes
(best picked from mid-
November onwards)
250g (9oz) caster sugar
500ml (18fl oz) gin or
vodka

1. Prick each sloe at least 4 times with a pin or the point of a sharp knife. Place the sloes in a 1.4 litre (2½ pint) Kilner jar and cover with the sugar. Top up with gin or vodka, then seal tightly and give the jar a good shake. Label and date, then store in a cool, dark place, shaking the jar every day for a week until all the sugar has dissolved.

2. Leave the jar in a cool, dark place for at least 3 months, then strain and bottle as described on page 212. Although you can drink the spirit at this point, it will be very strong. The longer you leave it, the better the flavour, because it mellows with time.

Makes 600ml (1 pint)
Takes 30 minutes, plus at least
3 months to mature
Christmas is just not the same without a bottle of home-made sloe gin (or vodka) to add to a cocktail or serve at the end of a meal. The rich ruby colour looks really festive, and the flavour is totally individual – both bitter and sweet.

Bullace gin

600g (1 lb 5oz) bullaces
250g (9oz) caster sugar
500ml (18fl oz) gin

1. Prick each bullace at least 6 times with a pin or the point of a sharp knife. Place the fruit in a 1.4 litre (2½ pint) Kilner jar and cover with the sugar. Add the gin, seal tightly, then give the jar a good shake. Label and date, then store in a cool, dark place, shaking the jar every day for a week until all the sugar has dissolved.

2. Leave the jar in a cool, dark place for at least 3 months, then strain and bottle as described on page 212. Although you can drink the spirit at this point, it will be very strong. The longer you leave it, the better the flavour, because it mellows with time.

Makes 1 litre (1¾ pints)
Takes 40 minutes, plus at least 3 months to mature
Bullaces are wild plums and can be either white or purple. They are larger than sloes (to which they are related), but smaller than damsons.

Crab apple schnapps

crab apples (enough to
three-quarters fill
a 1.4 litre (2½ pint)
Kilner jar)
200g (7oz) caster sugar
3 cinnamon sticks
peel from 1 orange
and 1 lemon
1 litre (1¾ pints) vodka

1. Blanch the apples for 1 minute in hot water. Allow to cool, then slice in half.

2. Put the fruit and all the other ingredients into a 1.4 litre (2½ pint) Kilner jar, seal tightly and shake well.

3. Label and date the jar, then store in a cool, dark place for 3 months, inverting it every couple of days.

4. Around Christmas-time, taste the schnapps and if it isn't quite sweet enough, add more sugar. Shake and invert as before, and store for a few more weeks.

5. Once you're happy with the flavour, strain and bottle as described on page 212. Although you can drink the spirit at this point, it will be very strong. The longer you leave it, the better the flavour, because it mellows with time.

Makes about 1 litre (1¾ pints)
Takes 25-60 minutes, plus at least 3 months to mature
Although sour beyond edibility in their natural state, crab apples make lovely drinks, none nicer than this warming spiced schnapps. If you make this recipe around mid-September, when crab apples are in season, the schnapps should be ready to drink by Christmas.

Elderflower cordial

800g (1lb 12oz) caster
sugar
800ml (28floz) boiling
water
zest and juice of 2 lemons
14 elderflower heads

1. Combine the sugar and water in a large bowl. Add the lemon zest and juice and the elderflowers, then mix well.

2. Cover and leave in a cool place for 5 days before straining through muslin and bottling in sterilized bottles.

Makes about 1 litre (1¾ pints)
Takes 30 minutes, plus 5 days to stand
This cordial will keep for several weeks in a cool dark cupboard. Make lots and you can have a taste of the summer long after the elderflowers have disappeared.

Elderflower 'champagne'

15–18 sweet-smelling elderflower heads, depending on how strong you would like the final flavour to be

4 unwaxed lemons

4.5 litres (8 pints) boiling water

800g (1lb 12oz) caster sugar

30ml (1fl oz) white wine or cider vinegar

½ tsp dried yeast mixed with 2 tbsp tepid water (optional)

1. Gently shake the elderflower heads to remove any debris or bugs, but don't wash them or you risk losing the natural yeasts.

2. Remove the zest from the lemons and set it aside. Now peel off and discard the white pith. Cut the lemon flesh into 6 wedges.

3. Pour the boiling water into a large, non-reactive container (a plastic bucket is ideal). Add the sugar and stir until dissolved. Pour in 2 litres (3½ pints) of cold water, then add the lemon zest and flesh and the vinegar.

4. Using kitchen scissors, carefully snip the little stems of elderflowers into the liquid. Stir well, then cover with muslin or a clean towel, tucking the cloth underneath the bucket. Leave in a cool place for 2 days.

5. If, after 2 days, the liquid looks foamy, it contains enough natural yeast to create the fizz. If it looks flat, add the yeast mixture and stir well. Cover and leave for 4 days.

6. Line a sieve with muslin and strain the liquid, discarding the solids. Decant into bottles, leaving a small gap at the top to allow for the build-up of gas. Seal tightly, then label and date. Store in a cool, dark place for at least 7 days before drinking.

Makes about 7 litres (12 pints)
Takes 40 minutes, plus 6 days to stand and 1-2 weeks to mature
This 'champagne' is delightfully refreshing and costs next to nothing to make. The fermentation process produces carbon dioxide, which builds pressure in the bottles, so store it in strong glass ones with a swing-top seal, or in strong plastic bottles that have been sterilized. It will keep for six months.

Blackcurrant schnapps

500g (1lb 2oz) blackcurrants (no need to remove stalks)

6 mint leaves

1 bay leaf

1 star anise

2 tbsp caster sugar

1 litre (1¾ pints) vodka, at least 40% proof

1. Using a large needle or sharp skewer, prick a hole in each berry. Place them in a 1.4 litre (2½ pint) Kilner jar (the stalks can go in too) and add all the other ingredients, topping up with a little extra vodka if necessary. Seal tightly and shake well. Label and date, then store in a cool, dark place for 2 months, inverting the jar every 2–3 days.

2. Strain and bottle as described on page 212. If kept in a cool, dark place, the schnapps will keep almost indefinitely. Serve over ice, either on its own, or topped up with lemonade or soda.

Makes about 1 litre (1¾ pints)

Takes 30 minutes, plus 2 months to mature

Although there is relatively little sugar in this recipe, it still makes a stronger drink than the other hedgerow spirits in this book.

If at all possible, avoid buying supermarket blackcurrants for this recipe as the cultivated fruits rarely have the depth of flavour you find in wild fruit. Either take advantage of a bountiful hedgerow in July/ August, or look out for wild berries at farmers' markets and in farm shops, selecting the plumpest and juiciest you can see.

Preserves, chutneys & pickles

1

Preserves: jams, jellies & marmalade

Making jams, jellies and marmalade is not difficult, but you do need to follow some basic rules to get a successful outcome.

Tips for making jams and jellies
• Always use beautifully ripe and fragrant fruit, when the starch contained in the flesh has converted to natural sugars. Unripe fruit just doesn't taste fruity enough and requires a lot of added sugar, so you are left with a sweet but fairly tasteless preserve.
• Never use damaged fruit – it can shorten the shelf-life of the finished product.
• Make sure all your equipment is scrupulously clean.
• Avoid making one huge pan of jam: it takes a long time to reach setting point, and by then the fruit will have broken down too much and the jam will have no variance in texture. If you have vast quantities of fruit, use several pans.
• Don't overcook a jam or jelly; if the sugars start to caramelize, you lose the fruity flavour. If this happens to you, don't throw it away – it still makes a fine roly-poly or steamed pudding.
• Sterilize jars and lids to prevent bacteria contaminating the contents (see below).

How to test for setting point
• Place a saucer in the fridge when you start making your jam. When the jam has boiled for the specified time, place a spoonful of it on the saucer and chill for 5 minutes; after that, if the jam wrinkles when you push it with your finger, it has reached setting point and can be potted up.
• Alternatively, use a sugar thermometer: jams set at 105°C/220°F; marmalade at 106°C/223°F; jellies at 104°C/219°F.

How to sterilize jars
It is essential to sterilize glass containers and their lids before use. There are two ways of doing this: either put them through a hot dishwasher cycle, timing it so they are ready when your preserve is, or wash them thoroughly and place in the oven at 140°C/275°F/gas mark 1 for 30 minutes.

How to pot up
• Allow jams and jellies to cool for 20 minutes before potting up. This ensures the fruit will be evenly distributed instead of floating to the top.
• Always add hot preserves to hot jars, and cover immediately with a hot lid. This will avoid the jar cracking, and also creates a natural vacuum as the jar cools, keeping the contents airtight.
• Use good jars with undamaged, tight-fitting lids and there should be no need for wax discs on top of the jam. If in doubt, though, they do no harm and help stop spoilage.
• Remember to label and date your jars so that you know which batch to eat first.

Blackcurrant jam

1.8kg (4lb) blackcurrants,
stalks and flowers
removed
2.7kg (6lb) granulated
sugar

1. Place the blackcurrants in a pan with
1.4 litres (2½ pints) of water and bring
to the boil.

2. Lower the heat and simmer until soft. Add
the sugar and stir until dissolved. Boil until
setting point is reached (about 10 minutes).

3. Allow to cool a little, then pot up in
sterilized jars. The jam will keep for 6
months in a cool, dark place.

Makes 4kg (9lb)
Takes 1 hour
*Blackcurrants contain a high level
of pectin, a natural setting agent,
so this recipe will give you beautiful
jam every time.*

*See page 222 for information
about testing for setting point,
sterilizing jars and potting up.*

Crab apple jelly

crab apples
granulated sugar
(see step 4)

1. Wash, weigh and halve the apples, place
in a preserving pan and pour on cold water,
allowing 1 litre (1¾ pint) of water per 1kg
(2¼lb) of fruit. Bring to the boil. Simmer.

2. Once soft, tip into a muslin bag and strain
overnight over a non-metallic bowl.

3. When it has drained out of the bag,
measure the liquid and return to the
preserving pan.

4. On a baking tray in the oven, warm 750g
(1½lb) of sugar for every litre (1¾ pint)
of fruit juice. Add this warm sugar slowly
to the juice over a low heat, stirring until
dissolved.

5. Once the sugar has dissolved, bring the
resulting syrup to a fast rolling boil (small
bubbles should almost reach the top of the
pan). At this stage, do not stir.

6. Boil until the jelly reaches 105°C and sets
on a plate (see page 222), cool slightly and
bottle in sterilized jars.

Makes (see below)
Takes 2 hours, plus overnight
straining
*The amount of jelly made depends
on how much fruit you have and the
amount of juice it produces when
cooked and strained. The jelly will
keep for up to 6 months in a cool,
dark larder.*

*Do not be tempted to squeeze the
bag as the fruit strains as this will
make your jelly cloudy.*

Julie's hedgerow jelly

selection of hedgerow berries and fruit (e.g. elderberries, blackberries, rosehips, crab apples, bullaces)

granulated sugar (see step 2)

1. Place the fruits in a pan and almost cover with water. Bring to the boil, then simmer gently for 1 hour.

2. Place the pulp in a sterilized jelly bag and strain for 8 hours. Do not squeeze the bag as this will make the jelly cloudy. Measure the juice and for every 600ml (1 pint), add 450g (1lb) of sugar.

3. Place the sugar and juice in a pan and heat gently, stirring until the sugar has dissolved. Increase the heat and boil for 10 minutes, until setting point is reached.

4. Allow to cool a little, then pot up in sterilized jars. These will keep for 6 months in a cool, dark place.

Makes 1kg (2lb 4oz) jelly from every 600ml (1 pint) juice mixed with 450g (1lb) sugar

Takes 4 hours

As in the recipe on page 225, the amount of jelly made depends on how much fruit you have and the amount of juice it produces when cooked and strained.

See page 222 for information about testing for setting point, sterilizing jars and potting up.

Wortleberry compote

500g (1lb 2oz) wortleberries, picked over to remove stalks and leaves

200g (7oz) caster sugar

zest and juice of 1 lemon

1. Place the wortleberries in a large saucepan with the sugar, lemon zest and juice. Cover the pan and heat very gently for 10 minutes, shaking occasionally. The berries should have burst and released their inky juice.

2. Pot up in sterilized jars (see page 222) and store in the fridge until needed. The compote will keep for 6 months in a cool, dark place.

Makes about 700g (1lb 9oz)

Takes 30 minutes

Also known as bilberries, wortle-berries are blue and flat-topped with fragrant flesh. They can be found on moorland in August, but are small and take a long time to collect. Here they are cooked in a sugar syrup to make a compote, which can be served warm or cold with thick yoghurt, whipped cream or ice-cream, used as a fruit layer in trifle or sponge cake, or spread on home-made Drop scones (see page 247).

Gooseberry curd

900g (2lb) gooseberries
350g (12oz) golden caster
sugar
250g (9oz) butter
3 eggs plus 3 egg yolks,
beaten together

1. Place the gooseberries in a pan with 100ml (3½fl oz) of water. Bring to the boil, then simmer for 15 minutes, until the berries have burst and are soft. Pass the mixture through a fine sieve.

2. Return the purée to a saucepan, add the sugar and butter and stir over a very low heat until the sugar has dissolved.

3. Place the gooseberry mixture in a bowl set over a pan of simmering water. Stir in the eggs, then keep stirring until the curd thickens. Pot up immediately in sterilized jars (see page 222). Stored in the refrigerator, the curd will keep for 2 weeks.

Makes 1.5kg (3lb 5oz)
Takes 40 minutes
Originally found wild in hedgerows, gooseberries were taken into cultivation by the Victorians, who developed a liking for them. They can be either blush red, pale yellow or cool green in colour. This curd is delicious on toast, and makes a fantastic base for the meringue pie on page 254.

Seville marmalade

900g (2lb) Seville oranges
2kg (4lb 8oz) granulated
sugar
juice of 2 lemons
knob of butter

Makes 4kg (8lb 13oz)
Takes about 4 hours plus
overnight standing and
2-24 months to mature
Bitter Seville oranges hit the shops in January, so what better to way to while away the long, dark evenings than by making some delicious tangy marmalade?

1. Peel the oranges, then finely shred or chop the rind. Chop the flesh and place in a bowl with the rind. Add 1.4 litres (2½ pints) of cold water and leave to stand overnight.

2. Strain the fruit mixture, reserving the liquid. Separate the peel, then wrap the fruit in muslin. Place both peel and fruit in a pan with the reserved liquid, bring to the boil, then simmer gently for 2 hours.

3. Allow the mixture to cool slightly, then lift out the muslin bag and squeeze all the juice into the pan.

4. Warm the sugar in the oven (5 minutes at 140°C/275°F/gas mark 1 will be enough), then add to the pan and stir until dissolved. Bring to the boil, then simmer for 20–30 minutes, until setting point is reached.

5. Once the mixture has reached setting point, stir in the lemon juice, then add the butter to disperse any froth on the surface.

6. Allow the marmalade to cool for 20 minutes, then pot up in sterilized jars and seal tightly. Store for at least 2 months before using. The marmalade will keep for 6 months in a cool, dark place.

Chutneys & pickles

Late summer and early autumn often bring an overwhelming abundance of seasonal fruits and vegetables, so it is the traditional time to get picking and preserve some of that glut for later in the year. Chutneys and pickles can be used to brighten many a meal in the darker months, when a taste of the summer is much appreciated.

At The Ginger Pig Pickle Pot all the ingredients we use are natural, which often results in a sharper taste and thinner consistency than most commercial products. We happen to like them this way as they cut through the fat on cold pork and other meats.

What's the difference between a chutney and a pickle?

Chutney is a sweet and sour relish made from fruit and/or vegetables cooked in vinegar with sugar and spices. It takes long, slow cooking and may be smooth or contain small chunks.

Pickle is vegetables and/or fruit preserved in spiced vinegar with or without cooking. The key difference from chutney is that the fruit or vegetable is pickled whole or in recognizable pieces. Some commercial brands have blurred this distinction by calling their product pickle when it is actually chutney.

Tips for making chutneys and pickles

• Use decent, naturally grown fruit and vegetables. If you're not growing your own or using produce from someone who is, avoid mass-produced fresh ingredients as these are often grown quickly and for quantity, rather than quality or taste. While jams and jellies are best made from perfectly ripe fruit, you want to avoid anything verging on overripe for a chutney or pickle, as the finished preserve can be mushy and unpleasant.
• Make sure any spices you add haven't been festering at the back of a cupboard for too long – they will lack punch and can even add a musty flavour to the finished chutney.
• Choose malt or white vinegar of at least 5% acetic content as it's fairly concentrated and will deliver the acidity needed to balance the sweetness without watering it down.
• Always salt or brine vegetables as indicated in each recipe. The salt draws out excess moisture, meaning that the finished chutney or pickle is less likely to spoil, and the vegetables stay crisp.
• Use a non-reactive pan made from stainless steel or enamel. Pans made from brass, iron or copper may react with the vinegar, spoiling the flavour and causing discoloration.
• Jars and lids should be sterilized (see page 222) to prevent contamination of the contents.
• Store chutneys and pickles for at least a couple of months before eating. This maturation time allows the vinegar sharpness to soften and all the other flavours to infuse.

Traditional chutney

1kg (2lb 4oz) brown sugar

600ml (1 pint) malt vinegar

1.5kg (3lb 5oz) tomatoes, peeled (see recipe introduction) and roughly chopped

1.5kg (3lb 5oz) apples, peeled and chopped

1kg (2lb 4oz) onions, peeled and chopped

1kg (2lb 4oz) dates, chopped

1kg (2lb 4oz) raisins

85g (3oz) ground ginger

10 cloves, tied in muslin

1. Place the sugar and vinegar in a large pan and stir over a low heat until dissolved. Add the tomatoes, apples, onions, dates, raisins and ginger and mix well.

2. Add the wrapped cloves to the pan and stir in. Bring the mixture to the boil, then reduce the heat and simmer for about 1 hour, stirring frequently until the liquid has evaporated and the mixture is thick enough to stand a spoon in.

3. Allow the mixture to cool a little, then pot up in sterilized jars (see page 222) and seal tightly. Store the chutney for 2 months before opening. If unopened, it will keep for up to 6 months in a cool, dark place.

Makes 4kg (9lb)

Takes 2 hours, plus 2 months to mature

The traditional formula for chutney is a mixture of sweet and savoury ingredients cooked in a tangy liquid. That's what we have here and is so good that it's worth making a lot. Enjoy it with cold meats and cheese. To peel tomatoes, place them in a roasting tin and heat in the oven at 180°C/350°F/ gas mark 4 for 4–6 minutes. This will make the skin split and be easy to peel off. Try to use Bramley apples for this recipe.

Beetroot & orange savoury

300ml (½ pint) malt vinegar

300g (10½oz) white sugar

350g (12oz) raw beetroot, peeled and grated

350g (12oz) eating apples, peeled and chopped

225g (½lb) red onions, peeled and chopped

1 garlic clove, crushed, peeled and diced

zest and juice of 2 oranges

1 tsp allspice

1 tsp sea salt

1. Place the vinegar in a saucepan, add the sugar and heat gently, stirring until dissolved.

2. Add all the remaining ingredients and bring to the boil, then simmer gently for 1 hour, stirring frequently to ensure it does not catch on the bottom of the pan. The liquid should evaporate so the mixture becomes good and thick.

3. Allow to cool a little, then pot up in sterilized jars (see page 222) and seal tightly. Store the chutney for 2 months before opening. If unopened, it will keep for up to 6 months in a cool, dark place.

Makes 1kg (2lb 4oz)

Takes 2 hours , plus 2 months to mature

At last, beetroots have come into their own and are no longer just found sliced and submerged in vinegar. Julie discovered this unusual savoury and, with its lovely rich colour and hint of orange, it makes a great addition to roast duck or to serve with cold meats.

Marrow & apple chutney

2kg (4lb 8oz) marrow, peeled and chopped into 1.5cm (¾in) pieces

75g (2½oz) coarse sea salt

1kg (2lb 4oz) cooking apples, peeled and chopped into 1.5cm (¾in) pieces

500g (1lb 2oz) onions, peeled and chopped

850ml (1½ pints) white wine vinegar

400g (14oz) white sugar

300g (10½oz) piece of fresh root ginger, peeled and smashed

6 red chillies, split open

1 tbsp black peppercorns

1. Place the marrow in a bowl, sprinkle with the salt and mix by hand. Leave overnight, then rinse in a colander and drain for 1 hour.

2. Place the drained marrow in a large pan with the apples, onions and 350ml (12fl oz) of the vinegar. Bring to the boil, then simmer for 10 minutes. Add the remaining vinegar and sugar, stirring until the sugar has dissolved.

3. Tie the ginger, chillies and peppercorns in muslin, add to the pan and simmer for a further 1 hour, until the chutney is nice and thick. Remove the muslin bag.

4. Allow the mixture to cool a little, then pot up in sterilized jars (see page 222) and seal tightly. Store the chutney for 2 months before opening. If unopened, it will keep for up to 6 months in a cool, dark place.

Makes 2kg (4lb 8oz)

Takes 3 hours, plus overnight salting and 2 months to mature

When marrows are abundant and you have stuffed, souped and mashed them to exhaustion, try making this lovely spicy chutney, which marries extremely well with cold meats.

Apple & mint chutney

1.25kg (2lb 12oz) apples (any variety), peeled and cored

1.25kg (2lb 12oz) red onions, peeled and chopped

300g (10½oz) sultanas

zest and juice of 1 lemon

300ml (½ pint) malt vinegar

500g (1lb 2oz) demerara sugar

75g (2½oz) mint leaves, finely chopped

1. Place the apples and onions in a large pan with the sultanas, lemon zest and juice and the vinegar. Bring to the boil and simmer gently for 25 minutes, stirring frequently.

2. Add the sugar and bring to the boil again, stirring until all the sugar has dissolved.

3. Simmer rapidly for 5 minutes, stirring often to prevent the mixture from catching.

4. Add the mint leaves and stir through. Allow the mixture to cool for 5 minutes, then pot up in sterilized jars (see page 222) and seal tightly. Store the chutney for 2 months before opening. If unopened, it will keep for up to 6 months in a cool, dark place.

Makes 2kg (4lb 8oz)

Takes 1½ hours, plus 2 months to mature

Mint adds a gentle freshness to this chutney, which goes really well with cheese and cold meats.

Classic tomato chutney

1kg (2lb 4oz) ripe
tomatoes, peeled (see page
232) and chopped into
2.5cm (1in) pieces
225g (½lb) onions, peeled
and chopped
225g (½lb) raisins
400g (14oz) white sugar
400ml (14fl oz) malt
vinegar

1. Place all the ingredients in a large
saucepan and stir well. Bring to boil, then
simmer very gently for 2 hours, uncovered,
stirring frequently to prevent the mixture
catching on the bottom of the pan.

2. When the liquid has evaporated and the
mixture is thick, allow to cool a little, then
pot up in sterilized jars (see page 222) and
seal tightly. Store the chutney for 2 months
before opening. If unopened, it will keep for
up to 6 months in a cool, dark place.

Makes 1.25kg (2lb 12oz)
Takes 3 hours, plus 2 months
to mature
*You can make this chutney with
cherry tomatoes if you happen to
have a glut of them. In that case,
I would recommend not peeling
them as it would take far too long.*

Red hot relish

800g (1lb 12oz) ripe
tomatoes , peeled (see
page 232) and quartered
450g (1lb) red onions,
peeled and chopped
3 red peppers, deseeded
and chopped
3 red chillies, deseeded
and sliced
200g (7oz) white sugar
200ml (7fl oz) red wine
vinegar
25g (1 oz) yellow mustard
seeds
3 tsp hot paprika
1 tsp sea salt
1 tsp dried chillies,
crumbled

1. Place the tomatoes in a pan with the
onions, peppers and fresh chillies. Bring to
the boil, then cover and simmer gently for 15
minutes.

2. Add the sugar and vinegar, stirring until
the sugar has dissolved. Add the mustard
seeds, paprika, salt and dried chillies, then
simmer for 45 minutes, stirring frequently,
until the liquid has evaporated and the
mixture is thick enough to stand a spoon in.

3. Allow the mixture to cool for a little, then
pot up in sterilized jars (see page 222) and
seal tightly. Store the chutney for 2 months
before opening. If unopened, it will keep for
several months.

Makes 1.25kg (2lb 12oz)
Takes 2 hours, plus 2 months
to mature
*As the name makes clear, this relish
is really hot, so use it with care. It
contains less sugar and vinegar
than other chutneys, and this allows
the chillies to take centre stage.
Try adding it when you are making
a casserole for a fiery supper.*

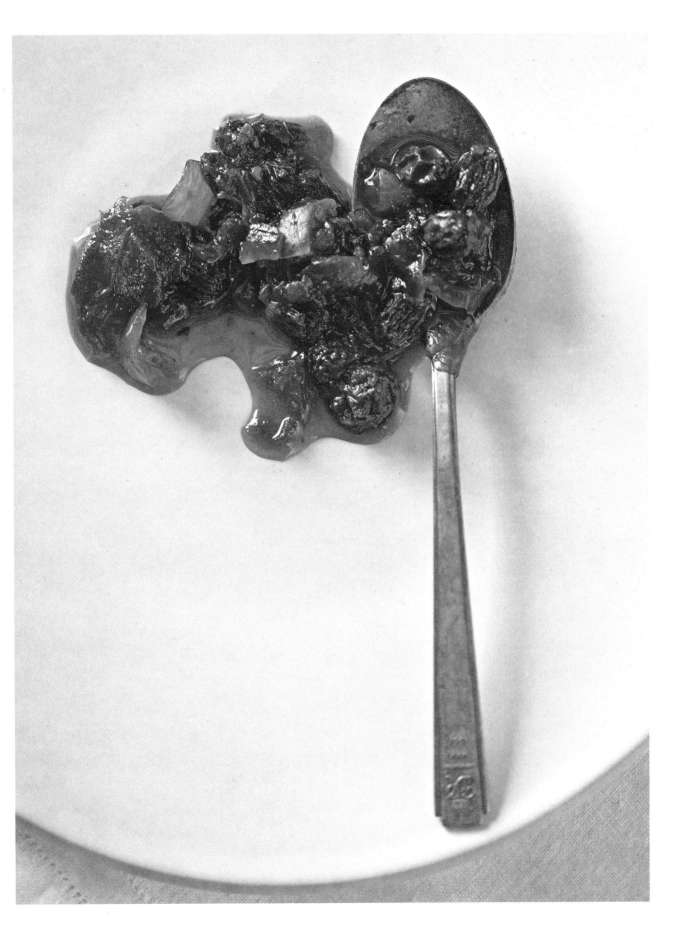

Spiced gooseberries

3.5kg (7lb) gooseberries, topped and tailed

1.8kg (4lb) brown sugar

600ml (1 pint) malt vinegar

½ tsp cloves, tied in muslin

1 tsp ground cinnamon

½ teaspoon allspice

2 tsp freshly ground nutmeg

1. Put all the ingredients into a large pan, place over a low heat and cook until the fruit is soft. Using a slotted spoon, remove the fruit from the pan, then boil the syrup rapidly until reduced by a third (about 10 minutes).

2. Return the fruit to pan and quickly bring to the boil. Take off the heat and pour immediately into sterilized jars (see page 222). Seal tightly. Store for 2 months before opening. Once opened, the gooseberries will keep for up to 6 months.

Makes 3kg (6lb 8oz)

Takes 1 hour, plus 2 months to mature

The spiced vinegar used in this recipe helps to soften the gooseberry skin, which is quite tough. Serve the fruit with rich meats, such as duck and pork.

Bread & butter pickle

2 large cucumbers, thinly sliced

1 mild Spanish onion, peeled and thinly sliced

coarse sea salt

150ml (¼ pint) white wine vinegar

150g (5½oz) brown sugar

1 tsp mustard seeds

1 tsp coriander seeds

½ tsp cayenne pepper

1. Put the cucumbers and onion in a bowl, mix with a good handful of coarse sea salt and leave overnight.

2. Transfer the cucumber mixture to a colander and rinse well in cold water. Allow to drain for at least 1 hour.

3. Place the vinegar, sugar and spices in a pan and bring to the boil. Add the cucumber and onion and cook until just tender. Pot up immediately in sterilized jars (see page 222) and seal tightly. Store the pickle for 2 months before opening. If unopened, it will keep for up to 9 months in a cool, dark place.

Makes 1kg (2lb 4oz)

Takes 2 hours, plus overnight salting and 2 months to mature

Delicate slivers of cucumber and onion gently pickled in white wine vinegar with a few choice spices – all the piquancy and acidity needed to cut through a juicy burger without the clumsiness of your common or garden gherkin. Delicious with cold cuts, hard cheeses, smoked fish or pies.

Spiced damsons

450g (1lb) caster sugar
2 blades of mace
6 cloves
900g (2lb) damsons

1. Put the sugar and 1 litre (1¾ pints) of water in a saucepan, bring to the boil and stir for 2 minutes, until the sugar has dissolved. Add the mace and cloves, then set the pan aside until the syrup is cold.

2. Place the whole damsons in sterilized jars (see page 222), packing them as tightly as possible without squashing or splitting. Pour the cold syrup over the fruit until completely covered. Tap the jars on a work surface to release any air bubbles, then put the lids on, but not tightly.

3. Place the jars on a trivet in a large saucepan – they must not touch one another. Add enough water to reach the level of the syrup, then heat gently to 85°C/185°F and maintain this temperature for 15 minutes. Remove the jars, tighten the lids and leave to cool overnight. Store for 2 months before opening. This will keep for up to 6 months in a cool, dark place.

Makes 3kg (6lb 8oz)
Takes 1 hour, plus cooling and 2 months to mature
It is important that the fruit you use for bottling is totally blemish-free, so always select the best. Serve these damsons with cold meats or simply spoon over ice-cream.

Piccalilli

1.5kg (3lb 5oz) mixed vegetables (we used cauliflower, peppers, courgettes, onions and fine green beans)

250g (9oz) coarse sea salt

1litres (1¾ pints) white vinegar

175g (6oz) white sugar

3 tsp ground turmeric

8 tsp dry mustard powder

4 tsp ground ginger

25g (1oz) cornflour

1. Chop the vegetables into small chunks and place in a bowl with the salt and 4 litres (7 pints) of water. Leave to soak overnight, then drain and rinse well.

2. Put the vinegar, sugar and spices in a pan, bring to the boil, then add the vegetables. Simmer until just tender, then strain, returning the liquid to the pan.

3. Mix the cornflour with a little water to make a smooth paste. Bring the strained liquid to the boil, then add the cornflour, stirring until thickened.

4. Pot up immediately in sterilized jars (see page 222) and leave until cold before sealing tightly. Store the piccalilli for 2 months before opening. If unopened, it will keep for up to 12 months in a cool, dark place.

Makes 2kg (4lb 8oz)

Takes 1 hour, plus overnight soaking and 2 months to mature

Bright yellow and deliciously piquant, piccalilli will brighten up all cold meats. It contains an array of vegetables often over-abundant at the end of the summer, so it's a great way of using them up. Don't forget to save a jar to serve with the cold remains of turkey or ham at Christmas.

Spiced plum & ginger pickle

750g (1lb 10oz) plums or damsons, stoned and roughly chopped

50g (2oz) piece of fresh root ginger, peeled and finely diced

2 onions, peeled and chopped

1 garlic clove, crushed, peeled and diced

125g (4½oz) sultanas

400g (14oz) demerara sugar

350ml (12fl oz) distilled vinegar

1. Put all the ingredients in a pan and bring to the boil. Lower the heat and simmer for 40 minutes, stirring frequently until the mixture becomes thick and glossy.

2. Allow the mixture to cool a little, then pot up in sterilized jars (see page 222) and seal tightly. Store the pickle for 2 months before opening. If unopened, it will keep for up to 6 months in a cool, dark place.

Makes approximately 2 large jars
Takes 1¼ hours, plus 2 months to mature
This pickle is a gorgeous mix of sweet and sour, and the ginger adds a gentle heat. Serve hot or cold with various meats, and try it with grilled cod or halibut – fantastic!

Italian mustard fruits

450ml (¾ pint) white wine vinegar

6 tsp mustard seeds

675g (1lb 8oz) granulated sugar

1kg (2lb 4oz) mixed stoned fruit, e.g. peaches, apricots, cherries and plums, stoned and larger fruits cut into 6 or 8 pieces

675g (1lb 8oz) granulated sugar

1. Place the vinegar and mustard seeds into a small saucepan, bring to the boil and simmer for 5 minutes. Turn off the heat, put a lid on the pan and leave for 1 hour.

2. Strain the vinegar, reserving the mustard seeds, and return the vinegar to the pan. Add the sugar and simmer until it has dissolved and the liquid is a little syrupy.

3. Starting with the hardest or least ripe pieces of fruit, place them in the syrup and poach gently until just soft. This will take 10–15 minutes for harder fruits, 5–10 minutes for softer or very ripe fruits.

4. Pack the fruit into clean, sterilized jars (see page 222), add a few of the reserved mustard seeds and cover with the poaching liquor. Leave to mature for 2 months.

Makes 2 large jars
Takes 1 hour, plus 1 hour to infuse and 2 months to mature
A beautiful accompaniment to cheeses and cured meats, this condiment is made with vibrant, summery stone fruits. The careful poaching means that the fruits retain their shape and colour, making the finished jars rather beautiful additions to your kitchen or gifts for friends. The fruits will keep for up to a year, though they will start to lose their colour a little after a few months.

Sweets

Sweets

At Grange Farm we like to be prepared for visitors.
If someone makes an unexpected appearance,
I feel embarrassed if there is no cake to offer or a light
lunch cannot be readily produced. This probably makes
me a little old-fashioned, but that's the way I was brought
up: it's only polite to offer visitors something to eat.

For this reason, we usually have something we can
offer with tea – maybe a cream-filled sponge cake freshly
baked that morning, or a fruitcake to be sliced and eaten
with Lancashire cheese. We also like to have these things
available at 10 a.m.,when the shepherds and stockmen
and women gather in the kitchen for a break and to
discuss what's going on in different parts of the farm.
With 1,300 acres of farmland, and our sheep grazing an
1,800-acre stretch of the North Yorkshire Moors, there's
a lot to be gained by sitting down to talk about things over
a piece of cake.

Eccles cakes

100g (3½oz) unsalted
butter
300g (10½oz) currants
150g (5½oz) soft brown
sugar
zest of 1 lemon
zest of 1 orange
1 tsp allspice
¼ tsp freshly ground
nutmeg
½ tsp ground cinnamon

For the pastry
450g (1lb) strong white
flour
1 tbsp caster sugar
1 tsp salt
150g (5½oz) chilled
unsalted butter, diced
85g (3oz) chilled lard,
diced
1 egg, beaten

For the glaze
1 egg white, beaten and
loosened with a little water
caster sugar, for dusting

1. First make the pastry. Mix the flour,
sugar and salt together in a large bowl. Add
the butter and lard and mix with a wooden
spoon (not your hands) to combine.

2. Pour in the egg and 185ml (6½fl oz)
of cold water. Mix well to produce a firm
dough. Cover the dough in clingfilm and
chill for 45 minutes.

3. Lightly flour a work surface and roll out
the dough to a thickness of 2.5cm (1in).
Fold into thirds, then wrap and chill again.
Repeat this process one more time, ending
with 30 minutes in the fridge.

4. While the pastry is chilling, make the
filling. Melt the butter, add the remaining
ingredients along with 30ml (1fl oz) of cold
water and stir well. Chill the filling.

5. Preheat the oven to 190°/375°F/gas 5.

6. Cut the dough in half and return one half
to the fridge. On a floured work surface, roll
the pastry into a rectangle 5mm (¼in) thick,
then cut into 12 squares. Place a dollop of
the cold filling in the centre of each square,
dampen the edges of the pastry, then fold in
the corners and sides to enclose the filling.
Turn the cake over and shape into a rough
circle or oval, pressing it down a little to seal
the folds. Place on a baking sheet lined with
parchment and repeat this step until all the
pastry and filling have been used up.

7. Using a sharp knife, make 3 small slashes
in the top of each cake, then brush with the
glaze and sprinkle with caster sugar. Bake
for 25 minutes until golden brown.

Makes about 24
Takes 1¼ hours, plus 2 hours to chill
*Flaky, buttery pastry filled with
spiced currants, Eccles cakes
– named after the town near
Manchester where they originated
– are as sustaining as they are
delicious. They also go wonderfully
with a piece of Lancashire cheese.*

Yorkshire ginger parkin

150g (5½oz) self-raising flour

2 tsp ground ginger

1 tsp ground mixed spice

1 tsp ground cinnamon

1 tsp bicarbonate of soda

175g (6oz) oatmeal

60g (2¼oz) black treacle

200g (7oz) golden syrup

150g (5½oz) butter

150g (5½oz) soft brown sugar

2 eggs, beaten

4 tbsp milk

1. Preheat the oven to 180°C/350°F/gas mark 4. Grease a 23cm (9in) square cake tin and line it with baking parchment.

2. Sift the flour, spices and bicarbonate of soda into a mixing bowl, add the oatmeal and mix well. Make a well in the centre.

3. Put the treacle, golden syrup, butter and sugar in a small pan and place over a low heat, stirring constantly, until melted.

4. Beat the eggs into the milk, pour into the flour mixture and add the treacle mixture too. Beat to a smooth batter.

5. Pour the batter into the prepared cake tin and bake for 1¼ hours.

6. Let the cake cool in the tin for 8 minutes, then turn onto a wire rack and allow to cool completely. Cover in clingfilm and store in an airtight container for 1 week before serving.

Serves 6–8

Takes 1 hour 40 minutes, plus 1 week to mature

There are umpteen variations of parkin in Yorkshire, each of them using differing quantities of oats, sugar, treacle and syrup. Whatever the proportions, it is the oats that make parkin stand out from other cakes, and they were probably included because they provide extra sustenance for manual workers in cold winter weather.

Drop scones

200g (7oz) plain flour

1½ tsp baking powder

pinch of salt

1 tbsp sugar

1 egg

250ml (9fl oz) milk

1. Sift all the dry ingredients into a large bowl and mix together. Make a well in the centre.

2. Whisk together the egg and milk, then slowly pour into the flour mixture, whisking to create a smooth batter.

3. Heat a flat griddle pan or a large, heavy frying pan until medium hot, then grease with a little butter. To see if the temperature is correct, drop in a little of the batter – it should set and rise in 2 minutes, and be a lovely golden colour when turned over.

4. When you are happy with the temperature of your griddle, drop tablespoons of the batter into it, spacing them so that they do not touch. (You will need to make several batches.)

5. Cook for 2 minutes, then turn with a palette knife and cook the other side for just under 2 minutes.

6. Keep the scones warm while you cook the remaining batches, then serve with butter and homemade jam.

Makes 12

Takes 30 minutes

When time is tight and the cake tin is empty, this recipe comes to the rescue. The scones are quick and easy to make, and a pleasure to eat with home-made preserves.

The Salt family's rich fruitcake

250g (9oz) sultanas

200g (7oz) currants

100g (3½oz) raisins

100g (3½oz) mixed peel

100g (3½oz) glacé cherries, quartered

50g (2oz) flaked almonds

3 tbsp sherry or brandy, plus more to feed

200g (7oz) soft butter

200g (7oz) soft dark brown sugar

3 large eggs, lightly beaten in 3 separate cups

2 tbsp black treacle

425g (15oz) plain flour

2½ tsp ground mixed spice

1. Put all the fruit and almonds in a large bowl, pour in the alcohol and mix well. Cover with a clean tea towel and leave to soak overnight.

2. The next day, preheat the oven to 170°C/325°F/gas mark 3. Butter a 20cm (8in) spring-form cake tin and line with baking parchment.

3. Cream together the butter and sugar until light and fluffy. Add the eggs one at a time, beating well after each addition. Stir in the treacle and beat again.

4. Sift in the flour and spice, then gradually fold into the egg mixture using a wooden spoon until evenly distributed.

5. Spoon the mixture into the cake tin and spread to the sides. Tap the tin sharply on a work surface to get rid of air bubbles, then use a spoon to make a dent about 2.5cm (1in) deep in the centre of the mixture: this will help it to rise evenly.

6. Place a double layer of greaseproof paper over the tin to prevent the cake over-browning, then bake in the centre of the oven for 1 hour. Reduce the heat to 150°C/300°F/gas mark 2 and bake for a further 2½ hours, until a skewer inserted into the middle of the cake comes out clean. Set aside to cool in the tin.

7. Once the cake is cold, turn it out and prick all over with a thin skewer or cocktail stick. Brush liberally with more alcohol, then cover in clingfilm and foil and place in an airtight container to mature. Wait at least 4 weeks before eating the cake, and repeat the 'feeding' process every fortnight or so, depending on how rich you like your cake.

Serves 8–10

Takes 4 hours, plus overnight soaking, cooling and at least 6 weeks to mature

Hester Salt, who works tirelessly pickling, preserving and making puddings and cakes for The Ginger Pig, has had this recipe in her family for many years. Rich and packed full of fruit, it goes perfectly with a piece of tangy cheese, such as Kirkham's Lancashire or Hawes Wensleydale.

Note that the cake needs to mature for at least 6 weeks before being cut, but it will keep for many months if well 'fed' with alcohol and securely wrapped.

Baked blackberry cheesecake

500g (1lb 2oz) cream cheese

1 egg plus 2 egg yolks

100g (3½oz) caster sugar

75ml (3fl oz) double cream

finely grated zest of 1 lemon

For the pastry

200g (7oz) plain flour

100g (3½oz) chilled butter, diced

For the topping

300g (10½oz) blackberries

50g (2oz) icing sugar

1 tsp gelatine powder

1. First make the pastry. Rub the flour and butter together in a bowl until the mixture resembles breadcrumbs. Pour in 40ml (1½fl oz) of cold water and mix with a knife, using a cutting motion, until a dough forms. Place it on a lightly floured surface and knead gently for 2 minutes until smooth.

2. Preheat the oven to 170°C/325°F/gas mark 3. Lightly butter a 23cm (9in) spring-form cake tin. On a lightly floured surface, roll out the pastry and use to line the prepared tin, trimming off the excess. Bake blind (see page 140) before filling.

3. Beat together the cream cheese, egg and egg yolks until smooth, then mix in the sugar, cream and lemon zest. Pour into the pastry case and bake for 1 hour. When ready, just switch the oven off and leave the cake to cool slowly inside it —this should prevent it from sinking in the middle. When cold, remove from the oven but leave in the tin.

4. Now make the topping. Place the blackberries in a pan with a very small amount of water and heat gently until the berries are soft and juicy. Strain the juice into a jug, then return the fruit to the pan and mix in the sugar.

5. Sprinkle the gelatine powder over the hot juice and stir until dissolved. Return this liquid to the blackberries and stir well.

6. Pour the blackberry mixture on top of the baked cheesecake and spread it out. Place in the fridge to set for 2 hours.

7. To remove the cheesecake from the tin, run a knife around the edge, release the fastening, then slide onto a plate and serve.

Serves 6

Takes 1¼ hours, plus cooling and 2 hours to chill

Many people think that baked cheesecake is an American idea, but in the past cheesecakes were always baked, and it's only in recent years that chilled cheesecakes seem to have become the norm. As a traditionalist, I'm giving you a baked cheesecake here, but incorporating a modern twist by covering the top with a luscious blackberry gloss. It's irresistible.

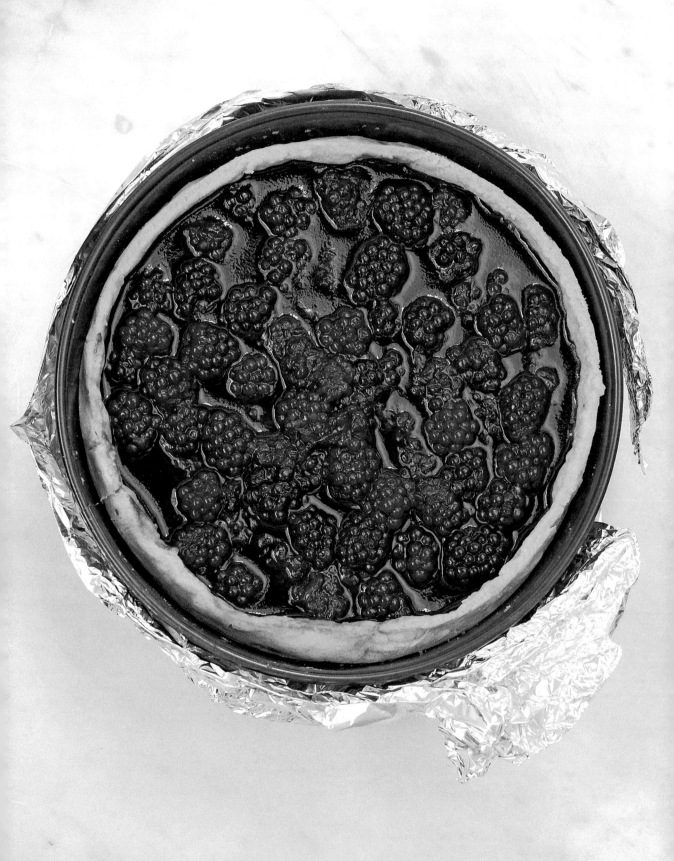

Custard tart

4 eggs

50g (2oz) caster sugar

seeds from 1 vanilla pod

450ml (¾ pint) creamy
milk, such as Jersey

freshly grated nutmeg

For the pastry

150g (5½oz) plain flour

80g (2¾oz) chilled butter,
diced

20g (¾oz) caster sugar

1 egg yolk

1. First make the pastry. Rub the flour and butter together in a bowl until the mixture resembles breadcrumbs. Stir in the sugar, then add the egg yolk and a tablespoon of cold water. Mix with a round-bladed knife, using a cutting motion, until a dough forms. Cover with clingfilm and place in the fridge for 10 minutes.

2. Roll out the pastry on a lightly floured surface and use to line a 20cm (8in) loose-bottomed flan tin. Place in the fridge for 15 minutes. Meanwhile, preheat the oven to 190°C/375°F/gas mark 5.

3. Line the chilled pastry case with crumpled baking parchment and fill with baking beans. Bake for 15 minutes, then remove the parchment and beans and bake for a further 5 minutes. Set aside and reduce the temperature to 170°C/325°F/gas 3.

4. Beat together the eggs and sugar. Add the vanilla seeds and milk and mix well. Pour into the prepared pastry case, grate some nutmeg over the top and bake for 1 hour, until the custard is set. Enjoy hot or cold.

Serves 6

Takes 2 hours

On some farms in the past custard tarts were made with cow's colostrum, the very rich milk that the mother produces to feed her newborn baby. In order to get this, the farmer would milk the mother from one side of the udder while the baby fed from the other. I believe you can get the same rich result as colostrum by using ordinary creamy milk.

Pop the unused vanilla pod into a jar of sugar. It will gradually infuse its flavour and be a lovely addition to your baking.

Orchard pear & almond bake

250g (9oz) soft butter

250g (9oz) unrefined caster sugar

5 eggs

100g (3½oz) ground almonds

300g (10½oz) self-raising flour

75 ml (3fl oz) milk

4 pears, halved, peeled and cored

For the topping

4 pears, halved, peeled and cored

60g (2¼oz) butter

80g (2¾oz) unrefined caster sugar

1. Lightly butter a 23cm (9in) ovenproof baking dish. Preheat the oven to 180°C/350°F/gas mark 4.

2. Cream the butter and sugar with a mixer, then add the eggs and ground almonds and whisk again.

3. Fold in the flour and milk using a large spoon, then pour the mixture into the prepared dish.

4. Arrange the pears on top, then bake for 40 minutes.

5. About 5 minutes before the time is up, to make the topping, put the butter, sugar and 3 tablespoons of water in a small pan. Heat gently, stirring until the sugar has dissolved, then bring to the boil, stirring constantly for 2 minutes.

6. Spoon the sticky syrup over the pears and bake for a further 20 minutes, until crispy and golden. Serve warm or cold.

Serves 6

Takes 1½ hours

Pears and almonds are natural bedfellows, and make a wonderful dessert in a buttery case. The best English varieties of pears to use are Comice, Conference, Concord or Williams.

Gooseberry meringue pie

1 jar Gooseberry curd
(see page 228)
2tsp cornflour
4 egg whites
200g (7oz) caster sugar

For the pastry
250g (9oz) plain flour
25g (1oz) caster sugar
140g (5oz) chilled butter,
diced
1 egg

1. First make the pastry. Combine the flour, sugar and butter until the mixture resembles breadcrumbs. Add the egg and mix again to form a dough.

2. Lightly butter a 26cm (10in) loose-bottomed tart tin. Roll the pastry out on a lightly floured work surface and use to line the pastry case, leaving a small overhang. (Do not stretch the pastry to fit as it will shrink while cooking.) Chill for 30 minutes.

3. Preheat the oven to 180°C/350°F/gas mark 4 and line the chilled pastry case with crumpled parchment. Fill it with baking beans and bake for 30 minutes. Remove the paper and beans, then bake for a further 8 minutes. Trim off the pastry overhang, then set the case aside to cool while you make the meringue.

4. Reduce the oven temperature to 170°C/325°F/gas mark 3. Whisk the egg whites into stiff peaks, add half the sugar and whisk until very glossy. Add the remaining sugar and whisk again. Mix the cornflour with a little water and blend into the curd carefully over a low heat, taking care not to let it catch. Allow it to cool slightly, then spoon into the pastry case.

5. Spoon the meringue mixture over the gooseberry curd, then use a palette knife to spread it to the edges and make a good seal all the way around. Fork the meringue into peaks, then bake for 15 minutes.

6. To remove the tart tin, centre it on an upturned glass or cup and push the outer ring downwards. Slide the pie onto a plate and serve with lashings of cream.

Serves 6-8
Takes 1 hour 20 minutes, plus 30 minutes to chill
The gooseberry curd is a tangy filling that beautifully offsets the sweetness of the meringue, but you can of course use any other fruity filling you like.

Walnut & salted caramel tart

75g (2½oz) caster sugar

40g (1½oz) butter

150ml (¼ pint) double cream

175g (6oz) shelled walnuts, halved

½ tsp sea salt

For the pastry

150g (5oz) plain flour

75g (2½oz) chilled butter, diced

25g (1oz) caster sugar

1 large egg, beaten

1. First make the pastry. Place the flour and butter in a bowl and rub together until the mixture resembles breadcrumbs. Stir in the sugar, then mix in the egg using a round-bladed knife until a dough forms. Cover in clingfilm and chill for 1 hour.

2. Preheat the oven to 190°C/375°F/gas mark 5.

3. Place the pastry on a cold work surface and press out a little with the heel of your hand. Roll out and use to line a 23cm (9in) loose-bottomed tart tin without stretching it to fit. Trim off the excess around the edge.

4. Line the pastry case with crumpled baking parchment, fill with baking beans and bake for 20 minutes. Reduce the temperature to 170°C/325°F/gas mark 3, remove the beans and parchment, and bake the pastry case for a further 15 minutes.

5. Meanwhile, make the filling. Place the sugar in a heavy-based, non-stick pan and heat until it caramelizes. Set aside to cool for 5 minutes, then add the butter and cream. Return to the heat and stir until smooth.

6. Scatter the walnuts in the cooked pastry case and pour the caramel over them. Sprinkle with the salt and leave to set for at least 1 hour before serving.

Serves 4–6

Takes 1 hour, plus 2 hours to chill and set

Sweet and nutty with a hint of salt, this tart is easy to make and is best accompanied by a cup of rich, dark coffee to cut through the sweetness.

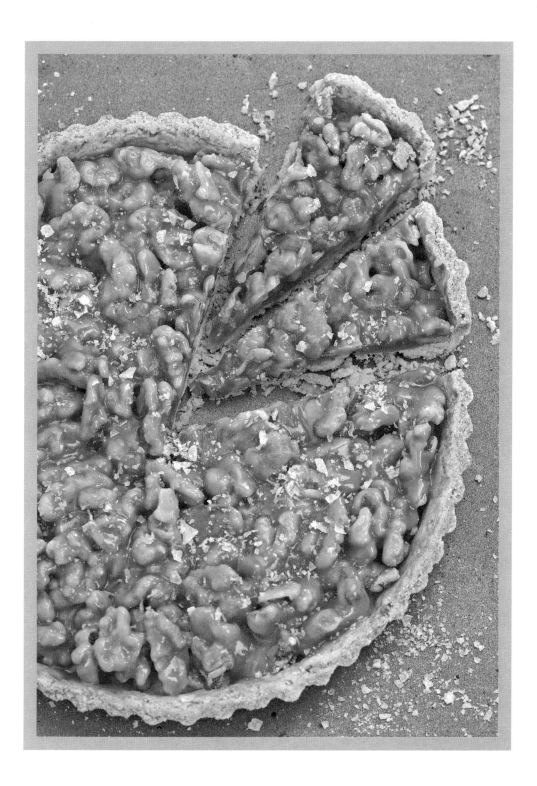

Les's mince pies

1 smallish Bramley apple,
peeled and grated

100g (3½oz) shredded
suet

125g (4½oz) raisins

125g (4½oz) currants

125g (4½oz) sultanas

125g (4½oz) mixed peel

zest and juice of 1 lemon

zest and juice of 1 orange

100g (3½oz) muscovado
sugar

50ml (2fl oz) rum

50ml (2fl oz) brandy

1 tsp mixed spice

½ tsp ground cinnamon

freshly grated nutmeg

For the pastry

450g (1lb) plain flour

250g (9oz) chilled butter,
diced

125g (4½oz) icing sugar

1–2 egg yolks

1 egg, beaten, for brushing
the pastry

1. First make the mincemeat. Mix the apple with all the other ingredients and stir well. Transfer to a sterilized plastic box or glass jar (see page 222), seal tightly and store in a cool, dark place for at least 2 months.

2. When the mincemeat is ready, make the pastry. Put the flour and butter in a large bowl and rub together until the mixture resembles breadcrumbs. Mix in the icing sugar, then add the egg yolks a little at a time until a dough forms. Knead until smooth, then cover in clingfilm and place in the fridge for 30 minutes.

3. Preheat the oven to 190°C/375°F/gas mark 5. Lightly butter a couple of bun tins.

4. Cut off one-third of the chilled pastry and set aside. On a lightly floured surface, roll out the remaining pastry to a thickness of 5mm (¼in). Using a 9cm (3½in) cutter, stamp out 12 circles. Use the circles to line the prepared tins. Place a scant tablespoon of the mincemeat in each 'hole', taking care not to overfill them.

5. Roll out the remaining pastry the same thickness as before. Using a 5cm (2in) cutter, stamp out 12 circles for the lids. Brush the edge of the pastry cases with a little beaten egg, place the lids on top and press the edges together, sealing the mincemeat inside.

6. Make a small hole in the centre of each pie, then place in the middle of the oven and bake for 20 minutes, until golden brown. Transfer the pies to a wire rack to cool, then dust with icing sugar and serve warm or cold with brandy butter or whipped cream.

Makes about 800g (1lb 12oz)
mincemeat and 12 pies
Takes 1½ hours plus 2 months for
the mincemeat to mature

Les, originally one of my butchers, but now our baker, assembles the sweet mincemeat filling in October so that it has two good months to mature before Christmas. It develops a rich, luxurious flavour, which is fantastic with the short, buttery pastry.

Steamed syrup pudding

125g (4½oz) soft butter

125g (4½oz) caster sugar

4 tbsp golden syrup

2 eggs

100g (3½oz) self-raising flour

50g (2oz) shredded suet

4 tsp milk

1. Butter an 850ml (1½ pint) pudding basin with a knob of the butter. Sprinkle in 2 teaspoons of the sugar and shake to coat all the sides. Pour in the golden syrup.

2. Choose a saucepan large enough to hold the pudding basin and fill it three-quarters full with water. Place on the heat.

3. Cream together the remaining butter and sugar until light and fluffy. Beat the eggs in one at a time. Fold in the flour and the suet, then mix in the milk.

4. Pour the mixture into the prepared pudding basin and cover with buttered greaseproof paper pleated in the middle. Tie in place with string, making a loop over the top to act as a handle.

5. Place on a trivet in the simmering water, cover tightly and steam for 1½ hours, checking the water level regularly and adding more if necessary.

6. When ready, carefully lift out the basin, remove the string and greaseproof paper and invert onto a large plate, shaking gently to dislodge the pudding. It should be a lovely golden colour with a topping of sticky syrup.

Serves 4

Takes 2 hours

After a cold, hard day on the farm, or a long winter walk, nothing beats a sticky steamed pudding. This one is made in 10 minutes from store-cupboard ingredients, but takes 1½ hours to cook, so put it in the steamer and get busy making something else while the steaming works its magic.

Queen of puddings

300ml (½ pint) milk

250ml (9fl oz) double cream

25g (1oz) butter

140g (5oz) breadcrumbs

zest of 1 lemon

4 eggs, separated

4 tbsp raspberry jam

250g (9oz) caster sugar

1. Lightly butter a 1.2 litre (2 pint) pie dish.

2. Place the milk and cream in a pan and bring to the boil. Remove from the heat and add the butter, breadcrumbs and lemon zest. Mix, then set aside for 30 minutes so that the breadcrumbs can absorb the liquid.

3. Preheat the oven to 180°C/350°F/gas mark 4.

4. Mix the egg yolks into the bread mixture, then place in the prepared pie dish. Bake for 20 minutes, until set. Set the dish aside and lower the oven to 150°C/300°F/gas mark 2.

5. Put the jam in a small pan and melt carefully over a low heat.

6. Meanwhile, whisk the egg whites until stiff, then add half the caster sugar. Whisk again until glossy, then quickly whisk in the remaining sugar.

7. Pour the melted jam over the contents of the pie dish and spread evenly. Pile the meringue mixture on top and bake for 15 minutes, until golden brown and set on the outside.

Serves 4–6

Takes 1½ hours

Aptly named, this is a great British pudding topped with crisp yet chewy meringue. Traditionally, this sits over a layer of raspberry jam, but other flavours can be used instead. You could even swap the jam for lightly poached fruit or preserved fruits.

Guards' pudding

175g (6 oz) wholemeal breadcrumbs

90g (3¼oz) vanilla caster sugar

2 tbsp self-raising flour

1 pot of home-made or best-quality strawberry jam, containing whole fruit

3 eggs, beaten

125g (4½oz) butter, melted

1 tsp bicarbonate of soda

1. Generously butter a 1.2 litre (2 pint) pudding basin.

2. Put the breadcrumbs and sugar in a large bowl, sift in the flour and mix together.

3. Gently melt the jam and pour it into the breadcrumb mixture, along with the eggs and butter. Stir well.

4. Dissolve the bicarbonate of soda in a little water and stir it into the breadcrumb mixture. Pour into the pudding basin and cover with a plastic lid or pleated foil secured with string.

5. Place the basin on a trivet or inverted metal cake tin in a heavy-based saucepan. Pour in enough boiling water to come halfway up the sides of the basin, then cover and simmer for 2 hours.

6. Invert the pudding onto a plate and serve with cream, custard or ice-cream.

Serves 4-6

Takes 2¼ hours

Although it sounds as though it has royal connections, this pudding was supposedly the one longed for by servicemen in the trenches during the First World War.

If you want to be lavish, you can heat a second pot of jam to pour over the pudding when you serve it.

Summer pudding

1kg (2lb 4oz) mixed soft red fruits, such as blackcurrants, redcurrants, blackberries, strawberries and raspberries, trimmed as necessary

150g (5½oz) caster sugar

10 thin slices of brown bread, crusts removed

1. Place the currants and blackberries in a saucepan with the sugar and add 50ml (2fl oz) of water. Warm gently for a few minutes, until the fruits are just soft.

2. Remove from the heat and gently mix in the strawberries and raspberries. Cover the pan and leave for 5 minutes.

3. Remove the crusts from the bread. Drain the fruit juice into a shallow dish. Dip the bread in the juices and use it to line a 1.2 litre (2 pint) pudding basin, leaving no bowl showing. Reserve a slice of bread for later.

4. Fill the lined basin with the warm fruit and cover with the reserved slice of juice-dipped bread. Reserve any leftover juice.

5. Cover the basin with clingfilm and put a saucer or small plate on top. Sit a weight on this, then place the basin in a shallow dish in the fridge overnight.

6. The next day, remove the weight, saucer and clingfilm. Invert the basin onto a serving dish and shake gently to release the pudding.

7. Spoon over any reserved juices and serve with pouring cream.

Serves 4-6

Takes 35 minutes, plus overnight steeping

Any type of berry can be used in this recipe, but do not use less than three different types or the final pudding will be slightly bland. The berries need to have a variety of textures and acidity, and of course lots of juice for the bread to absorb. Soft brown bread has the best absorption, but it must sit overnight to steep thoroughly in the juice; never rush it or your pudding will be disappointing. One final important flourish – it must be served with lots of thick pouring cream.

Apple snow layer crunch

75g (2½oz) butter
400g (14oz) breadcrumbs
75g (2½oz) demerara sugar
1 kg (2lb 4oz) apples (cookers, eaters or a mixture), peeled and cored
75g (2½oz) caster sugar
2 egg whites
300ml (½ pint) double cream, whipped
ground cinnamon, for dusting

1. Melt the butter in large frying pan and fry the breadcrumbs, turning constantly, until golden. Take off the heat, mix in the demerara sugar and set aside to cool.

2. Meanwhile, cook the apples with a little water until soft. Mash until smooth, then stir in the caster sugar and leave to cool.

3. Whisk the egg whites until stiff. Mix the cream and apple purée together, then quickly fold into the egg whites.

4. Layer the apple snow and the bread-crumbs in a serving bowl or individual glass dishes, making 3 layers of each, and finishing a layer of apple. Dust with cinnamon and chill for 2 hours.

Serves 4
Takes 30 minutes, plus cooling and 2 hours to chill
If you want a simple dessert to help use up a glut of cooking or eating apples, this recipe is ideal. The puréed fruit is layered with sweet fried breadcrumbs and is deliciously moreish.

Rumtopf

1kg (2lb 4 oz) strawberries
500g (1lb 2oz) sugar
rum
other seasonal fruit as available (see recipe)

1. As strawberries are the first fruits of the summer, hull them and place a layer in your pot (any wide-necked glass or ceramic container will do). Pour the sugar over them, then add enough rum to come 5cm (2in) above the fruit. Cover and store in a cool, dark place, turning every day.

2. As the summer continues, add any of the following to your pot: cherries, raspberries, redcurrants, gooseberries, plums or pears. Each time you add fruit, always weigh it first and add half the weight in sugar. Top up the rum so that it always sits 5cm (2in) above the fruit and keep it covered to stop the alcohol evaporating.

Makes as much as you like
Takes 30 minutes, plus up to 3 months to mature
Rumtopf is the German word for 'rum pot', a ceramic lidded container in which seasonal fruits are macerated in alcohol. Different fruits are added to the pot as they come into season, and the alcohol is topped up each time. The boozy fruit can be added to rum babas, or served with waffles or ice-cream, and a small amount of the ruby liquid is also lovely in a glass of champagne. Keep the fruit until late autumn for the best flavour.

Rum babas with Rumtopf

250g (9oz) strong flour

2 tsp dried yeast

50ml (2fl oz) warm milk

4 eggs

2 tsp sugar

125g (4½oz) chilled unsalted butter, diced

2 tbsp dried currants

2 tsp lard

For the syrup

50ml (2fl oz) rumtopf liqueur or rum

400g (14oz) caster sugar

zest and juice of 1 orange

2 cloves

1 cinnamon stick

For the glaze

200g (7oz) apricot jam

1. Sift the flour into a mixing bowl and make a well in the centre. Combine the yeast and milk, then whick in the eggs and sugar and pour into the well. Mix until smooth. Scatter the butter over the dough and cover the bowl in clingfilm. Leave in a warm place until the dough has doubled in size (about 30 minutes).

2. Add the currants to the risen dough and beat until they and the butter are incorporated and you have a smooth, elastic dough. (It will be quite soft and loose.)

3. Grease 8 individual savarin rings or dariole moulds with the lard. Fill each one with dough to a third of its depth, cover and leave in a warm place until the dough reaches the top of the moulds (about 45 minutes).

4. Preheat the oven to 230°C/450°F/gas mark 8. Bake the babas for 15 minutes, then turn onto a wire rack and leave to cool.

5. To make the syrup, place 450ml (¾ pint) water, alcohol, sugar, zest, juice, cloves and cinnamon in a saucepan, bring to the boil and strain.

6. Place the cooked babas in a single layer in a shallow container and spoon over the syrup. Leave them to soak up the liquid for 1 hour.

7. Gently heat the apricot jam and 40ml (1½fl oz) of water in a small pan until melted and blended. Brush each baba carefully with this glaze.

8. Serve each baba with whipped cream and, for a real treat, a spoonful of fruit and liquor from the Rumtopf (see opposite).

Serves 8

Takes 1 hour, plus cooling and 2¼ hours to prove and soak

If you have made the rumtopf opposite, this is a really decadent and delicious dessert to make with it. If not, you can make it with any fruits steeped in alcohol.

Rhubarb & ginger oat crumble

125g (4½oz) chilled butter, diced

125g (4½oz) plain flour

50g (2oz) ground almonds

50g (2oz) soft brown sugar

50g (2oz) rolled oats

700g (1lb 9oz) rhubarb, coarse strings removed

20g (¾oz) fresh root ginger, peeled and grated

50g (2oz) unrefined caster sugar

1. Preheat the oven to 180°C/350°F/gas mark 4.

2. Rub the butter and flour together in a bowl until the mixture resembles breadcrumbs. Add the ground almonds, sugar and oats and mix well.

3. Chop the rhubarb and place in an ovenproof dish with the ginger. Add 4 tablespoons of water, sprinkle with the caster sugar, then evenly spoon the crumble mixture over the top.

4. Place the dish on a baking sheet and bake for 40 minutes, until golden and bubbling.

Serves 4–6

Takes 1 hour

Apart from being one of the great comfort foods, crumbles are amazingly versatile and lend themselves to almost any combination of fruit, so don't be afraid to experiment. And when fresh seasonal fruit is beginning to run low, try mixing it with a bag of frozen berries to make it go further.

Brioche & butter pudding

75g (2½oz) soft butter

400g (14oz) brioche, sliced

4 apples, peeled, cored and thinly sliced

3 eggs plus 2 egg yolks

700ml (22fl oz) double cream

75g (2½oz) caster sugar

1. Preheat the oven to 170°C/325°F/ gas mark 3. Lightly butter a 25 x 25cm (10 x 10in) ovenproof baking dish.

2. Spread the butter on the sliced brioche and place a layer of the brioche in the bottom of the prepared dish. Arrange a layer of apple on top. Repeat these layers, finishing with a layer of brioche.

3. Put the eggs, yolks, cream and half the sugar in a jug or bowl and beat together. Pour over the bread. Sprinkle with the remaining sugar and bake for 45 minutes.

Serves 8

Takes 1 hour

Beware – this pudding is very creamy and totally addictive. The cream can be replaced with milk if you wish, but it won't deliver the same luscious result.

Plum cobbler

500g (1lb 2oz) British plums

75g (2½ oz) light muscovado sugar

75g (2½oz) chilled butter, diced

125g (4½oz) self-raising flour

½ tsp baking powder

75ml (3fl oz) milk

1. Preheat the oven to 180°C/350°F/gas mark 4.

2. Put 2 plums aside, then cut the remaining plums in half and remove the stones. Cut the halves into quarters if large.

3. Divide the fruit between 4 ramekins, then sprinkle with 25g (1oz) of the sugar. Add 1 tablespoon of water to each dish.

4. Place the remaining sugar in a bowl with the butter, flour and baking powder and rub together until the mixture resembles breadcrumbs.

5. Make a well in the centre, pour in the milk and mix with a round-bladed knife until a dough forms. Place on a lightly floured surface and knead for 2 minutes until smooth.

6. Cut the dough into 4 equal pieces. Roughly shape to fit the top of the ramekins and place a circle of dough on each one.

7. Cut the reserved plums in half, remove the stones and place half a plum on top of each dish. Place the ramekins on a baking sheet and bake for 25–30 minutes, until golden.

Serves 4

Takes 1 hour

British plums are great, but are only in season for a short period, so get cooking and make these pretty individual plum cobblers. To store plums for later use, stone the fruit, poach in a little water for 5 minutes, then freeze.

Stocks, sauces & extras

Stocks, sauces & extras

The success or failure of a dish can rest on a sauce, so it's really important to get it right. We start with stock recipes in this chapter because these are the foundation of many classic sauces, but favourite English sauces, such as tangy mint or apple to go with roast lamb or pork, and a steadying parsley sauce to offset the saltiness of ham, also have their place in these pages.

A few choice condiments, a well-stocked larder and some herbs are enough to pull together a large range of accompaniments. Our kitchen is rarely without onions, celery, carrots, garlic, a few jars of mustard, various spices and vinegars, plus fats and flours of course. And from the garden I can pick bay leaves, mint, rosemary and thyme. With these ingredients, plus a few fruits or a good stock, it's easy to make most of the sauces in the chapter.

Classic stock

The classic way to make a stock is to simmer raw bones (never mix your animals), vegetables (such as onion, carrot and celery) and herbs (traditionally parsley, thyme and bay leaf) in a pan of water. The heat should be so low that the stock barely quivers, and it should remain on that heat for several hours, until all flavours from the bones and vegetables have been extracted. At that point, it should be strained, the solids discarded and the liquid reduced over a high heat to intensify the flavour.

It is also possible to make stocks out of cooked bones. Although they will not yield such depth of flavour as raw bones, I simmer them in the same way, adding herbs and any vegetables that might need using up, to extract every last drop of goodness and flavour. In our kitchen, stock like this often forms the basis of a beginning-of-the-week soup.

Herbs are very important in stocks, and the French love their bouquet garni, which is simply a bundle of herbs tied together. As the stock is strained, it is not essential to tie the herbs, but it is traditional. Finally, always add a few peppercorns, but never salt because it can intensify when the stock is reduced and end up over-salting any recipe it's added to.

Given the long simmering time, it is worth making a large batch of stock and freezing what you cannot use quickly. It's often useful in small amounts – ice-cube trays and yoghurt pots are ideal for this – but if you know you'll be needing larger amounts too, put a large plastic bag inside a measuring jug, then fill and freeze it, removing the bag from the jug when it's solid.

Is it worth making your own stock? Absolutely! Although the quality of shop-bought stock has vastly improved, it's not a patch on home-made. I find commercial products contain too much salt and never have the freshness and depth of flavour I want. To add insult to injury, they are also rather pricey. As butchers will often give you bones for free, it's madness not to make your own stock – so get cooking!

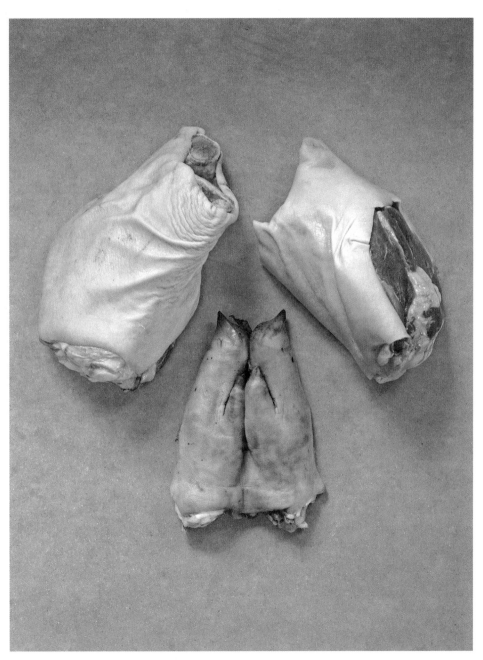

Veal stock

3kg (6lb 8oz) veal bones, chopped and excess fat removed (ask your butcher to do this)

250g (9oz) carrots, peeled

250g (9oz) onions, peeled

250g (9oz) leeks, chopped

250g (9oz) celery, chopped

1 bouquet garni

4 peppercorns

1. Place the bones in a stock pot, add 5 litres (8¾ pints) of water and bring to the boil. Skim as necessary.

2. Add all the remaining ingredients to the stock pot, then cover and simmer very gently for 4 hours.

3. Strain the stock, discarding the solids, and set aside to cool. Store in the fridge for up to 4 days or freezer for up to 2 months.

Makes about 4 litres (7 pints)

Takes 5 hours

A delicate-flavoured fine stock that can also be used in chicken recipes.

Vegetable stock

1 tbsp olive oil

3kg (6lb 8oz) mixture of chopped vegetables – carrots, onions, leeks, celery, fennel, button mushrooms

1 bouquet garni

4 peppercorns

6 tomatoes, chopped

1. Heat the oil in a large saucepan, add the chopped vegetables and sweat for 5 minutes.

2. Pour in enough water to generously cover the vegetables, add the bouquet garni, peppercorns and tomatoes, and bring to the boil. Lower the heat and simmer gently for 45 minutes.

3. Strain the stock, discarding the vegetables, and set aside to cool. Store in the fridge for up to 4 days or freezer for up to 2 months.

Makes about 2 litres (3½ pints)

Takes 1 hour

This is a lightly flavoured clear stock, which is good for all savoury cooking.

Beef stock

3kg (6lb 8oz) beef bones, chopped and excess fat removed (ask your butcher to do this)

250g (9oz) carrots, peeled

250g (9oz) onions, peeled

250g (9oz) leeks, chopped

250g (9oz) celery, chopped

1 bouquet garni

4 peppercorns

250g (9oz) tomatoes, chopped

250g (9oz) mushrooms, chopped

1. Preheat the oven to 200°C/400°F/gas mark 6.

2. Place the bones in a large roasting tin and roast for 25–30 minutes, until browned.

3. Drain off the fat and place the bones and juices in a large stock pot. Add 5 litres (8¾ pints) of water and bring to the boil. Skim as necessary.

4. Meanwhile, fry the vegetables in a little of the beef fat until browned. Add them to the stock along with the bouquet garni, peppercorns, tomatoes and mushrooms, then cover and simmer for 4 hours.

5. Strain the stock, discarding the solids, and set aside to cool. Store in the fridge for up to 4 days or freezer for up to 2 months.

Makes about 4 litres (7 pints)

Takes 5½ hours

Richly flavoured distinctive stock that gets its deep rich colour from pre-roasting the bones before cooking in the stock pot. You know how good a cook you are by the quality of your stock, so some chefs say.

Chicken stock

3kg (6lb 8oz) chicken bones, chopped (ask your butcher to do this)

250g (9oz) carrots, peeled

250g (9oz) onions, peeled

250g (9oz) leeks, chopped

250g (9oz) celery, chopped

1 bouquet garni

4 peppercorns

1. Place the bones in a stock pot, add 5 litres (8¾ pints) of water and bring to the boil. Skim as necessary.

2. Add all the remaining ingredients to the stock pot, then cover and simmer very gently for 2 hours.

3. Strain the stock, discarding the solids, and set aside to cool. Store in the fridge for up to 4 days or freezer for up to 2 months.

Makes about 4 litres (7 pints)

Takes 3 hours

This stock adds a distinctive taste and depth of flavour not only to gravies and casseroles but also to soup, and best of all, chicken and leeks.

Béarnaise sauce

140g (5oz) butter

2 shallots, peeled and finely diced

50ml (2fl oz) white wine vinegar

2 egg yolks

leaves from 1 bunch of tarragon, finely chopped

leaves from 1 bunch of chervil, finely chopped

freshly ground black pepper

1. Melt a knob of the butter in a pan and sauté the shallots until soft but not brown.

2. Add the vinegar and the remaining butter, and allow the butter to melt gently.

3. Whisk the egg yolks in a bowl, then very slowly drizzle in the butter mixture, whisking vigorously as you do so, until an emulsion forms.

4. Add the chopped herbs and pepper, stir well and serve at once.

Serves 4

Takes 20 minutes

Traditionally served with steaks, this French sauce has a beautiful creamy texture. It is usually flavoured with tarragon, but other soft herbs may be used if you prefer.

Fine herbes butter

100g (3½oz) soft butter, cut into pieces

75g (2½oz) finely chopped herbs, such as basil, parsley, tarragon, chives, coriander or chervil

4 garlic cloves, crushed, peeled and diced

freshly ground black pepper

1. Mash the butter with a fork until smooth. Add the herbs, garlic and black pepper and mix well.

2. Place the butter on a sheet of baking parchment and roll the paper around it to form a log shape. Twist the ends of the paper to secure, then chill for 1 hour before use.

Serves 6–8

Takes 15 minutes, plus 1 hour to chill

A pat of this butter is lovely on a grilled steak, the ultimate easy supper. The log can be frozen if you wish – just slice with a hot knife whenever you need it.

Parsley sauce

50g (2oz) butter

1 onion, peeled and finely diced

50g (2oz) flour

600ml (1 pint) milk

2 cloves

1 bay leaf

pinch of cayenne pepper

sea salt

freshly ground black pepper

leaves from 1 bunch of flat-leaf parsley, chopped

1. Melt the butter in a saucepan, add the onion and sauté gently for 4 minutes, until just soft.

2. Take off the heat and stir in the flour to make a smooth paste. Slowly pour in the milk, stirring as you do so, until combined. Add the cloves and bay leaf, then set aside for 15 minutes.

3. Place the infused mixture over a medium heat and bring to the boil, stirring constantly. Add the cayenne and seasoning, then stir in the parsley and serve.

Makes 600ml (1 pint)

Takes 30 minutes

Parsley sauce is quite delicately flavoured, so it goes perfectly with salty ham.

Onion sauce

25g (1oz) butter

200g (7oz) onions, peeled and finely sliced

50ml (2fl oz) red wine

50ml (2fl oz) red wine vinegar

300ml (½ pint) beef stock

1. Melt the butter in a pan, add the onions and sauté until just golden.

2. Add the wine and vinegar and simmer rapidly until reduced by half, about 5 minutes.

3. Pour in the stock, stir well and simmer for a further 5 minutes before serving.

Serves 6

Takes 15 minutes

Easy to make, this sauce adds great flavour to sausages, roast mutton or liver. If you want to add a kick, stir in a teaspoon of mustard to the finished sauce.

Horseradish sauce

140g (5oz) fresh
horseradish root
2 tbsp white wine vinegar
100ml (3½fl oz) double
cream

1. Peel and finely grate the horseradish.

2. Mix with the vinegar, then blend with the double cream before serving.

Serves 4–6
Takes 15 minutes
Horseradish sauce is fabulous when freshly made, and a must with roast beef or in savoury sandwiches. You can also add a little to vinaigrette for a punchy and unusual dressing.

Tewkesbury sauce

100g (3½oz) fresh
horseradish, peeled and
finely grated
100g (3½oz) mustard
(English mustard is
traditional, but use your
favourite if you prefer)

1. Combine the horseradish and mustard in a bowl and mix well. Serve with roasts, chops or sausages.

Makes 125ml (4fl oz)
Takes 10 minutes
First made during medieval times, and mentioned by Shakespeare in one of his plays, this sauce really packs a punch.

Devilled sauce

2 shallots, peeled and
chopped
5 peppercorns, crushed
1 bay leaf
1 sprig of thyme
50ml (2fl oz) white wine
100ml (3½fl oz) white
wine vinegar
500ml (18fl oz) beef stock
50g (2oz) butter
pinch of cayenne pepper

1. Put the shallots, peppercorns, herbs, wine and vinegar in a small pan and heat gently until most of the liquid has evaporated.

2. Add the stock and simmer for 10 minutes, uncovered, until reduced by half. Take off the heat, add the butter and cayenne and whisk until slightly thickened and glossy.

Serves 4–6
Takes 20 minutes
This piquant sauce is great for spicing up grilled meat. Once tried, it could well become a staple in your kitchen. It will keep for three or four days in the fridge.

Spiced bullace sauce

500g (1lb 2oz) bullaces, stemmed and stoned

caster sugar (see step 2)

4 tbsp red wine vinegar

1 tsp Chinese five-spice powder

1 star anise

5cm (2in) piece of fresh root ginger, peeled and grated

1 red chilli, chopped

1. Put the bullaces in a saucepan with 5cm (2in) of water. Cover and simmer for 5 minutes, stirring occasionally. Set aside to cool for 2 hours.

2. Weigh the fruit mixture and add half its weight in sugar. Add all the remaining ingredients, then bring to the boil and simmer for 40 minutes, stirring frequently. When thick enough to coat the back of a spoon, pour into sterilized jars (see page 222), seal tightly and store in a cool, dark place for 2 months to mature. .

Makes 500g (1lb 2oz)

Takes 1½ hours, plus 2 hours to cool and 2 months to mature

Bullaces are small wild plums, best picked when just soft and not too dark a colour. This spicy sauce will keep for six months if stored in a cool, dark place. Serve it with roast duck.

Cumberland sauce

1 orange

1 lemon

5 tbsp redcurrant jelly

5 tbsp port

1 tsp mustard powder

1 tsp ground ginger

1. Peel the orange and lemon, cut the rind into long, thin strips, then cut these into matchsticks. Place in a pan of boiling water, simmer for 5 minutes, then drain, discarding the liquid.

2. Juice the orange and add to the softened rind along with the remaining ingredients. Simmer very gently until the jelly has melted and everything is well combined.

Serves 6

Takes 30 minutes

This classic sauce goes very well with ham, lamb, duck and all kinds of game. It can be served hot and somewhat runny, or cold and thick. If kept in a sterilized jar in the fridge, it will keep for 2 weeks.

Mint sauce

50g (2oz) mint leaves, finely chopped

25g (1oz) caster sugar

50ml (2fl oz) white wine vinegar

1. Put all the ingredients in a screwtop jar and shake vigorously until all the sugar has dissolved.

2. Leave to steep for 2 hours before using.

Makes 125ml (4fl oz)

Takes 20 minutes, plus 2 hours to steep

A lovely mixture of sharp and sweet, this sauce is a must with roast lamb or mutton.

Apple sauce

500g (1lb 2oz) Bramley apples, peeled and cored

zest and juice of ½ lemon

1 tsp honey

15g (½oz) butter

1. Place the apples in a small saucepan along with the lemon, honey and 2 tablespoons of water. Cover and cook on a very low heat for 30 minutes, until the apples are soft.

2. Beat in the butter, then serve the sauce hot or cold.

Serves 6–8

Takes 45 minutes

When apples are abundant, it's a good idea to make a lot of this sauce and pot it up in sterilized jars (see page 222). It will keep for six months in a cool, dark place.

Cambridge sauce

3 hard-boiled egg yolks

5 preserved anchovy fillets

2 tsp capers

1 tsp chopped chervil

1 tsp chopped tarragon

2 tsp English mustard powder

100ml (3½fl oz) ground-nut or sunflower oil

1 tbsp white wine vinegar

freshly ground black pepper

1 tsp chopped chives

1 tsp chopped parsley

1. Place the egg yolks, anchovies, capers, chervil, tarragon and mustard in a blender and whiz until combined.

2. With the motor running, slowly pour in the oil until you have an emulsified sauce. Add the vinegar, a twist of pepper, the chives and parsley and give it a final whiz before serving.

Serves 4

Takes 30 minutes

Although not frequently seen these days, Cambridge sauce is English cooking at its most traditional. Both sharp and hot, it makes an unusual accompaniment to cold meats.

Cranberry sauce

375g (13oz) fresh or frozen cranberries

zest and juice of 2 oranges

175g (6oz) brown sugar

1 tsp allspice

1. Place all the ingredients in a small pan and warm very gently, stirring frequently, until jam-like (about 20 minutes).

2. Cool and serve straight away, or store in the fridge for up to a week.

Serves 8

Takes 30 minutes

The sweet/sharp flavour of this sauce goes well with with roast turkey, but is also good with other cold white meats.

Fats and oils

Fat is crucial in the kitchen: it flavours, cooks, binds, preserves and emolliates. We go into more detail about its importance in particular recipes and techniques, but these pages offer just a simple guide to its use in everyday cooking. In the past, a farm used to run on animal fats alone: butter from milk; lard, dripping and suet from livestock. Now, though, even the most old-fashioned of farmhouses probably has a bottle of oil somewhere, so we have included a couple of those too.

Butter

The fat solids obtained from milk by churning are what we know as butter. For table use, it should be kept at room temperature if climate allows; otherwise, it should be stored in the fridge or larder, well wrapped to prevent tainting by strong odours. Butter has a very low smoking point (the temperature at which it breaks down and becomes acrid), so it is unsuitable for high-temperature frying. Use it instead for baking sponges and biscuits, sautéeing at low temperatures (which helps to add colour and a nutty flavour), butter- and roux-based sauces, such as hollandaise and béchamel, and, of course, for spreading onto bread, toast and teacakes.

Caul fat

A soft, thin, web-like membrane that is found around the internal organs of cattle, sheep and pigs, caul fat melts away to almost nothing as it cooks, leaving little more than a bit of extra flavour. Veal and pork caul fat are the best for texture and flavour. Use them for encasing home-made faggots or paupiettes, or for lining a terrine dish to keep the pâté deliciously moist during cooking.

Dripping

As the name suggests, dripping is the fat that drips from a roasting joint as it cooks. It is very flavoursome, so well worth saving. Simply strain it while hot, then store somewhere cool. Use dripping for browning meat or onions, or making a delicious fry-up of leftover potatoes, cubes of bacon and eggs.

Goose and duck fat

Widely used throughout France, goose and duck fat are both excellent for frying and impart lots of their flavour to the finished dish. They set with relative firmness, so are useful preservatives. A layer of fine-flavoured goose or duck fat will seal a dish or stock and keep it airtight, thus prolonging its life.

Lard

When pork fat is rendered (heated until it melts, then cooled again) it is called lard. This is usually made from the flare fat around the kidneys, or the subcutaneous fat found underneath the skin of a pig's back. When taken from around the kidneys, it has very little flavour of pork, so is ideal for baking. The fat can be smoked before rendering, which makes it excellent for frying base vegetables for sauces – the smokiness adding a depth of flavour that makes all the difference to a finished sauce. Use lard for frying at high temperatures, for making savoury dumplings and for adding a wonderful shortness to pastry.

Suet

The raw fat surrounding the kidneys of cattle or sheep is called suet and has a high melting point, making it excellent for baking and frying. Raw suet is as perishable as meat, so must be kept refrigerated and used quickly. Suet bought in packets has a longer life because it has been dehydrated and flour has been added. Use suet when making pastry for savoury puddings, as on pages 60–63, for steamed puddings (see page 259) and for mincemeat and dumplings. Fresh suet is also brilliant for deep-frying chips.

Tallow
Rendered suet is called tallow, and the process of rendering makes it suitable for lengthy storing at room temperature. Use tallow for deep-fat frying and for making 'fat balls' (fat mixed with seeds) to feed the birds. At one time, tallow was used to make candles because it was much cheaper than beeswax, but it was smoky and smelly, so never very popular.

Groundnut oil
A light, flavourless oil with a high smoking point, so it is suitable for frying.

Olive oil
Extra virgin olive oil is excellent for dressing salads and vegetables, and is also tasty enough to use as a dip with good bread. (The flavour can range from smooth and grassy to slightly bitter and peppery, so do experiment.) Use a lighter olive oil for cooking and making mayonnaise.

Rapeseed oil
A neutral-flavoured oil, though some say it can taste cabbagey. Having a high smoking point, it is ideal for deep-frying.

Sunflower oil
A moderately healthy oil with a high smoking point. Use it for frying and for preserving dried vegetables, such as peppers and tomatoes.

Fat or lean?

If you buy meat from a good butcher, it should already have been trimmed of everything unnecessary, unless your recipe or diet specifically calls for more trimming. A covering of fat on a loin of pork or rib of beef, for example, is essential in protecting the meat from drying out as it cooks, while the fat and connective tissue found on stewing cuts break down during long, slow cooking to give succulence and flavour. Essentially, refrain from trimming meat unless absolutely necessary.

Meat cuts

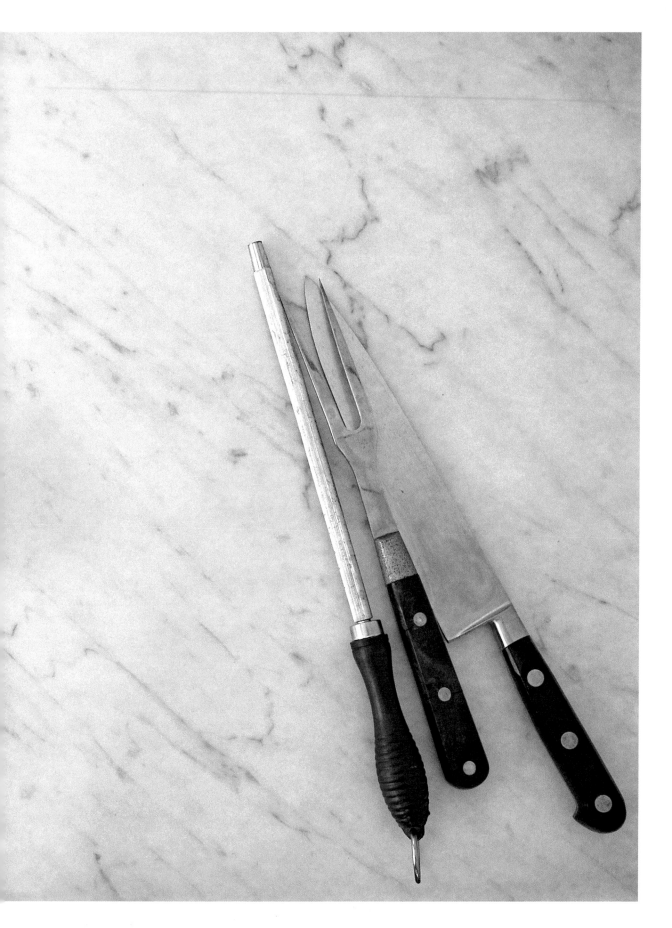

British pork cuts

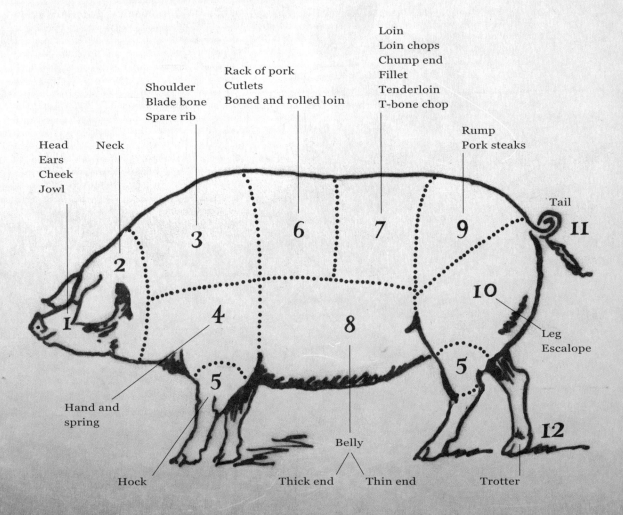

Loin
Loin chops
Chump end
Fillet
Tenderloin
T-bone chop

Shoulder
Blade bone
Spare rib

Rack of pork
Cutlets
Boned and rolled loin

Rump
Pork steaks

Head
Ears
Cheek
Jowl

Neck

Tail

Head
Ears
Cheek
Jowl

Leg
Escalope

Hand and
spring

Belly

Hock

Thick end

Thin end

Trotter

Fore end

1: Head

The head is traditionally used to make brawn (also known as 'headcheese') by pot-boiling. The brains and tongue can also be extracted and cooked separately.

1: Ears

Frequently eaten in France but not so popular here – yet. Simmer to soften, then dip in butter and breadcrumbs and fry until crisp.

1: Cheek|Jowl

Exactly as it says, this sweet nugget of meat comes from the cheek and is traditionally called a Bath Chap.

2: Neck

A cut with many muscles. Good for sausages, pies and stews

3: Shoulder

Whole (or boned) and slow-roasted, this is a very juicy cut, good for a large gathering as it's pretty big. Diced or minced, it makes excellent casseroles, sausages, terrines and pies.

3: Blade bone

The top side of the shoulder, this can be boned and stuffed, slow-roasted or braised.

3: Spare ribs

Cut from the upper part of the shoulder with 4/5 ribs. Tasty sweet and succulent due to the generous amount of marbled fat. Cook whole, boned and rolled, and slow roast, diced and casseroled or cut in cutlets to barbecue or grill. Versatile and economical.

4: Hand and spring

This cut comes from the lower part of the shoulder/upper part of the front leg. It is good slow-roasted, or braised with vegetables, and is often minced or diced and used in pies, terrines and sausages.

5: Hock

The lower part of the leg, which has sweet-flavoured meat. This cut is best braised or pot-roasted.

Middle end

6: Rack of pork

Since this cut comes from the rib area of the loin, it contains more fat, adding flavour. Can be tied to form a crown roast, similar to that you make using rack of lamb.

6: Cutlets

Taken from the front of the loin, these should be grilled or fried.

6: Boned and rolled loin

Classic premium boned and rolled joint, with lean meat and a good coating of crackling.

7: Loin

Running along the back of the pig from the shoulders to the rump, this is served on the bone (ask your butcher to remove the backbone to make it easier to carve).

7: Loin chops

Taken from the middle of the loin, these should be grilled or fried.

7: Chump end

The very rear of the loin. Roast it whole, or cut into chump chops for grilling or frying.

7: Fillet|Tenderloin

This cut lies inside the ribs along the length of the loin. It is removed as one piece of meat and, as the name says, it's tender! Grill, fry or roast.

7: T-bone chop

This is a butcher's cut that is not commonly known in the UK.

8: Belly, thin end

Best left on the bone, this makes wonderful crackling when roasted. Great for sausages, pies and terrines.

8: Belly, thick end

This is the part of the belly from the shoulder end, and benefits from its thickness. Roast or braise. Good for barbecues.

Hind end

9: Rump

Large lean muscle that is tasty when roasted. Also cube and skewer for grilling or barbecue.

9: Pork steaks

Large lean muscle that can be sliced to make pork steaks.

10: Leg

The classic roast. Ask your butcher to score the skin to help create crisp crackling. It makes a great pot-roast, braise, or boned, rolled and roasted. Your butcher can also slice it into steaks to grill or fry. It's sometimes considered dry, but a good-quality leg of pork should have enough fat marbling to keep its meat juicy.

10: Escalope

Cut from the leg and beaten to flatten them, these are usually bread-crumbed and fried.

11: Tail

Great when used in the stock pot, the tail is also deep-fried and eaten by enthusiasts.

12: Trotter

The foot makes great gelatine when braised. Trotters are also highly nutritious and used in cold meat pies. The whole foot can be breaded and cooked until crisp, or Michelin star chefs skilfully de-bone, stuff and braise them slowly, allowing the sinews to melt into a fabulous, gelatinous dish or for making gelatine.

Pork offal

Liver

Strong flavour, used in pâtés and terrines.

Kidneys

Left in a loin chop for a real treat, or in steak and kidney pies, or grilled or fried.

Other

Back fat|hard fat
From the length of the pig, this fat is vital in sausage production. While the meat cooks, the fat keeps its form and moistens it. It is also sliced into sheets for barding lean roasting joints of pork and beef.

Soft Fat|flair fat|leaf fat
From inside the carcass, this fat is rendered down to make lard.

British beef cuts

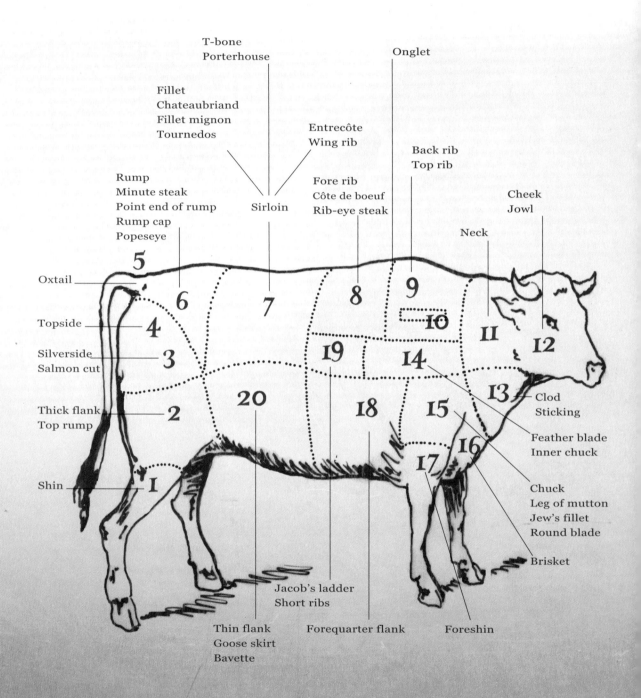

T-bone
Porterhouse

Onglet

Fillet
Chateaubriand
Fillet mignon
Tournedos

Entrecôte
Wing rib

Back rib
Top rib

Rump
Minute steak
Point end of rump
Rump cap
Popeseye

Fore rib
Côte de boeuf
Rib-eye steak

Cheek
Jowl

Sirloin

Neck

Oxtail

5

6

7

8

9

Topside

4

10

11

Silverside
Salmon cut

3

19

14

12

Thick flank
Top rump

2

20

18

15

13

Clod
Sticking

Feather blade
Inner chuck

16

17

Shin

1

Chuck
Leg of mutton
Jew's fillet
Round blade

Brisket

Jacob's ladder
Short ribs

Thin flank
Goose skirt
Bavette

Forequarter flank

Foreshin

Hind end

1: Shin
From the top of the back legs, with lean muscles and much connective tissue, for casseroles.

2: Thick flank|Top rump|Rump cap (6)
From the upper back legs, good for braises, casseroles or pie, or can be flash-fried in thin strips.

3: Silverside
For pot-roasts, braises or casseroles, a favourite for salt beef.

3: Salmon cut
A 1.5kg (2lb 12oz) joint to roast quickly at a high heat, rest andserve pink.

4: Topside
For pot-roast, casserole or braising. Well hung and barded, a good roast to be served pink.

5: Oxtail
Buy this sliced into 7cm (3in) thick rounds. An excellent braise or casserole, as it needs long, slow moist cooking. A tender meat packed with flavour, and has gelatine to enrich and flavour cooking juices.

6: Rump
The upper part of the rear, this cut sits next to the sirloin. Ask for a slice from the upper end. It must be well hung and will deliver a great-tasting steak, or roast it fast at a high heat and serve pink.

6: Minute steak
Finely sliced, this should be fried.

6: Point end of rump
Has great flavour, though some say it's a little tough. Needs be cooked medium-well and rested.

6 Popeseye
A large muscle from the rump, this joint represents great value. Roast quickly on a high heat, leave to rest, carve and serve rare.

Middle

7: Sirloin
Top-quality roast on or off the bone, or steaks to grill or fry.

7: Entrecôte
Steaks cut from the sirloin.

7: Wing rib
An excellent cut roasted on the bone, or boned and rolled.

7: T-bone
Cut with the sirloin steak on one side and the smaller fillet on the other. Grill or fry. You'll never get a perfect result as the fillet needs shorter cooking than the sirloin.

7: Porterhouse
Steaks cut from the wing rib.

7: Fillet Roast, fry or grill.

7: Chateaubriand
For Beef Wellington, roasts or steaks.

7: Fillet mignon
The lower, narrower end of the fillet, slice into small steaks.

7: Tournedos
Small rounds of fillet. The tail end of fillet should be half the price of the rest and is good for stir-fries.

7: Côte de boeuf
French name for trimmed fore rib of beef.

8: Fore rib
Upper part of the back. Makes a great roasting joint, due to the layer of fat that bastes the meat in the oven. Best cooked on the bone, but can be boned and rolled.

8: Rib-eye steak
Juicy, due to its marbling of fat.

9: Back rib|Top rib
Good-value, tasty cut best for slow pot-roasting, and great boned and rolled and slow- or pot-roasted.

Fore end

10: Onglet
A barrel-shaped muscle running along the spine, tasty for flash cooking or long braising.

11: Neck
Economical cut of meat used for stewing, braising and casseroling.

12 Cheek|Jowl
A large nugget of muscle that needs slow cooking. It has a similar flavour to oxtail.

13: Clod|Sticking
Very rich. For casseroles or mince.

14: Feather blade|Inner chuck
Very tender, richly flavoured and well marbled. Must be quickly seared or used for slow, moist cooking – anything in between just does not work well.

15: Chuck
Braise, casserole, pot-roast or mince.

15: Leg of mutton
Often diced and called chuck or braising steak and used as such, this cut can also be cooked whole, which needs long slow-roasting.

15: Jew's fillet|Round blade
A small, tasty fillet-shaped cut from the top rib, with gristle that melts with slow cooking running through its centre. Great value.

16: Brisket
From the lower shoulder, this cut is good for pot-roasting, braising and pies. Well wrapped in fat, adding flavour, and the classic cut for salting.

17: Foreshin
A cut with connective tissue that, when cooked slowly, makes a sticky, rich and unctuous casserole sauce.

18: Forequarter flank
Cut taken from the lower chest running into the upper belly.

19: Jacob's ladder|Short ribs
These cuts are very popular in the USA and becoming better known in the UK. Braise for tasty, big ribs.

20: Thin flank|Goose skirt|Bavette
A flat sheet of meat with a coarse texture. It either needs long, slow cooking (good for casseroles or mince) or marinating and flash cooking and slicing into thin, tasty ribbons with a good texture.

Beef offal

Liver
Very strongly flavoured, slice and braise with vegetables.

Kidneys
A speciality cooked whole with sauce or used for steak and kidney pie.

Heart
Slice and casserole slowly.

British lamb cuts

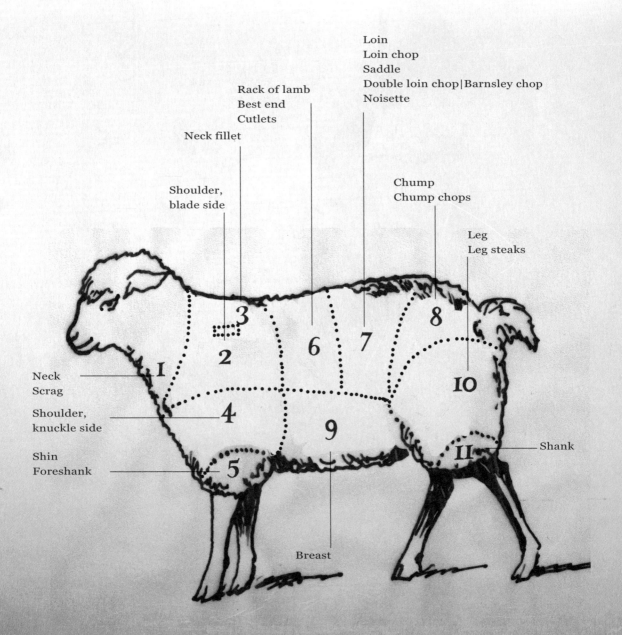

Loin
Loin chop
Saddle
Double loin chop|Barnsley chop
Noisette

Rack of lamb
Best end
Cutlets

Neck fillet

Shoulder,
blade side

Chump
Chump chops

Leg
Leg steaks

Neck
Scrag

Shoulder,
knuckle side

Shin
Foreshank

Shank

Breast

3

2

1

6

7

8

10

4

9

11

5

Fore end

1: Neck|Scrag

From the top of the neck, this cut is ideal for braising (long, slow cooking in liquid). If you cook it on the bone, it will add extra flavour to your pot.

2: Shoulder, blade side

This has the most flavour and is very succulent, perfect for slow-roasting on the bone for added flavour. Boned and rolled, the joint lends itself to stuffing before being slow-roasted or pot-roasted; the natural fat bastes the meat while cooking. It can be minced or diced.

3: Neck fillet

This cut runs along top of the shoulders. The small, marbled fillet used to be great value but is now pricier due to demand. It is versatile and can be roasted, fried or casseroled.

4: Shoulder, knuckle side

Again flavoursome, great for slow-roasting or ask you butcher to cut into 5/5 chunks, we call them 'henrys' or 'trunks'.

5: Shin|Foreshank

From the front leg, this cut can be sold as part of the shoulder or on its own for braising or pot-roasting.

Middle

6: Rack of lamb|Best end

The first seven ribs of the back. When trimmed this cut becomes a French dressed rack. Two racks shaped into a circle and stuffed, become a Crown Roast, which delivers wow factor at the table. Serve pink.

6: Cutlets

There are seven cutlets on each side of the animal. They are individual ribs cut from best end of neck. Grill or fry and serve pink.

7: Loin

From the middle of the back, this is a good roasting joint. Very tender, sweet meat and one of the tenderest cuts of lamb – so serve it pink. Boned and rolled, it is great for those who do not like coping with bones!

7: Loin chop

From the rib end of the joint, perfect for grilling and frying. Serve pink.

7: Saddle

This cut is made from both sides of the loin still joined by the backbone. A great celebration joint to roast and serve pink.

7: Double loin chop|Barnsley chop

This comes from the loin, with chops from both sides. For the hungry eater. Grill or fry.

7: Noisette

This is boned, rolled loin that can be sliced into perfect rounds. Noisettes are often served at dinner parties as they are easy-to-cook, tender portions. Grill or fry and serve pink.

8: Chump

The end of the back where it joins the leg, this cut can come on the bone or boned. It is a perfect small roasting joint, or can be sold as part of the leg.

8: Chump chops

Sliced on the bone at the top of the leg, these chops are generous in size. Grill or fry.

9: Breast

This can be cooked whole, or boned, stuffed and rolled. As a roast or braise it is fatty, but gives great value with sweet, tasty meat.

Hind end

10: Leg

The most popular cut of lamb, the leg can be boned, stuffed or rolled. Roast, cook pink, or slow-cook until the meat is falling off the bone. Butterflied and boned, the leg is wonderful for the barbecue.

10: Leg steaks

Sliced from the leg, these steaks are great to fry or grill.

11: Shank

From the end of the leg, this is a larger joint than the front leg. It is normally left on the leg to sell as a whole roast but if removed it will need braising.

Offal

Lamb's liver

Really fresh, this is almost as good as calves' liver but at a fraction of the price. Do check with your butcher that the meat is really fresh. Lightly pan-fry or grill.

Kidneys

Often overlooked, these are sweet and tasty nuggets. Grill them, fry or cook in a creamy, spiced sauce.

Characteristics of breeds

In the past British chickens were leggy, a body shape that delivers the most flavoursome meat, but with smaller breasts. The modern-day consumer desires larger breasted poultry and we have bred our chickens to accommodate this market demand. The French still produce a leggy, smaller breasted bird as they still demand flavour over lean white meat.

Welsummer

With flecked, rich, dark-brown feathers, originally from Holland, this breed was imported to the UK in 1928. It is an ideal bird for free ranging and produces large brown eggs.

Rhode Island Reds

Boasting a dark, rich, glossy red coat, this breed was originally from the USA and imported to the UK in 1903. It is a very popular, heavy breed and a good layer. When crossed with the Light Sussex cockerel, the males make a wonderful roast table bird. The most known breed around the world.

Light Sussex

Mostly white with speckled grey and silver head and tail feathers, this is Britain's oldest breed and is good for both meat and eggs.

Araucana

Its black feathers have a green sheen and white spots that develop with age. This breed was imported from Italy in 1888. These are good layers, producing a beautiful blue/green egg that results in a reasonable-sized bird.

Leghorn

This elegant black or white bird was imported from Italy in the late 1800s. A typical and prolific laying bird, it is also slender and not ideal for the table.

Marans

With 'cuckoo patterned' dark grey to silver feathers, this breed was originally from Marans in France and arrived in UK in 1800. It is a good breed for both meat and speckled-chocolate-coloured eggs, although the birds need space as they are prone to laziness and easily become fat. When crossed with an Old English game bird, Marrans make wonderful pot-roast table birds.

Master Gris

This brown-feathered bird was originally from France and has all the French characteristics of being leggy and smaller breasted. But they are packed with flavour and therefore make great table birds.

Dorking

A silver-grey-feathered bird from Sussex, it was bred in the nineteenth century for the London market. The ultimate broad-breasted English table bird.

British chicken cuts

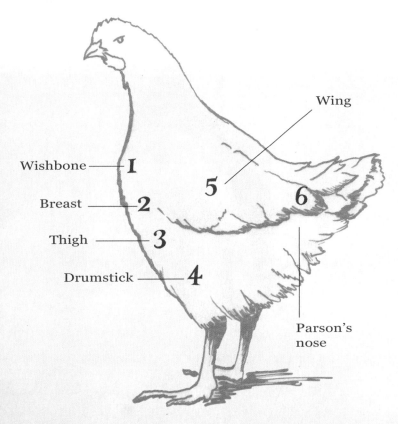

Wishbone — *1*

Breast — *2*

Thigh — *3*

Drumstick — *4*

5

6

Wing

Parson's nose

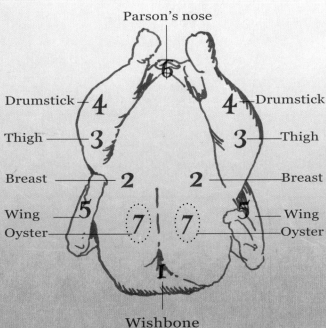

Parson's nose

Drumstick — *4*

Thigh — *3*

Breast — *2*

Wing — *5*

Oyster — *7*

6

4 — Drumstick

3 — Thigh

2 — Breast

5 — Wing

7 — Oyster

1

Wishbone

1: Wishbone

This bone is traditionally snapped at the table. Before it is snapped, two people make a wish and the receiver of the larger part will have their wish come true!

2: Breast

This cut provides lean, white meat and is very popular. With its mild taste, it can be grilled, fried, roasted, braised in liquid or barbecued.

3: Thigh

A cut that has dark. tasty meat that can be grilled, fried, roasted, braised in liquid or barbecued.

4: Drumstick

The meat from this cut is similar to that of the thigh (see above) and, when joined to the thigh, forms the chicken leg.

5: Wing

With brown meat, this cut is usually marinated for extra flavour and succulence, roasted and then eaten with one's fingers.

6: Parson's nose

By some, this is considered a sweet and tender delicacy; by others, this part of a chicken is totally disliked.

7: Oysters

These are two oval discs of sweet brown meat that lie on either side of the spine just under the wings.

Offal

Chicken livers are small, soft and inexpensive. They are principally used for pâtés or quickly fried for inclusion in salads.

Game cuts

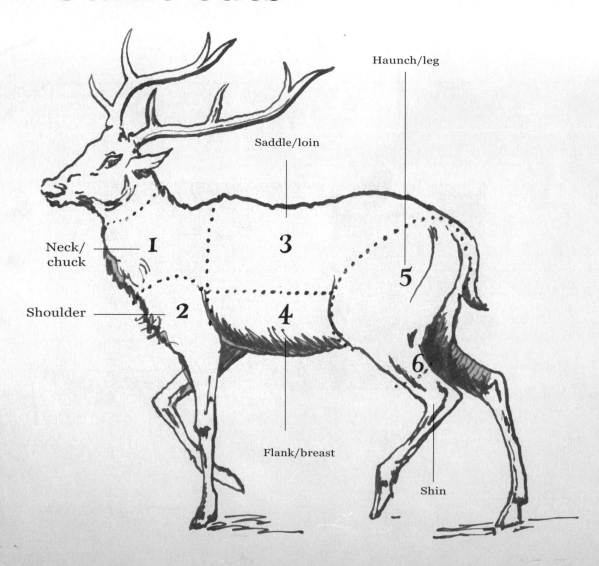

Haunch/leg

Saddle/loin

Neck/chuck

1

3

Shoulder

2

4

5

6

Flank/breast

Shin

Venison

1. Neck/chuck

A hardworking cut best suited to casserole, pot roast or braise. Commonly diced for cooking, made into sausages or minced for a leaner alternative to beef.

2. Shoulder

From the forequarter of the animal, ideal left on the bone for a long slow roast or diced, marinated and skewered for the barbecue.

3. Saddle/loin

Often referred to as 'saddle' when left on the bone and 'loin' when taken off, this is a very lean cut that is best cooked hot and fast and served pink. Leave on the bone for an impressive roast or take the eye of the loin for cut similar to fillet of beef.

4. Flank/breast

Not an awful lot of meat to be had, often used in sausage and pies making to add extra fat. Can be taken off the bone, rolled and slowly braised for a warming, sticky dish for two.

5. Haunch/leg

Makes a very fine roast either left on or taken off the bone (which is best left a little pink in the middle). It's wise to bard the joint with fat from the breast or streaky bacon, so that it doesn't dry out.

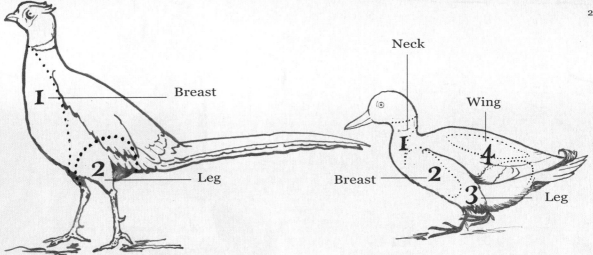

Pheasant

You can remove the leg and breast from a pheasant, for different cookery methods, however pot-roasting the bird whole is what we would most recommend. If you do remove the legs and breast, ensure you use the carcass for a rich, well-flavoured game stock.

1. Breast fillet

Very lean fillets, which don't handle over cooking. Season and pan fry until just cooked and serve in a salad.

2. Leg

Best slow cooked with a little moisture; pot-roasting is ideal. Pheasant legs also confit well, though are rather smaller than duck.

Duck

1. Neck and 4.Wing

Neither have much meat on them, but they make a brilliant addition to a game stock pot.

2. Breast

Lean, almost gamey meat with a covering of fat-rich skin. Cook quickly at a high temperature to leave the flesh slightly pink and the skin beautifully crisp.

3. Leg

Rich, succulent meat which needs long slow cooking such as pot-roasting or a braise. Perfect for confit, in which it is salt cured then cooking slowly in fat.

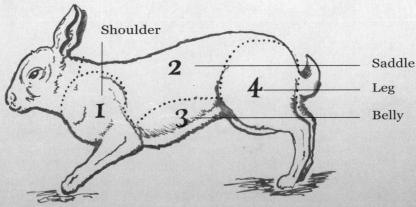

Rabbit

We would generally recommend that a whole rabbit be jointed for a pot roast or casserole, however if you're feeling ambitious you can cook each piece separately in the way which suits it best.

1. Shoulder

The front legs of the rabbit are fairly small and work a little harder than the back, and are best casseroled, pot roasted or confit.

2. Saddle

Essentially the loin of the rabbit, which should not be overcooked as it becomes dry. Often stuffed with forcemeat or mousse and wrapped in bacon or pancetta.

3. Belly

A fattier area, without much meat but still tasty marinated and grilled or barbecued.

The belly is often left attached to the saddle so that it can be wrapped around the leaner meat to secure a stuffing and add succulence.

4. Leg

Can be slow cooked in a casserole, pot roasted or marinated and barbecued or deep fried.

Index

Publisher's Acknowledgements

The Publishers would like
to thank everyone who helped
so generously in the preparation
of this book and, in particular:
Richard Sinclair of
The Warehouse Studio
(www.warehousestudio.co.uk);
Plain English
(www.plainenglishdesign.co.uk)
for their kind help with location
shots; and Sticks & Stones
(www.sticks-stones.co.uk) for
the provision of backgrounds.

Acknowledgements

We start by acknowledging one of our own, Nicola Swift, who joined the Ginger Pig team long after this book began; you ran with this project remarkably well, and your ideas, enthusiasm and determination have helped to ensure a book worthy of any keen cook's bookshelf.

Enormous thanks to the team at Octopus: to Denise Bates who envisioned this book as a whole, long before it was finished, and for her necessary intervention to keep us along the right path; to Tracey Smith, our wonderfully talented editorial director with a fantastic eye for detail, whose unfalteringly cheery and unflappable demeanour has been essential to everyone involved; to project editor Joanne Wilson, who has the brilliance and ability to pull together fourteen things at once; to our wonderful senior production manager, Katherine Hockley; and not least to Trish Burgess and Jo Murray for their eagle-eyed and tenacious editing and proofreading and to Hilary Bird for the index that completes the package.

To Anna Power of Johnson and Alcock, whose idea it was for us to write a book in the first place; her inspiration, determination, and ability to join the dots at each step along the way have been invaluable.

Of course there would be nothing to write about without our farmers, stockmen, butchers, bakers, drivers, shop staff, accounts and customer service team, together with our tremendous livestock. You have all made the whole thing possible; thank you for your loyalty, enthusiasm and hard work. A special nod to the following people: to Julie Howe and Hester Salt, our preserve and pudding-making experts in Thornton-le-Dale, who ensure that our shops are filled with delicious handmade condiments, and who provided several recipes for this book; to Les Bowes, head baker, who has been on-hand throughout to advise on pies, pates, terrines and pastry; and to Sarah Clubley, who gets on with whatever needs doing without ever batting an eyelid.

To our art director Pene Parker and photographer Kristin Perers; mavericks, both of you. You captured beautifully the life of the farm on the pages of our first book and we are delighted with the natural style and elegance you've given to this one. You are the only people we wanted for the job and the look and feel of this book bears testament to why.

Finally, thank you to the patrons of our shops, and to the readers of our books. Your enthusiasm for our meat and for making the most of it is overwhelming; we hope you get as much satisfaction from cooking with our produce and recipes as we get in providing them.

For Octopus Publishing

Group Publishing Director: Denise Bates

Art Director: Jonathan Christie

Head of Editorial: Tracey Smith

Senior Production Manager: Katherine Hockley

For Ginger Pig Farmhouse Kitchen

Design, Art Direction and Styling: Pene Parker

Photographer: Kristin Peres

Illustration: Pene Parker

Food stylist: Katie Giovanni

Project editor: Joanne Wilson

Copy editor: Trish Burgess

Proofreader: Jo Murray

Indexer: Hilary Bird

First published in 2013 by Mitchell Beazley, an imprint of Octopus Publishing Group Ltd, Endeavour House, 189 Shaftesbury Avenue, London, WC2 8JY.

An Hachette UK Company. www.octopusbooks.co.uk
Copyright © Octopus Publishing Group Ltd 2013
Text copyright © Tim Wilson and Fran Warde 2013

The authors have asserted their moral rights.

A CIP catalogue record for this book is available from the British Library.

ISBN: 978 1 84533 724 7

Colour reproduction in Singapore
Printed and bound in China